The Impact of ICT on Quality of Working Life

Christian Korunka • Peter Hoonakker
Editors

The Impact of ICT on Quality of Working Life

Springer

Editors
Christian Korunka
Faculty of Psychology
University of Vienna
Vienna, Austria

Peter Hoonakker
Center for Quality and Productivity Improvement (CQPI)
University of Wisconsin-Madison
Madison, WI, USA

ISBN 978-94-017-7850-3 ISBN 978-94-017-8854-0 (eBook)
DOI 10.1007/978-94-017-8854-0
Springer Dordrecht Heidelberg New York London

Printed on acid-free paper

Springer is part of Springer Science+Business Media (www.springer.com)

A word cloud of the contents of the book

Contents

About the Contributors

Sebastiano Bagnara Professor of Cognitive Psycholgy at the University of of Sassari, Alghero, Italy and Research Associate at the National Research Council, Institute for Cognitive Sciences

Research interests: interaction design, high reliability organization design, and human error. sebastiano.bagnara@gmail.com

Arnold B. Bakker Professor of Work and Organizational Psychology, Erasmus University Rotterdam, the Netherlands. Adjunct Professor at the department of Sociology and Social Policy, Lingnan University, Hong Kong. President of the European Association of Work and Organizational Psychology

Research interests: positive organizational phenomena such as work engagement, flow, and happiness at work. bakker@fsw.eur.nl; www.arnoldbakker.com

Pascale Carayon Procter and Gamble Bascom Professor in Total Quality in the Department of Industrial and Systems Engineering and Director of the Center for Quality and Productivity Improvement at the University of Wisconsin-Madison, Madison, WI, USA

Research interests: human factors and ergonomics, sociotechnical systems and macroergonomics, healthcare quality, and patient safety. carayon@engr.wisc.edu; www.engr.wisc.edu/ie/faculty/carayon_pascale.html

Erin K. Chiou Graduate Research Assistant for the Cognitive Systems Laboratory and Ph.D. student at the University of Wisconsin-Madison, Madison, WI, USA

Research interests: trust and reciprocity, interruptions, and healthcare systems. chiou2@wisc.edu; sites.google.com/site/erinchiou

Evangelia Demerouti Professor of Organizational Behavior and Human Decision Processes, Eindhoven University of Technology, the Netherlands

Research interests: occupational well-being (burnout, work engagement, flow), work characteristics, work-family issues, job crafting, and job performance. E.demerouti@tue.nl

Daantje Derks Assistant Professor of Work and Organizational Psychology, Erasmus University Rotterdam, the Netherlands

Research interests: work-family conflict, smartphone use, job crafting, and new ways of working. Derks@fsw.eur.nl

Cornelia Gerdenitsch Mag., Graduate Student and University Assistant at the Department of Applied Psychology: Work, Education, and Economy at the University of Vienna, Austria

Research interests: new ways of working, flexibility, and personal resources. cornelia.gerdenitsch@univie.ac.at

Nathalie Greenan Researcher at the Centre d'études de l'emploi (CEE), Noisy-le-Grand, France. nathalie.greenan@cee-recherche.fr; www.cee-recherche.fr/

Peter Hoonakker Associate Director of Research and Scientist at the Center for Quality and Productivity Improvement at the University of Wisconsin-Madison, Madison, WI, USA

Research interests: implementation and evaluation of health information technology, quality of care, and patient safety. phoonakker@cqpi.engr.wisc.edu; cqpi.engr.wisc.edu/hoonakker

Jörn Hurtienne Professor of Psychological Ergonomics at the University of Würzburg, Germany

Research interests: time and work pressure, design for intuitive use, inclusive design, the psychology of knowledge work. joern.hurtienne@uni-wuerzburg.de; psyergo.uni-wuerzburg.de

Gisa Junghanns Scientific Member of the Federal Institute for Occupational Health and Safety in Berlin, Germany. Unit: Mental Workload, Occupational Health Management

Research interests: time and work pressure, creativity, mental workload, and changing world of work. junghanns.gisa@baua.bund.de; www.baua.de

Christian Korunka Professor of Work and Organizational Psychology at the University of Vienna, Austria

Research interests: effects of organizational change on employees, new job demands, ICT and quality of working life, burnout, and engagement. christian.korunka@univie.ac.at; www.univie.ac.at/christian.korunka

Bettina Kubicek Mag., Dr., Postdoctoral Researcher at the University of Vienna, Austria

Research interests: new job demands, work stress, retirement, and emotional labor. bettina.kubicek@univie.ac.at

Susana Llorens Associate Professor of Work and Organizational Psychology and Research Coordinator of WoNT Research Team at Universitat Jaume I, Castellon, Spain

Research interests: positive psychology, healthy and resilient organizations, work/team engagement, organizational justice, work emotional intelligence, organizational/team trust, technology, and health. llorgum@uji.es; www.wont.uji.es

Patrizia Marti Professor of Culture-Based Design, Eindhoven Technical University, the Netherlands, and Senior Researcher, University of Siena, Italy

Research interests: interaction design, embodied cognition, and phenomenology. patrizia.marti@unisi.it; www.patriziamarti.it

Enid Montague Professor of General Internal Medicine and Geriatrics and Technology and Social Behavior at the Northwestern University, Chicago, IL, USA

Research interests: human factors and ergonomics, health information technology, human-computer interaction, and trust in technology. enid.montague@northwestern.edu; www.enidmontague.com

Mathieu Narcy Researcher at the Centre d'études de l'emploi (CEE), Noisy-le-Grand, France. mathieu.narcy@cee-recherche.fr; www.cee-recherche.fr/

Matea Paškvan Mag., Graduate Student and University Assistant at the Department of Applied Psychology: Work, Education, and Economy at the University of Vienna, Austria

Research interests: new job demands, challenge-hindrance occupational stress model, organizational resources, burnout, and engagement matea.paskvan@univie.ac.at

Simone Pozzi is Human Factors and Safety R&D expert at Deep Blue Consultancy and Research, Rome, Italy

Research interests: interaction design, human-computer interaction, and human performance in safety critical systems. Simone.pozzi@gmail.com

Roman Prem Mag., Graduate Student and University Assistant at the Department of Applied Psychology: Work, Education, and Economy at the University of Vienna, Austria

Research interests: new job demands, diary studies, self-control, vitality, and engagement. roman.prem@univie.ac.at

Hartmut Rosa Professor of Social Thought and Sociological Theory at the University of Jena, Germany

Research interests: sociology of time, sociology of modernity, and critical theory. Hartmut.rosa@uni-jena.de; www.soziologie.uni-jena.de/HartmutRosa.html

Marisa Salanova Full Professor of Work and Organizational Psychology and Director of WoNT Research Team (www.wont.uji.es) at the Jaume I University, Spain

Research interests: positive psychology, healthy organizations, work/team engagement, technology, and health. Marisa.Salanova@uji.es; www.wont.uji.es/en/salanova

Michael Smith Professor Emeritus at the Department of Industrial Engineering, University of Wisconsin-Madison, Madison, WI, USA

Research interests: occupational safety and health, stress, and quality of working life. mjsmith@cae.wisc.edu

Ulrike Stilijanow Research Assistant at the Federal Institute for Occupational Health and Safety in Berlin, Germany. Unit: Mental Workload, and Occupational Health Management

Research interests: time and work pressure, leadership and health, and time and stress management. stilijanow.ulrike@baua.bund.de; www.baua.de

Lieke L. ten Brummelhuis Assistant Professor at the Beedie School of Business, Simon Fraser University, Vancouver, BC, Canada

Research interests: cover topics related to employee well-being including employee recovery, workaholism, work-life balance, and flexible work designs. lieke@wharton.upenn.edu

Mercedes Ventura Manager Consultant at WoNT Research Team (www.wont.uji.es) at the Jaume I University, Castellon, Spain. mventura@guest.uji.es; www.wont.uji.es/en

Serge Volkoff Director of the Centre de recherché et d'études sur l'age et les population au travail

Research interests: population aging, working conditions, and health. Serge.volkoff@cee-recherche.fr; www.cee-recherche.fr

Harald Weber Board Member and Researcher at the Institut für Technologie und Arbeit (ITA), Kaiserslautern, Germany

Research interests: inclusive system design, accessible and usable design of information and communication technology, and vocational and social inclusion of people with disabilities. harald.weber@ita-kl.de; www.ita-kl.de

Klaus J. Zink Senior Research Professor for Human Factors and Industrial Management at the University of Kaiserslautern and Scientific Director of the Institut für Technologie und Arbeit (ITA), Kaiserslautern, Germany

Research interests: stakeholder-oriented assessment and design of organizations, integrative management concepts, change management and participation, and inclusive design concepts including life-cycle aspects. klaus.j.zink@ita-kl.de; www.ita-kl.de

Chapter 1
Introduction

Peter Hoonakker and Christian Korunka

There is no doubt that the development and implementation of information and communication technology (ICT)[1] during the last decades has had – and still has – a major impact on all levels of society. One only has to think of the Arab Twitter Revolution in the spring of 2011. Both society as a whole and individual lives have changed dramatically as a result of ICT implementation. In this book, the focus is on the effects of ICT on work and, more in particular, on quality of working life. That ICT has had an impact on working life is without a doubt: whole jobs that had been around for "ages" have disappeared (e.g., the teller at a bank, the stenotypist) and have been replaced with other, new sort of jobs (e.g., database manager, information technology specialist, web designer, etc.). Apart from jobs that have disappeared, nearly all existing jobs have changed tremendously. Even in "old-fashioned jobs" such as the agricultural industry or construction industry, ICT has a major impact. Most of the jobs have changed tremendously because access to and exchange of information have become many times faster. Only 20 years ago, if we needed specific information from colleagues and friends, such as a copy of a recent published journal article, we sent letters by postal mail, which would take at least 2 days to arrive, and it would last at least another 2 days before the response would get back to the sender. Nowadays, the exchange of information is almost instantaneously. Instead of having to go to the library and use all kinds of antiquated search systems to find a certain article or book, we use Google and the results are shown in

[1] Information and communication technology (ICT) is the term often used in Europe; in the United States, the term IT (short for information technology) is often used.

P. Hoonakker (✉)
Center for Quality and Productivity Improvement (CQPI), University of Wisconsin-Madison, Madison, WI, USA
e-mail: phoonakker@cqpi.engr.wisc.edu

C. Korunka
Faculty of Psychology, University of Vienna, Vienna, Austria
e-mail: Christian.korunka@univie.ac.at

C. Korunka and P. Hoonakker (eds.), *The Impact of ICT on Quality of Working Life*,
DOI 10.1007/978-94-017-8854-0_1, © Springer Science+Business Media Dordrecht 2014

milliseconds. The big question however is: does this instantaneous access to and exchange of information make us happier? Does it improve the quality of our working lives? In this chapter, we briefly describe the development of information and communication technology (ICT) and the effects of ICT in particular on work.

1.1 Communication and Information

One of the things where people have a great advantage over other living beings is the ability to communicate with each other. History shows us that people have communicated for a long time in one form or another, although at the beginnings of mankind, it was not possible to record the content of the communication, and the information that was potentially useful had to be remembered. Later, clay tables were used to record communication, followed by papyrus, parchment (sheepskin), vellum (calfskin), and later paper. The invention of the printing press in 1440 allowed information to spread quickly and accurately and played by the way an important role in the Reformation, a role which was to be repeated by the Twitter revolution during the Arabian Spring Revolutions 600 years later. However, the speed of communication and written information was still dependent on the fastest mode of transportation (horses on land, sailships on the seas, and oceans), until the invention of the telegraph in 1844 which enabled people to communicate faster over distances.

It is hard to imagine, but before Claude Shannon (1948), the word information hardly existed, let alone that we knew how to measure it. In 1948, Shannon published his seminal work "The Mathematical Theory of Communication" in the *Bell System Technical Journal*. Shannon's publication coincided with another crucial development, in the same year, also at the Bell Telephone Laboratories: the invention of a tiny electronic semiconductor, the transistor. In order to be able to measure information (words, pictures, movies, etc.), Shannon had to strip it from all of its meaning and reduce it to binary digits or, more briefly, bits. Using this unit of measurement, Shannon tried to imagine the greatest amount of information, expressed in bits. A punch card was 10^3 bits; a typed page 10^4; the information on a gramophone record 10^6; the content of a scientific journal 10^7; the content of the *Encyclopedia Britannica* 10^9; and the largest source of information he could think of, the Library of Congress, 10^{14} or 100 trillion. This enormous amount of information in the Library of Congress (more than 152 million items, including 32 million books) represents about 10 terabytes (one byte consists of 8 bits), as Shannon correctly guessed (Gleick 2011). Sixty years later, the largest computer hard disks one can buy for a few 100 dollars are currently about one or two terabytes, which gives us some idea of the enormous amounts of information we can use in daily life. The invention of semiconductors and its application in computers has an enormous impact on how we access and exchange information and communicate with each other.

1.2 Technology and Condensation of Time and Space: Intensification

Before the invention of the steam engine, when most distances were covered by the fastest way available, the horse, it would take someone 12 days to make the 400-mile trip from Edinburgh to London. After the invention of steam engine, and the train, it would take someone 12½ h in 1848. Air travel further reduced the amount of time to travel between the two cities to a little bit more than an hour. The introduction of technology caused a condensation of space and time: it took considerably less time to travel greater distances. Subsequent technologies such as the telegraph, the telephone, radio, and television condensed space and time even further. For example, radio (and later television) reporters were able to bring something that happened at the other side of the world almost instantaneously in our living rooms. In the late 1960s, the Defense Advanced Research Projects Agency (DARPA) succeeded in linking several computers together (ARPANET) and figured out a way to send messages back and forth (the same technology is still being used today as the Internet). In 1991, Timothy Berners-Lee, while working at the European Organization for Nuclear Research (CERN), implemented the first successful communication between a HyperText Transfer Protocol (HTTP) and a server via the Internet and in that way created the World Wide Web (WWW). The invention of the Internet condensed space and time even further, because it allowed people in different places and in different time zones to share the same information almost instantaneously. In short: ICT has changed the way people experience space and time. Distances seem shorter, and things seem to be happening much quicker. Everything appears to be more intense. In other words: an intensification has and still does take place.

All the technological acceleration that happened over the past centuries has left us with a paradox (Rosa and Scheuerman 2009). Technological acceleration decreases the time needed to carry out processes, communication, and transportation. That would possibly mean that it should cause an increase in free time. In 1930, John Maynard Keynes imagined a world in which, a hundred years later, work would be to a large extent replaced by leisure. He speculated about a 3-hour shift and a 15-hour working week by 2030. However, more and more people have the idea that they have less and less time. A good example of how ICT has affected our daily lives is e-mail. The advantages of e-mail are obvious. As described above, compared to postal mail, e-mails reduced the time of information exchange with days, and we now can exchange information almost instantaneously. However, e-mail also has distinct disadvantages: the enormous increase in the number of e-mails that we receive every day. Hartmut Rosa in Chap. 4 compared dealing with e-mails as the labor of Sisyphus: when we think that we are nearly done with responding to all the e-mails in our in-box, the mail program will link to the server, and a new batch of e-mails will appear in our in-box, and we can start all over again. Estimates show that in 2011, on an average, 228 corporate e-mails were sent and received per person, per day. That is nearly double the amount of the number of e-mails only 5 years earlier (142 in 2007) (Idinopolous 2008). According to the Radicati Group, in 2010, a typical corporate e-mail user sends and receives about 100 e-mails per day. If one assumes that it takes on an average about 1 min to read, react, or compose a new e-mail, that means that on an average people are nearly 2 h per day working on their e-mails. Interestingly, relatively little research has been conducted on how people feel about this. According to the results of a recent study by Intermedia among 2,000 adults in the United States, people can deal with a maximum of 50 e-mails per day without feeling overwhelmed (Heusner 2010).

1.3 Intensification and Quality of Working Life

The concept of quality of working life (QWL) was introduced in the 1970s in an attempt to integrate the values of organizational members in the process of organizational design. It meant a shift from the traditional approach of selecting people with certain qualities for a certain job (recruitment and selection) to adapting jobs to fit the qualities of employees (Levine et al. 1984). Quality of working describes the broader job-related experience that an individual has in his or her work. It involves positive components such as job satisfaction, work involvement, use of one's skills, possibilities for development, a meaningful future at work, and work-family balance but also negative components such as anxiety and job strain. In short, it refers to well-being of employees.

Much has been written about the explosive growth of ICT, but less attention has been paid to the impact of ICT on workers. What does ICT do to the quality of working life of workers? The Job Demands-Resources (JD-R) model postulates that job demands on the one hand and the availability of resources on the other determine QWL (Evangelia Demerouti, Daantje Derks, Lieke ten Brummelhuis and Arnold Bakker in Chap. 8). With the JD-R model in mind, on the one hand, one might expect that ICT places more demands on workers, but on the other hand, workers have more resources available. In this book several authors try and answer this question: what is the impact of ICT on QWL?

In the second chapter, Peter Hoonakker provides background information about the development of ICT and the past years and, using data from the European Foundation, examines whether ICT has an impact on satisfaction with working conditions and stress in several European countries.

In Chap. 3, Bettina Kubicek, Christian Korunka, Matea Paškvan, Roman Prem, and Cornelia Gerdenitsch, using data from several surveys such as the European Working Conditions Survey and the American General Social Survey, examine intensification and job security at the individual level. They examine how individual factors such as age and education determine how employees cope with an increase in use of computers.

Hartmut Rosa (Chap. 4) describes acceleration from a sociological perspective and explains how different forms of acceleration (technological acceleration, acceleration of social change, and acceleration of the pace of life) have accumulated into a self-propelling system that does no longer need external driving forces. Especially illustrating is his example, how we, like Sisyphus, try to respond to our daily e-mails only to discover that when we nearly reach the top of the list, we can start at the bottom again.

Jorn Hurtienne, Ulrike Stilijanow, and Gisa Junghanns examine in Chap. 5 the root causes of the increase in work and time pressure in the past decades. They show that several factors play a certain role, such as increased competition and globalization, performance-based goal setting, computerization, and acceleration. These factors lead to a decrease of resources, rapidly outdated skills and qualifications, and as a consequence a devaluation of expertise and experience, and an increasing need for permanent learning and adapting to the (social) environment.

In Chap. 6, Marisa Salanova, Susana Llorens, and Mercedes Ventura describe the darker side of information and communication technology: techno-addiction, techno-stress, and techno-strain. They describe these concepts and describe how to measure them and examine possible causes and consequences and propose different coping strategies to deal with techno-stress.

In Chap. 7 Pascale Carayon and Michael Smith also focus on the darker side of ICT: job stress and on ways to deal with it. They argue that we need a better balance between the positive and negative aspects of jobs, and that jobs need to be designed in such a way that stressors can be reduced or eliminated. They describe how interventions at several levels (society, company, and individual) can help to better balance the impact of ICT.

Information and communication technologies have deeply influenced the way we work. Organizations and employees have for the most part adapted to the challenges that ICT can create, and overall work and the way it is done has become more flexible, also known as the "new ways of working" (NWW). However, apart from the plus side (more flexibility), NWW has also drawbacks. For example, the boundaries between work and family life can be crossed much easier. Demerouti et al. describe in Chap. 8 how these new ways of working, and in particular e-mail, have effects on work-family balance.

In Chap. 9 Enid Montague and Erin Chiou focus on a specific aspect of working with ICT: trust. They describe how different types of trust mediate the acceptance of ICT and how trust can identify appropriate design features and implementation strategies for ICT use in the workplace.

The next two chapters focus on the effects of ICT on vulnerable populations. In Chap. 10, Nathalie Greenan, Mathieu Narcy, and Serge Volkoff focus on the effects of technical and organizational changes on the elderly. They explain that changes affect young employees differently than older employees but that the changes have less of an impact on quality of working life of older employees than is often assumed.

In Chap. 11, Harald Weber and Klaus J. Zink focus on the impact of ICT-vulnerable populations. Although ICT has the potential to empower vulnerable populations, such as people with a disability, at the same time ICT and its acceleration might be an essential factor in producing new vulnerabilities in parts of the population, i.e., creating new groups unable to participate in ICT-based activities.

Many studies and publications are concerned that ICT interrupts workflow, and they do not support us in the tasks and processes that we need to accomplish. For example, most e-mail programs list incoming messages by the time they have arrived in our in-box and do not help us to prioritize between the many e-mails that we receive every day. Further, "in the old days," one would receive the postal mail, go through it, and if necessary reply to requests, but other than that, the mail would not interrupt our daily activities. E-mail, on the other hand, arrives in our in-box continuously throughout the day and can distract us from our activities. Much effort is spent on optimizing the different processes that are interrupted by IT, and adapting IT in such a way that it supports us in our daily activities, instead of hindering, by creating an optimal flow. The chapter by Sebastiano Bagnara, Simone Pozzi, and Patrizia Marti (Chap. 12) examines this phenomenon from a completely different perspective and emphasizes that interruptions in our daily activities should invite us to take a pause and use these moments for reflection. The authors even suggest that IT should be designed for more pauses, detachment, serendipity, action, and eventually more reflection!

In the conclusion Chap. 13, Christian Korunka and Peter Hoonakker aim to integrate the different perspectives on ICT and quality of working life, as they are presented in the chapters of this book. We develop a comprehensive framework aiming to integrate the potential effects of ICT on different levels. When combining the different perspectives, it becomes quite obvious that ICT do have a strong potential to affect our lives in many ways. There can be many benefits of ICT implementation, but there can also be many new challenges and risks. Many efforts are needed to deal with the potential risks and to enable the many potentially positive effects of ICT.

Finally, when we contemplated the idea of editing a book about acceleration, we were afraid that the world around us might have already accelerated too much to ask our coauthors to contribute to this book. After all, we all have more than enough to do already without having to write a book chapter! To our pleasant surprise, we found many excellent authors willing to contribute to this book and spend part of their precious time to write the different chapters. Evidently, without their time and effort, this book would not have been published, and therefore we would like to express our gratitude to our coauthors. Especially the diversity and different backgrounds of the authors have made this a book, to use the words of Bagnara, Pozzi, and Marti, that invites us to take a pause and use these moments for reflection. We would like to thank all our authors for contributing their interesting thoughts and bringing in their different perspectives on ICT and quality of working life. We would also like to thank Elisabeth Dorfinger and Springer publishers for their valuable help and support when finalizing this book!

References

Gleick, J. (2011). *The information: A history, a theory; a flood*. New York: Vintage Books.

Heusner, K. M. (2010). *Tech stress: How many emails can you handle a day*. http://abcnews.go.com/Technology/tech-stress-emails-handle-day/story?id=11201183#.UOHAt6xuLYW. Accessed 25 Feb 2013.

Idinopolous, M. (2008). *Email overload: What went wrong?* http://michaeli.typepad.com/my_weblog/2008/01/the-plague-of-e.html. Accessed 25 Feb 2013.

Levine, M. F., Taylor, J. C., & Davis, L. E. (1984). Defining quality of working life. *Human Relations, 37*(1), 81–104. doi:10.1177/001872678403700105.

Rosa, H., & Scheuerman, W. E. (Eds.). (2009). *High-speed society: Social acceleration, power, and modernity*. University Park: Pennsylvania State University Press.

Shannon, C. E. (1948). A mathematical theory of communication. *The Bell System Technical Journal, 27*, 379–423.

Chapter 2
Information and Communication Technology and Quality of Working Life: Backgrounds, Facts, and Figures

Peter Hoonakker

2.1 Introduction

In this chapter, I will describe how communication and information technologies (ICT) have evolved in the past decades and examine whether the use of ICT has had an impact on quality of working life (QWL). I use data from the European Union (EU) and, more specifically, data from several countries in different stages of ICT adoption within the EU to tentatively examine this relationship. Tentatively because the data is reported on an aggregated level: averages from the different countries. I examine whether an increase in the use of ICT in a country also shows an increase or decrease in quality of working life in those countries over time. However, examining the data on such an aggregated level can disguise developments at the individual level. Even if the data at an aggregated level does or does not show a relationship between ICT and QWL, this does not necessarily mean that at the individual level, this relationship is the same. But examining the data at an aggregated level does provide us with a broad picture of how ICT and QWL have developed in those countries in the past decades. Kubicek et al. have analyzed data from the European Union and the USA at the individual level and describe the results in this book (Chap. 3).

2.2 Communication Technology

In the beginning was the word (Genesis, 1:1). People have communicated for a long time and over time have used different methods to increase the speed of communication, varying from sending messages by runners, horses, pigeons, etc. However,

P. Hoonakker (✉)
Center for Quality and Productivity Improvement (CQPI), University of Wisconsin-Madison, Madison, WI, USA
e-mail: phoonakker@cqpi.engr.wisc.edu

C. Korunka and P. Hoonakker (eds.), *The Impact of ICT on Quality of Working Life*,
DOI 10.1007/978-94-017-8854-0_2, © Springer Science+Business Media Dordrecht 2014

Table 2.1 Main phases of telecommunication development

Technology	Period
Telegraphy	1830s–1920s
Telephone	1870s–now
Radio	1920s–now
Television	1950s–now
Space technologies, e.g., satellite-based communications	1960s–now
Digital technologies	1990s–now

Adapted from Norris (2002)

the speed of communication was always limited to the speed of the fastest carrier and the limitations of those carriers. Only relatively recently, technology has been used to increase the speed of communication (see Table 2.1).

Especially with invention of the computer, and the reduction in the size of computers to such a format that they could be used for personal use in the early 1980s, and the invention of the Internet in the early 1990s, the speed of communication has increased to nearly the speed of light.

For example, the telephone seems to have been around "forever." However, if you would try and explain to a teenager how the telephone system worked only 25 years ago, she/he would stare at you in disbelieve. Dial a number? What do you mean no voice mail? And no number recognition? Then how do you know who is calling? Especially with the development of cell phones in the 1990s, things went very fast (see Fig. 2.1).

The numbers in the figure show the explosive growth of number of cell phones per capita in the period 1997–2007. In 2007 the United Arab Emirates (UAE) had the highest number of cell phones per 1,000 people: 1,709 cell phones. Ten years earlier, in 1999, the UAE had "only" 329 cell phones per 1,000 people. Brazil had 26 cell phones per 1,000 people in 1997, 256 in 2002, and 637 in 2007. Burma, the last country on the list (#212), had 0.2 cell phones per 1,000 inhabitants in 1997, 1.3 per 1,000 in 2002, and 4.2 per 1,000 in 2007. The USA (#72 on the list in 2007) had "only" 847 cell phones per 1,000 inhabitants in 2007, up from 564 in 2002 and 251 in 1997. At the end of 2011, six billion people worldwide had a cell phone subscription. One billion of those cell phones are smart phones (phones that enable communication and information technology).

To summarize, nowadays, about everybody in the developed world has at least one cell phone (and in some countries even two); and many people in developing countries have cell phones too. That means that we can always be contacted, no matter where we are, with whom we are, or what we are doing. Evidently this has many advantages, but it has also distinct disadvantages.

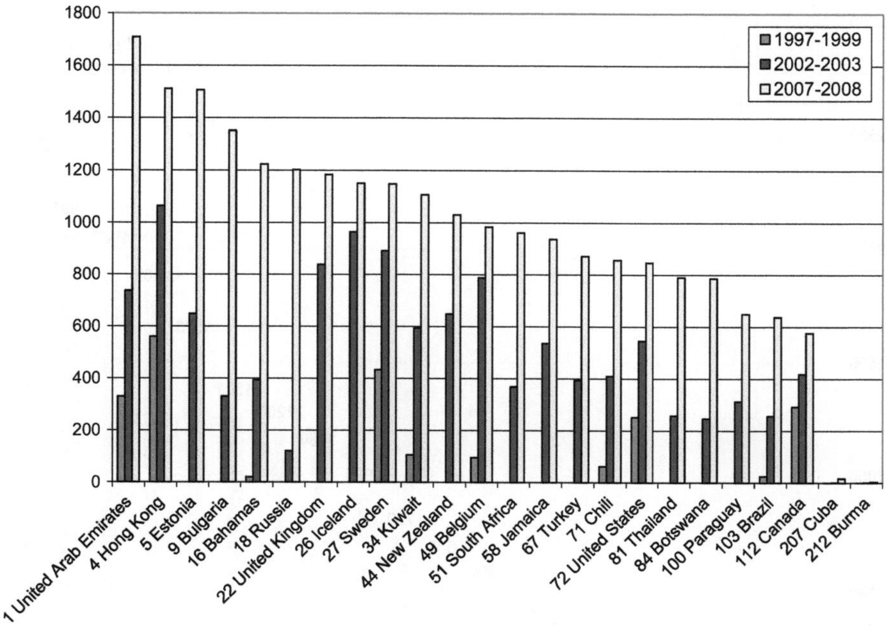

Fig. 2.1 Cell phones per 1,000 people in the period 1997–2007, selected countries CIA Factbook (2013), Nationmaster (2012)

2.3 Information Technology

Already in the 1960s researchers succeeded to connect several computers to each other and thus established the so-called ARPANET. It would take time to develop the protocols needed for the computers to properly "communicate" to each other and even longer before this "service" became available to the general public. The breakthrough occurred in the early 1990s: with the introduction of HyperText Markup Language (HTML), the World Wide Web became an interactive medium. The very first web browser (1989) was written by Tim Berners-Lee while at CERN (a European center for physics research). The year 1991 meant the birth of what we now know as the World Wide Web (WWW). In 1993 the WWW opened to nontechnical users. After 1993, the situation changed dramatically as Fig. 2.2 shows.

While in 1994 only three million people had access to the World Wide Web, this number had increased to 605 million users in 2002 (NUA 2002) and 925 million users in 2004 (ClickZ Networks 2005) and the latest estimates show that – at year-end 2012 – there were 2,405,518,376 people connected to the Internet (Internet World Stats 2012). To give another example of the tremendous growth of the Internet: in 1995 100 billion e-mails were sent annually; in 2002 this number had increased to 5.5 trillion e-mails, spam not included (PCWorld 2003); and in 2010 to 107 trillion e-mails, of which 89 % were spam (Pingdom 2011).

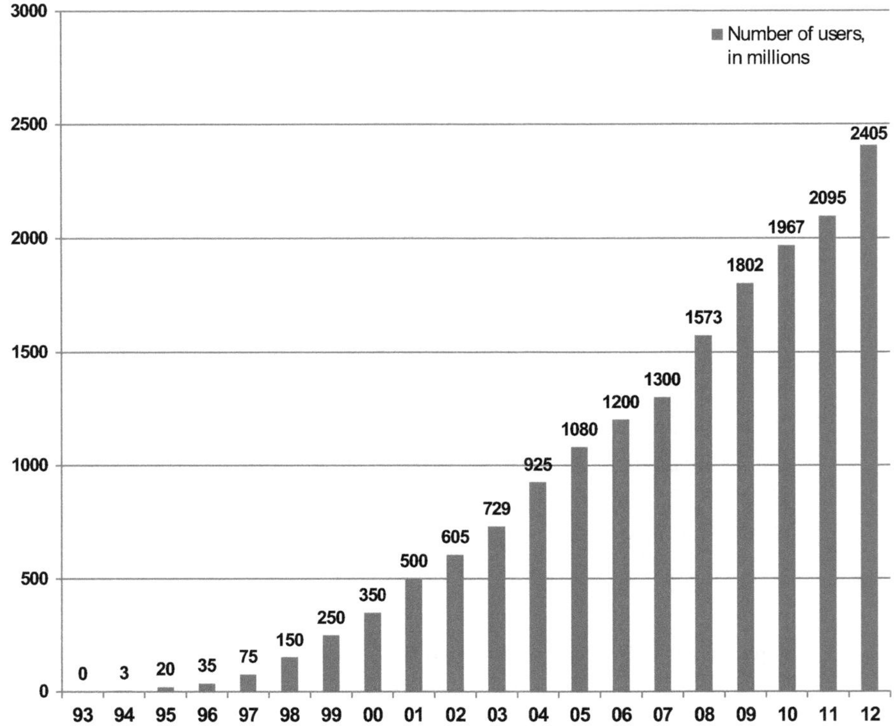

Fig. 2.2 Estimate of Internet users worldwide, in millions (Sources: ClikZ, Computer Industry Almanac, Global Research, Internet World Stats, NUA)

2.3.1 Internet Use in Different Countries Around the World

Results in Fig. 2.3 show the internet connections per 100 people in selected countries, based on statistics provided by the Organisation for Economic Co-operation and Development (OECD 2012).

In 1991, the USA had 3,000,000 Internet users or 1.2 users per 100 people. Most other countries had no Internet connections at all, with an exception for the countries in Northern Europe. In 1995, the situation started changing: in the USA there were 25 million Internet users (nearly 10 per 100 people) and in most other countries – apart from Northern Europe, where there were more users – there were in between 0 and 1 users per 100 people.

In 2000 the situation had changed drastically: in the USA there were 44 people per 100 people connected to the Internet, and in most developed countries, a quarter to a third of every 100 people was connected. In developing countries, the growth was slower: in 2000 between 1 and 5 people were connected to the Internet. For example, in China, in 2000, only 1.8 people per 100 were connected to the Internet.

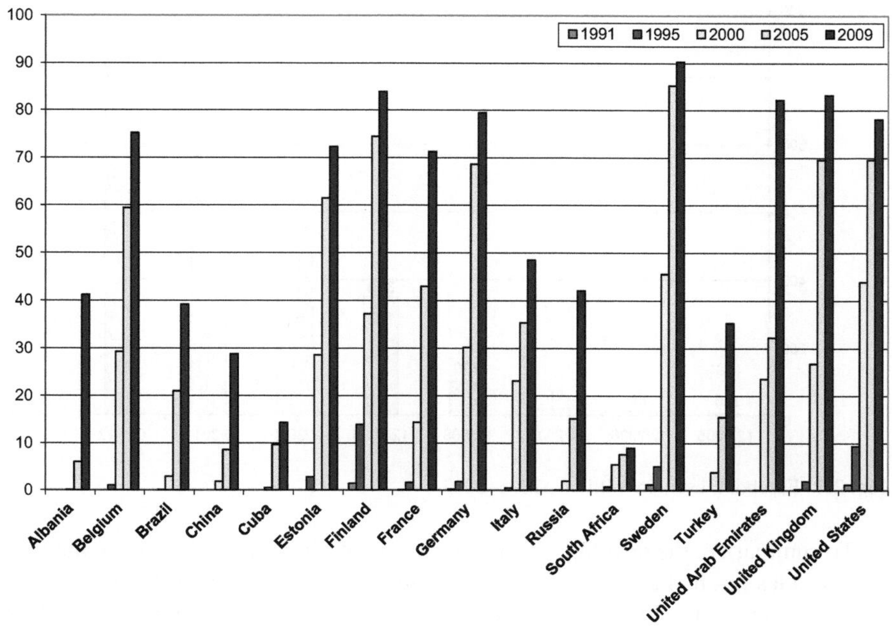

Fig. 2.3 Internet users per 100 people, selected countries, 1991–2009

In 2005, Sweden had surpassed the USA as the country with the most Internet users per 100 people (85.2 vs. 69.6). Other countries in the developed world were still behind the USA but not by far. In developing countries between 6 and 20 people per 100 were connected to the Internet in 2005.

In 2009 China has surpassed the USA in absolute numbers of Internet users (384 million vs. 240 million), but only 28.8 people per 100 were connected to the Internet in China versus 78.1 in the USA. Sweden had the highest number of Internet connections per 100 people in 2009: 90.3. Albania, which had started very slowly and had still only 6 users per 100 people in 2005, had 41.2 users per 100 people in 2009.

2.3.2 Social Media

An even more recent phenomenon is social networking. Internet but nowadays also smartphone users can use software such as LinkedIn, Facebook, Twitter, etc. to inform others about their activities, to keep in touch, and to make new friends. Some of these social media are more work oriented such as LinkedIn, others are more "friend"-related or are just gossipy. The growth of the social media has been astonishing as well. See Fig. 2.4 for the enormous growth of the number of Facebook users in the past 7 years.

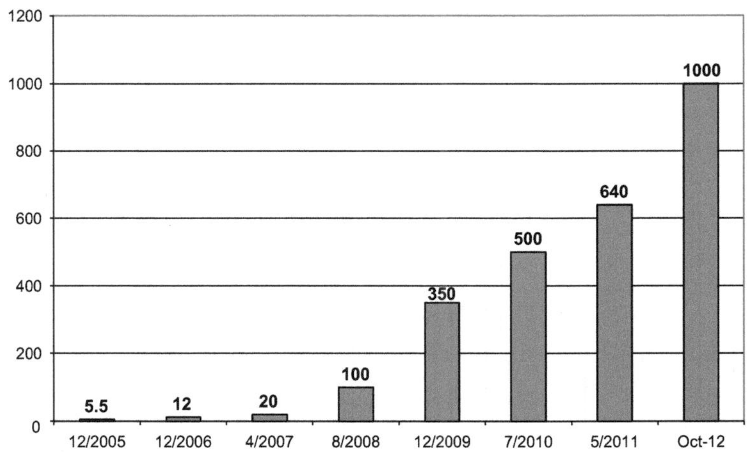

Fig. 2.4 Facebook users in millions, 2005–2012

To summarize, the development and adoption of digital technologies in the past two decades has had an enormous impact. Billions of people around the world are now connected via either cell phones or the Internet to information and to other people. The new technologies have had an impact on our private life but also a huge impact on our work life.

2.4 ICT and Work

The introduction of computers in the workplace in the 1980s and 1990s has had a major impact on work. Jobs such as typists (and real carbon copies with them) have all but disappeared. Other jobs such as bank tellers are still around, but because of automatization, there are fewer people working in them. It is easier these days to get money "out of the wall" (ATMs) than having to go to a bank, fill out the forms, wait in line, etc. In the past 20 years, millions of jobs have disappeared, but millions of other jobs, especially in information technology (IT), have been created. Apart from jobs having become obsolete and new jobs created, computers and IT have had an impact on nearly all other jobs (see Fig. 2.5). Even in historically manual jobs such as jobs in agriculture and construction, computers have become part of the job.

In order to describe the developments and adoption of ICT, and its impact on quality of working life, I use data collected by the European Union in the period 1995–2010. The data was collected by the European Foundation for the Improvement of Living and Working Conditions (European Foundation: http://www.eurofound.europa.eu/). The European Foundation conducts several regularly repeated surveys among the countries of the European Union (EU). The European Working Conditions Survey (EWCS) is the longest running survey and has become an established source of information about employment, working conditions, and

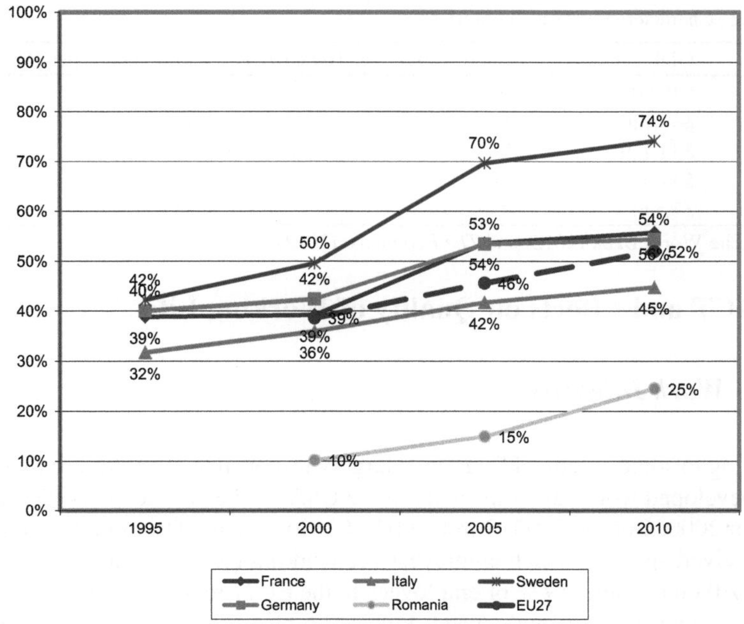

Fig. 2.5 Working with computers at least 25 % of the time, by selected countries and EU27

quality of working life in Europe (European Foundation for the Improvement of Living and Working Conditions 2010; Paoli 2000; Paoli and Merllié 2001; Parent-Thirion et al. 2007). Since 1990, 5 rounds of data have been collected. The most recent survey took place in 2010 in the 27 countries of the EU (EU27) and 44,000 employees were interviewed. The EWCS enables monitoring of long-term trends in working conditions in Europe. Topics covered in the EWCS include employment status, working time, work organization, learning and training, physical and psychosocial risk factors, health and safety, worker participation, work-life balance, earnings and financial security, as well as work and health.

I selected five countries from the EU27 in different phases of development and ICT use: Sweden, Germany, France, Italy, and Romania. The first four countries have been members of the EU since 1995; Romania submitted its official application for membership in 1995 and officially joined the EU in 2007 (Table 2.2).

In the 27 countries belonging to the EU (EU27), the percentage of people working at least 25 % of their time with a computer has increased from 39 % in 2000 to 52 % in 2010. Working with computers is not yet as widespread in the countries belonging to the former East Bloc, such as Romania, but especially in the Nordic countries, such as Sweden, nearly three-quarters of employees work with a computer at least 25 % of their time. More than one-third of employees in Sweden work with computers almost all of the time.

Table 2.2 Characteristics of the countries

	GDP per capita	Internet users per 100 citizens	Cell phones per 100 citizens
Sweden	$48,000	91	116
Germany	$40,120	83	127
France	$39,450	77	101
Italy	$34,080	57	150
Romania	$7,540	44	115

Source: The World Bank (2012) and *The Economist* (2012)

2.5 ICT and Effects on Quality of Working Life

2.5.1 Work Intensity

According to some authors, IT has been largely responsible for productivity growth in the developed world, and especially in the USA, in the past 20 years (Dewan and Kraemer 2000; Gordon 2000; Stiroh 2002). Obvious is that IT has had an impact of the perceived speed at which employees are working (see Fig. 2.6).

In 2010 on average, 59 % of employees in the EU27 report that, at least 25 % of their time, they work at high speed. Figure 2.6 also shows how working at high speed has increased in countries such as France, Germany, and Italy but that in Sweden, where in 2005 85 % of employees reported to work at high speed at least 25 % of their time, that number has decreased to 77 % in 2010. In Romania, there has been a decrease in working at high speed in the last 10 years.

Working with tight deadlines has – on an average – also increased in the EU during the past 15 years (see Fig. 2.7).

Working with tight deadlines at least 25 % of the time has increased from 59 to 62 % in the EU27, from 45 to 58 % in France, and from 58 to 73 % in Germany. In Sweden the percentage has increased to 85 % in 2005, but has since seen a decrease to 77 %. In Romania working with tight deadlines has decreased in the last 10 years.

2.5.2 Satisfaction with Working Conditions

One can wonder whether the digitalization of society and work has made people happier. On the one hand, everyone is "connected" and it has become very easy to communicate with each other. On the other hand, we have seen that in the workplace, ICT has caused more working with computers and more often working with tight deadlines. Figure 2.8 shows satisfaction with working conditions in selected countries in the EU27 in the period 1995–2010.

Over the past 15 years, satisfaction with working conditions has remained relatively stable: in the EU27, in 2000 82 % of employees were satisfied or very satisfied with their working conditions; in 2005, 82 %; and in 2010, 84 %. Satisfaction with working conditions is – overall – highest in Germany, with nearly 90 %

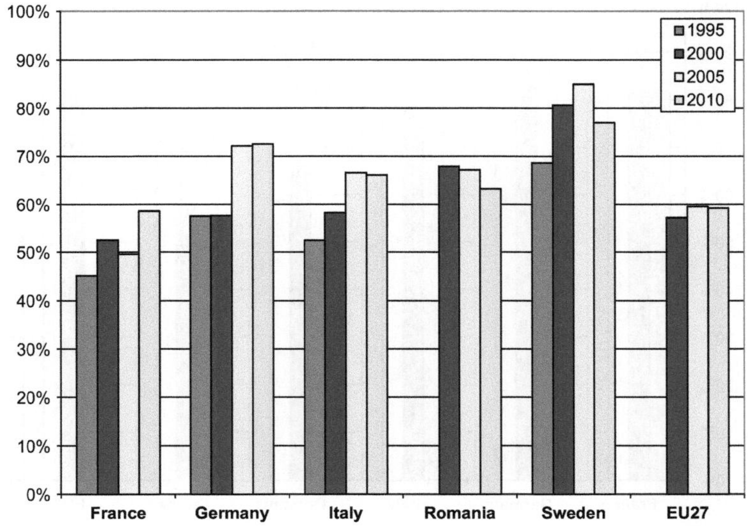

Fig. 2.6 Working at high speed, at least 25 % of the time, 1995–2010, selected countries

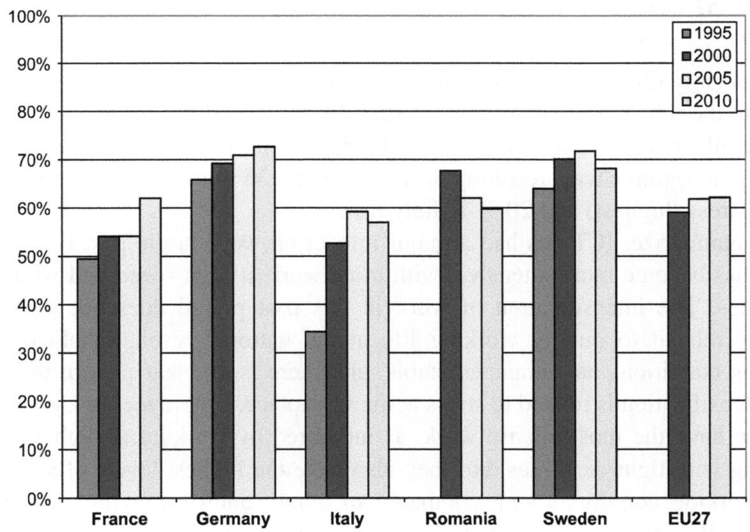

Fig. 2.7 Working with tight deadlines at least 25 % of the time, 1995–2010, selected countries

of employees satisfied or very satisfied with their jobs and lowest in Romania (75 % in 2010). Satisfaction with working conditions in Sweden has decreased in the past 15 years: from 91 % in 1995 to 87 % in 2010.

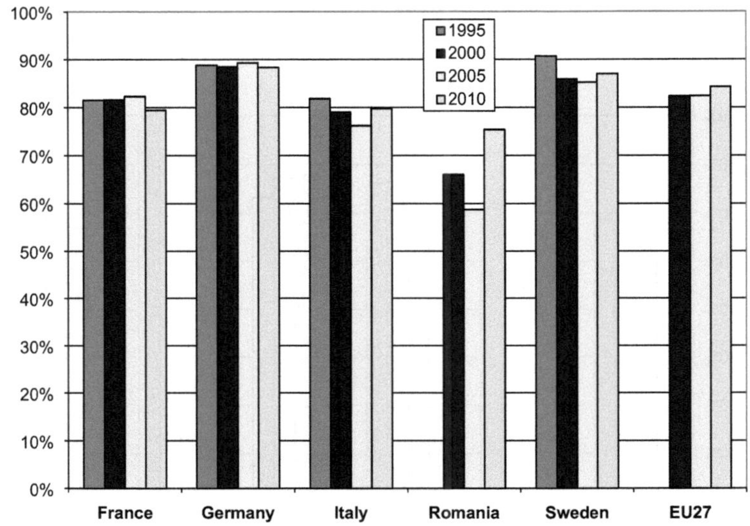

Fig. 2.8 Satisfied or very satisfied with working conditions, selected countries, 1995–2010

2.5.3 Stress

Only recently (2010), the European Foundation has started asking questions about stress in the job on a national level. Figure 2.9 shows the results.

Overall, about 25 % of employees in the EU27 report that their work affects their health in a negative way, resulting in stress. Nearly 35 % of employees in Romania report stress (highest) and 20 % in Italy (lowest).

To summarize, ICT has had a major impact on work in the past two decades. Work has become more intensive, with more work at high speed and with tighter deadlines. The intensification of work in this past period does not seem to be directly related to quality working life at the national level. Satisfaction with working conditions has remained stable, and there is no clear pattern that shows that intensification is related to stress at the workplace. Employees in Germany and Sweden have the most intense work, as measured by working at high speed and working with tight deadlines, but they also have the highest levels of satisfaction with working conditions and, compared to other countries, do not report more stress. In Romania, relatively few employees work with computers; they do report lower levels of work intensification as compared to other countries, but they report less satisfaction with working conditions and more stress.

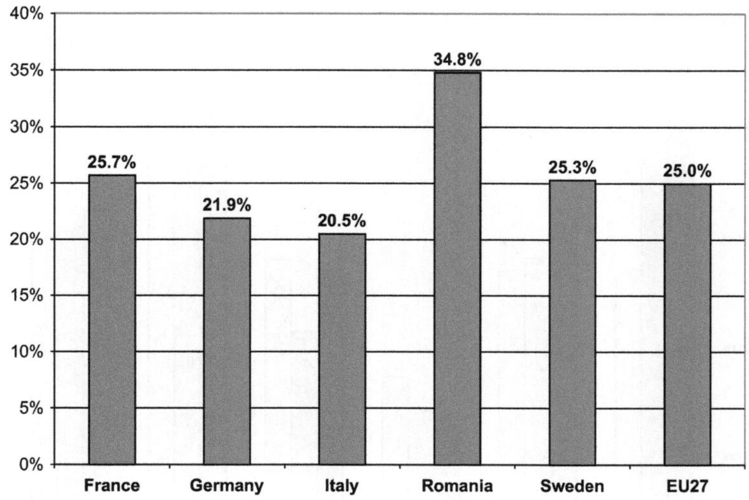

Fig. 2.9 Work affects health in a negative way resulting in stress

2.5.4 *ICT Work and Family*

The introduction of ICT has made it increasingly easier to work in other places than the workplace. Work nowadays can be done from home, in hotels, at the airport, and even on vacation. Evidently this has huge advantages. However, it also means that the boundaries between work and family life have become less transparent. To exaggerate a little bit to make the point, 25 years ago, people had nine-to-five jobs, and after the work was done at 5 PM, they would "close the door behind them" and go home. Evidently, tight schedules and deadlines also existed in those days, and employees used overtime to meet their demands, but the work took place at the workplace, whether an office or a factory, because the tools and the information they needed for the job was linked to the workplace. Nowadays, information has become portable as well as the tools to perform the work (laptop computers and smart phones). This has caused the borders between work and family to disappear.

For example, results of a recent (unrepresentative) poll by Xobni (Inbox spelled backwards) among 2,200 adults ages 18 and older showed that 72 % of Americans and 68 % of Brits check their e-mail on vacation, when they are taking time off, on weekends, and/or on other nonwork days (Xobni 2010). Thirty-seven percent of the American respondents and 45 % of respondents in the UK are afraid to go without checking their e-mail because they might miss something important. Many of the American respondents (43 %) who check work email outside of regular business hours indicate that they do so in order to ease their workload, and 18 % feel the need to check email outside of work hours in order to have a successful career.

Upon returning from vacation, more than a quarter (26 %) of the American respondents who take vacation/time off of work either feels that they get too many emails to respond to all of them or are too overwhelmed by the volume of emails

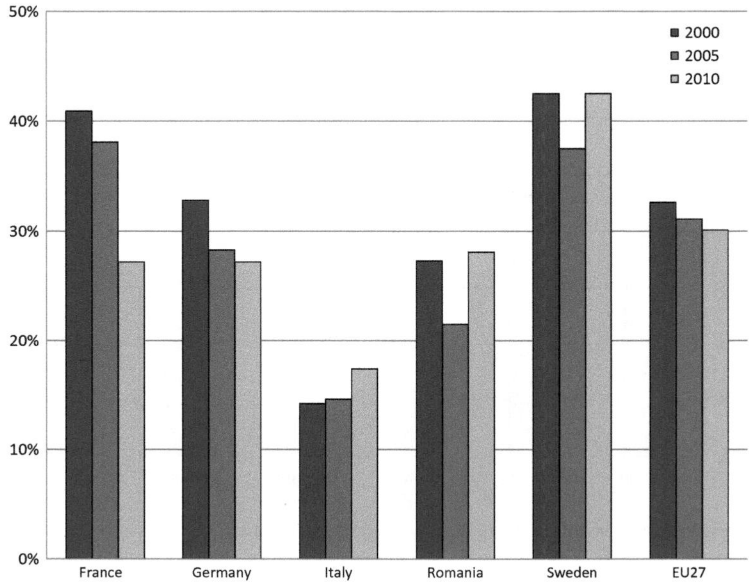

Fig. 2.10 Working hours fit family or social commitments very well, selected countries, 2000–2010

upon returning from vacation as compared to 86 % of British respondents. There is some evidence in the data from the European Foundation that work, and more in particular working hours, has an impact on family life (see Fig. 2.10).

Results in Fig. 2.10 show that in the EU27, the percentage of respondents who say that their working hours fit their family or social commitments very well has decreased from 32.6 % in 2000 to 30.1 % in 2010. The work-family fit is highest in Sweden where 42.5 % of employees report a good fit between working hours and family and social commitments in 2010 and lowest in Italy, where only 17 % of employees report a very good fit between working hours and family and social commitments in 2010. Chapter 8 by Demerouti et al. describes in detail the impact of ICT on working conditions and work-life balance.

2.6 ICT and Quality of Working Life over Time

The results of the surveys of the European Foundation in 2000 and 2010 are summarized in Table 2.3. In the table the percentages of employees who report working with computers at least 25 % of their time, working at high speed at least 25 % of the time, and working with tight deadlines at least 25 % of the time report that their work affects health negatively, resulting in stress, and the percentages of employees who are satisfied or very satisfied with working conditions in 2010 are shown. Further, the changes between 2000 and 2010 for four out of the five topics

Table 2.3 Summary table developments in ICT, working conditions, and quality of working life in selected countries of the EU, period 2000–2010

	WWC 2010 (%)	Δ WWC 2000–2010 (%)	WHS 2010 (%)	Δ WHS 2000–2010 (%)	WWD 2010 (%)	Δ WWD 2000–2010 (%)	SWC 2010 (%)	Δ SWC 2000–2010 (%)	WAH 2010 (%)
France	56	+16.5	59	+6.1	62	+7.9	79	−2.2	26
Germany	55	+12.0	73	+14.9	73	+3.4	88	−0.2	22
Sweden	74	+25.5	77	+7.9	68	+4.3	87	+1.1	25
Italy	45	+8.9	66	−4.7	57	−8.0	80	+0.8	21
Romania	25	+14.3	63	−3.6	60	−1.9	75	+9.4	35
EU27	52	+13.4	59	+2.0	62	+3.1	84	+2.0	25

Δ: difference between 2000 and 2010. WWC 2010: working with computers more than 25 % of the time 2010; WHS 2010: working at high speed at least 25 % of the time 2010; WWD 2010: working with tight deadlines at least 25 % of the time 2010; SWC 2010: satisfied or very satisfied with working conditions 2010; WAH 2010: work affects health: stress 2010

are shown. The question about working conditions negatively impacting health and causing stress was only asked in the 2010 survey.

Results in Table 2.3 show that Sweden has the highest percentage of employees working with a computer at least 25 % of their time (74 % in 2010). Sweden has also seen the highest increase in employees working with a computer in the past decade (+25.5 %). Romania has the lowest percentage of employees working with a computer, at least 25 % of their time (25 %). This percentage has increased with 14.3 % in the past decade. Overall, in the EU27, more than half of employees (52 %) work with a computer, at least 25 % of their time. This number has increased from 38.6 % in 2000, an increase with 13.4 %.

Sweden is also the country with the highest percentage of workers who reported working at high speed at least 25 % of their time in 2010 (77 %). This percentage has increased with nearly 8 % since 2000. France is the country with the lowest percentage of workers who report that they have to work at high speed at least 25 % of their time in 2010 (59 %). This percentage has increased with 6.1 % since 2000. The percentage of France (59 %) is comparable to that of the EU27 (59 %). The increase in employees working at high speed is lower in the EU27 (+2.0 %) than in France (+6.1 %). The relatively lower increase in the EU27 can be explained by the fact that the percentage of employees who report to working with high speed has actually decreased in the past decade in some of the countries in the EU27, such as Italy (−4.7 %) and Romania (−3.6 %).

Germany has the highest percentage of employees who reported that they work with tight deadlines at least 25 % of their time in 2010 (73 %). This percentage has increased with 3.4 % since 2000. A bigger increase in percentage of employees who work with tight deadlines took place in France (+7.9 %). On the other hand, countries such as Italy (−8.0 %) and Romania (−1.9 %) showed a decrease in the percentages of employees who report working with tight deadlines.

Romania is the country where in 2010 the highest percentage of employees report that work affects health negatively, resulting in stress. In Italy the percentage of employees reporting stress is much lower than in Romania: 21 % vs. 35 %.

Finally, Germany has the highest percentage of employees that report being satisfied or very satisfied with the working conditions in their job (88 %), closely followed by Sweden (87 %). However, satisfaction with working conditions decreased slightly in Germany (−0.2 %) and France (−2.2 %) in the last 10 years. The largest increase in satisfaction with working conditions was reported in Romania: the percentage of employees who reported to be satisfied or very satisfied with their working conditions increased from 66 % in 2000 to 75 % in 2010, an increase of 11 %.

2.7 Conclusion

Information and communication technology (ICT) has a major impact on many aspects of our life, ranging from family to work life. In this chapter I have provided some examples of the explosive growth of ICT worldwide, and I have compared survey data collected in the period 1995–2010 in several countries in the EU27 about use of computers at work and the impact it has on quality of working life. The 5 European countries that I compared are in different stages of ICT adoption (see Table 2.2). The results show how rapidly computers have been introduced in the workplace in the past 20 years. In 2010, more than half of employees in the EU27 worked with a computer at least 25 % of their time. I examined whether this increase in use of computers had an impact on quality of working life in those countries. Results show that in most countries working at high speed has increased in the past decade, as well as working with tight deadlines. However, overall, most employees in the EU27 are satisfied or very satisfied with their working conditions. The EU27 average was, respectively, 82.3 % in 2000, 82.4 % in 2005, and 84.3 % in 2010.

The results show that there is no direct relationship between ICT use and quality of working life at the national level. On the one hand, working at high speed and working with tight deadlines is higher in countries with a high percentage of employees working with computers, such as Sweden and Germany, but on the other hand, employees in those countries are more satisfied with their working conditions and report less stress. Further, an increase in computer use in the past decade does not always "translate" in an increase in working at high speed, working under tight deadlines, or employees reporting less satisfaction with working conditions. However, the data that I used at an aggregate level can mask relationships at the individual level. Further, evidently other factors can play an important role.

ICT has had a major impact on how our work is organized and how we perform our jobs. Statistics show that employees more and more use computers for their work, but also that work has intensified, as measured by working at high speed and with tight deadlines. ICT obviously has advantages and disadvantages. Among the advantages are that we are better connected and that we can be reached everywhere and anytime, that many of us can do their work wherever and whenever they want to. One of the disadvantages is that the boundaries between work and family have become less transparent and that work has permeated our private life.

References

Central Intelligence Agency (CIA). (2013). *The world factbook 2012–2013*. Retrieved February 25, 2013, from https://www.cia.gov/library/publications/the-world-factbook/rankorder/2151rank.html

ClickZ Networks. (2005). *Trends & statistics: The web's richest source*. http://www.clickz.com/stats/web_worldwide/. Accessed 5 Oct 2005.

Dewan, S., & Kraemer, K. L. (2000). Information technology and productivity: Evidence from country-level data. *Management Science, 46*(4), 548–562.

European Foundation for the Improvement of Living and Working Conditions. (2010). *Changes over time – First findings from the fifth European Working Conditions Survey*. Luxembourg: European Foundation for the Improvement of Living and Working Conditions.

Gordon, R. J. (2000). Does the 'new economy' measure up to the great inventions of the past? *Journal of Economic Perspectives, 14*, 49–74.

Internet World Stats. (2012). *Internet usage statistics*. http://internetworldstats.com/stats.htm. Accessed 4 July 2012.

NationMaster.com. (2012). *Media statistics*. Retrieved December 27, from http://www.nationmaster.com/graph/med_tel_mob_cel_percap-telephones-mobile-cellular-per-capita#source

Norris, A. C. (2002). *Essentials of telemedicine and telecare*. New York: Wiley.

NUA. (2002). *How many online*. http://www.nua.ie/surveys/how_many_online. Accessed 11 Oct 2005.

Organisation for Economic Cooperation and Development (OECD). (2012). *OECD key ICT indicators*. http://www.oecd.org/document/23/0,3746,en_2649_37441_33987543_1_1_1_37441,00.html. Accessed 4 July 2012.

Paoli, P. (2000). *Second European survey on working conditions in The European Union*. Luxembourg: European Foundation for the Improvement of Living and Working Conditions.

Paoli, P., & Merllié, D. (2001). *Third European survey on working conditions 2000*. Luxembourg: European Foundation for the Improvement of Living and Working Conditions.

Parent-Thirion, A., Fernández Macías, E., Hurley, J., & Vermeylen, G. (2007). *Fourth European working conditions survey*. Luxembourg: European Foundation for the Improvement of Living and Working Conditions.

PCWorld. (2003). 20 years of software. *PC World, 21*, 101.

Pingdom. (2011). *Internet 2010 in numbers*. http://royal.pingdom.com/2011/01/12/internet-2010-in-numbers/. Accessed 4 July 2012.

Stiroh, K. J. (2002). Information technology and the US productivity revival: What do the industry data say? *American Economic Review, 92*(5), 1559–1576.

The Economist. (2012). *Pocket world in figures: 2013 edition*. London: Profile Books Ltd.

The World Bank. (2012). *Internet users (per 100 people)*. http://data.worldbank.org/indicator/IT.NET.USER.P2. Accessed 28 Dec 2012.

Xobni. (2010). *New survey from Xobni on email overload shows there is no such thing as a day off for Americans and Brits*. https://www.xobni.com/press/09022010_harris_survey. Accessed 29 Dec 2012.

Chapter 3
Changing Working Conditions at the Onset of the Twenty-First Century: Facts from International Datasets

Bettina Kubicek, Christian Korunka, Matea Paškvan, Roman Prem, and Cornelia Gerdenitsch

3.1 Introduction

There is general agreement that work has changed considerably since the introduction and dissemination of information and communication technologies (ICTs) in the 1980s and that political and economic transformations, such as the rise of globalization, altered the context of today's industrial relations (Cascio 1995). Yet, there is still debate on how these changes affect employees' working conditions. We argue that the technical and societal changes put more pressures on employees by contributing to work intensification and increased job insecurity.

New technologies, in particular computerization, enable companies to increase their efficiency in producing goods as well as in delivering services. Just-in-time production, optimal timing for the ordering and delivering of goods and services, and immediate access to customer information are but a few examples for how ICTs make work more efficient. For employees, this can result in a speeding up of the work process and in work intensification (Green and McIntosh 2001). When goods are produced just in time, then periods of stoppage and wasted time jeopardize production outputs and can generate high costs for companies. Therefore, pressures may be put on employees to work at higher speed (Green 2004) and to reduce the time taken for breaks (Roberts 2007), thus contributing to work intensification.

On the other hand, ICTs enable global interconnectedness (Castells 2000) and allow the coordination of economic activities across different locations. This potential of ICTs can be used to set up and control plants and services in foreign

This research was partly supported by grant no.: P23377-G17 from the Austrian Science Fund.

B. Kubicek (✉) • C. Korunka • M. Paškvan • R. Prem • C. Gerdenitsch
Faculty of Psychology, University of Vienna, Vienna, Austria
e-mail: bettina.kubicek@univie.ac.at; christian.korunka@univie.ac.at; matea.paskvan@univie.ac.at; roman.prem@univie.ac.at; cornelia.gerdenitsch@univie.ac.at

C. Korunka and P. Hoonakker (eds.), *The Impact of ICT on Quality of Working Life*, DOI 10.1007/978-94-017-8854-0_3, © Springer Science+Business Media Dordrecht 2014

markets. But with the opening up of new production and sales markets, global interconnectedness also increased competition. These days, production firms and service providers compete not only against local but also against international competitors. To ensure competitive advantages, companies may be pressed to speed up decision processes, shorten product cycles, and accommodate to fluctuations in service need and work cycles (Smith 1997). They try to meet these new demands by implementing more flexible organizational structures (Cascio 2003) and by supplementing permanent staff with a temporal workforce. For employees, this restructuring of the workforce makes permanent positions and stable employment less certain (Beck 2009; Blossfeld et al. 2005), contributing to increased job insecurity (Burchell et al. 2002).

We therefore argue that employers have reorganized work and employment structures in response to greater global competition and the availability of new technologies. The main outcomes of the reorganization are work intensification and job insecurity.

Although increases in work intensity and job security are frequently discussed in the public media and in academia, empirical evidence is still scarce. If empirical evidence exists, as in the case of work intensification, analyses are mainly based on trend data from the late twentieth century. More recent evidence is needed to find out whether work intensification holds on to the present and whether changes in job security are indeed observable. In the present chapter, we provide such evidence and add to previous research on changing working conditions in three ways: First, we take a closer look at more recent data on work intensity. Second, we not only examine trends in work intensity but also trends in job insecurity, thus contributing to a more comprehensive understanding of changing working conditions and their relations to ICTs. Third, we complement trend analyses in working conditions with the modeling of change patterns, thus sensitizing to the importance of disentangling general trends into more specific constellations that take trajectories of change and stability into account.

3.2 Work Intensification and Rising Job Insecurity: Previous Evidence

3.2.1 Work Intensification

Work intensity refers to the amount of effort an employee invests during a working day. It thus needs to be differentiated from the hours spent at work. Working longer hours does not necessarily imply that work intensity has increased. Rather, the amount of work during a working day can remain the same but interruptions or a long hours culture (Chatzitheochari and Arber 2009) may prompt employees to stay longer. By contrast, work intensification or an increase in work intensity occurs if employees feel pressed to complete more tasks within one working day.

This pressure may result, for instance, from tighter deadlines or the pressure to pursue and meet ever-higher goals.

To figure out whether the intensity of work has changed over time, researchers have thus far relied on two different ways of measuring work intensification. They either compared data from comprehensive longitudinal studies in the working domain or asked employees how their effort or pace of work has changed over the past years (e.g., Burchell et al. 2002; Green 2004; Green and McIntosh 2001; Paoli and Merllié 2005). In the first set of studies, work intensification is measured indirectly by comparing employees' self-reported levels of work intensity at different points in time. This can be achieved either by using repeated cross-sectional measures (i.e., trend data) such as the European Working Conditions Surveys (EWCS) or by using repeated measures from the same respondent (i.e., panel data) such as the General Social Survey (GSS) or the International Social Survey (ISS). In the second set of studies, work intensification is measured directly. Employees are asked to indicate whether they experience an increase in the speed of work or in the effort they put into their jobs. This measure was used, for example, in the British Job Insecurity and Work Intensification Survey (JIWIS; Burchell et al. 2002).

Although the way of measuring work intensification varies between these two sets of studies, their results are strikingly similar. Using data from the EWCS, researchers have identified an intensification of work in Europe during the 1990s (Green 2004; Green and McIntosh 2001; Paoli and Merllié 2005). In the EWCS, work intensity was measured by two items named working at high speed and working to tight deadlines. For both items, Paoli and Merllié (2005) reported that intensity of work has increased from 1990 to 2000, yet this intensification was higher between 1990 and 1995 than between 1995 and 2000. In 2000, more than half of the employees reported working at high speed and to tight deadlines (Paoli and Merllié 2005). Using the same empirical data as Paoli and Merllié (2005), Green and McIntosh (2001) additionally analyzed national differences in work intensification between 12 European countries. Work intensification in the 1990s was the strongest in Great Britain followed by Ireland and France. West Germany was the country with the lowest levels of intensification (Green and McIntosh 2001; Paoli and Merllié 2005).

Bringing together the American and European context, Olsen and her colleagues (2010) analyzed trends in perceived job quality focusing on four industrial countries, namely, West Germany, Norway, Great Britain, and the United States. They used data from the ISS to assess job quality which was defined by five dimensions named extrinsic rewards, intrinsic rewards, work intensity, working conditions, and interpersonal relationships. With regard to work intensity, the authors found an increase in all countries in at least one period.

Burchell and his colleagues (2002), who did not compare longitudinal data but asked their respondents directly whether they had experienced an increase in work effort, also found an intensification of work in the JIWIS. They asked employees of manufacturing or service companies located in Great Britain whether the speed of work or the effort they put into their job had changed over the last 5 years. The responses to both items were remarkably similar. In fact, over 60 % of the respondents reported increases, compared to only 5 % who reported decreases.

In sum, researchers have identified an intensification of work in Europe and in the United States in the 1990s with the highest levels in Great Britain. This intensification is described by tight deadlines, working at high speed, and requirements to work hard or under great tension. The main reasons for this intensification are an increased use of ICTs and the force of the product market (Green 2004; Green and McIntosh 2001). Still it is unclear if this intensification holds on to the present, in other words to the first decade of the twenty-first century. To answer this question, we analyzed data from Europe and America collected between 2000 and 2010. Additionally, we focused on groups of employees which are more or less affected by intensification and potential sources of group differences.

3.2.2 Rising Job Insecurity

Apart from contributing to work intensification, international competition and the resulting restructuring of organizations may increase the risk of losing one's job. We therefore also look more closely at job insecurity as another working condition employees might increasingly face. Job insecurity is defined as the subjectively experienced threat of involuntary job loss (Cheng and Chan 2008; Sverke et al. 2002). Within this definition, there are two main elements we want to underline here. First, we want to point out that job insecurity is subjectively experienced. This implies that two employees in the same situation might experience different degrees of job insecurity. Second, we separate job insecurity from actual job loss. Job loss can be described as an immediate situation, whereas job insecurity is experienced on a daily basis over a longer period of time. To examine whether employees perceive job insecurity, most studies use single-item measures asking employees about the perceived likelihood of a job loss in the near future (Sverke et al. 2002).

Research on job insecurity primarily focuses on the effects of perceived job insecurity on psychological and physical variables, showing that high levels of perceived job insecurity negatively affect employees' well-being (for a comprehensive overview, see Cheng and Chan 2008; Sverke et al. 2002). Moreover, employees that feel insecure in their job are more likely to change the job than employees that perceive their job as secure. Those findings indicate that the feeling of a nonsecure job results in various negative outcomes for employees and employers. In contrast to studies on the consequences of job insecurity, less research investigated if levels of perceived job insecurity have changed over time. Yet, there is one central finding, which was reported by the OECD in 1997. Based on data from 21 OECD countries, the report shows that there was a large increase in the number of employees perceiving job insecurity during the 1980s and the 1990s. These findings have been replicated by several researchers (Gottschalk and Moffitt 1999; Green 2003; Green et al. 2000). Green (2003) also compared changes in job insecurity within European countries (Germany and the United Kingdom) and the United States. For all three countries, he found that the amount of perceived job insecurity increased in the early 1990s and fell from 1997 to 2002 (Green 2003).

In sum, researchers have identified a rise in the level of perceived job insecurity in Europe and the United States in the 1980s and the 1990s, followed by a slow decline. As for work intensification, research on trends in perceived job insecurity has not yet been extended beyond the 1990s. The existing studies indicate that employees in the United States experience rather high levels of job insecurity, as do employees in the United Kingdom, who are also those most strongly affected by work intensification. Similar to our approach to work intensification, we analyzed if job insecurity again increases at the beginning of the twenty-first century in Europe and America.

3.3 Changing Working Conditions: New Evidence

We used different sources of empirical data describing working conditions in Europe and America to analyze changes in work intensity and job insecurity. More specifically, we relied on the European Working Conditions Surveys (EWCS), the German Socio-Economic Panel (G-SOEP), and the Health and Retirement Study (HRS).[1]

3.3.1 Work Intensification: Changes in Work Pace and Deadline Rush

To investigate whether work intensity has increased over the past years, we first looked at data from the EWCS. Following Esping-Andersen's (1990) typology of welfare states, we included Germany, Spain, and France as conservative welfare states, Finland as a social democratic welfare state, and the United Kingdom as a liberal welfare state into the analyses. These countries differ with regard to the "de-commodification," the social stratification, and the interplay of the public and the private sector in providing social security. In social democratic welfare states, de-commodification, that is, the degree to which social rights "permit people to

[1] Based on the nature of the data, we pursued two different analytical strategies. The cross-sectional data from the EWCS were analyzed using trend analyses. The longitudinal panel data from the G-SOEP and the HRS were analyzed using growth mixture modeling techniques (Jung and Wickrama 2008; Muthén 2004; Wang and Bodner 2007). For more information about the datasets, see the Appendix.

make their living standards independent of pure market forces" (Esping-Andersen 1990, p. 3), is much stronger than in liberal welfare states. In addition, social benefits are an important political tool in social democratic welfare states because these benefits are thought to diminish inequalities between social classes. Employment protection legislation is also much stronger in social democratic states than in liberal states. We assume that employee rights reduce the pressures that management can impose on their workforce and therefore prevent or slow down work intensification and increasing job insecurity. For example, if dismissal is made difficult by the law, this may reduce employees' perceived job insecurity and management's ability to use the dismissal threat as a means of obtaining more effort from their workforce. We therefore expect that increases in work intensity and job insecurity are stronger in liberal than in social democratic welfare states. Conservative welfare states should be located between liberal and social democratic welfare states because they also have established social rights in order to ensure a living independent of market forces but do not aim at reducing social inequalities as much as social democratic welfare states.

In complementing previous evidence indicating an intensification of work between 1991 and 2000, we investigated data from 2000 onwards. We selected two items focusing on work intensity that were identical in wording and response format in 2000, 2005, and 2010. In these items, participants were asked whether their job involves working at very high speed or to tight deadlines.

Table 3.1 presents means and standard deviations for both work intensity items. As can be seen, trends in work intensity varied among countries. In Germany, Spain, and France, the general trend points towards an increase in work intensity. In these countries, work has intensified between 2000 and 2010. Not only did the pace of work speed up for employees, but also did employees experience the increasing need to work to tight deadlines. For Finland, no general trend in work intensity was observable. Rather, employees' perceptions of work speed and deadline rush fluctuated around relatively high levels. For the United Kingdom, the general trend pointed towards a decrease in work intensity. Although the mean level of employees' work speed did not vary a lot between 1995 and 2000 in the United Kingdom (Paoli and Merllié 2005), it constantly declined thereafter. Likewise, the need to work to tight deadlines decreased constantly from 2000 to 2010.

Since trends in work intensity may not only vary across countries but also across employees' educational level, we also examined the data separately for different skill levels. We used the ISCO code (occupational classification) to differentiate between four skill levels: (1) primary education, (2) secondary education, (3) tertiary education, and (4) tertiary education with university degree. Employees with primary education experienced the strongest increase in work intensity between 2000 and 2010. For example, average levels of reported work speed rose from 3.5 in 2000 to 3.8 in 2010. Likewise, average levels of deadline rush increased from 3.5 in 2000 to 3.8 in 2010 for this group of employees.

Although the European Foundation study contains a large dataset designed to be representative for the participating countries, it does not follow respondents over time. Rather, trend data was collected that does not allow to model individual

Table 3.1 Work intensity in Germany, France, Spain, Finland, and the United Kingdom, 2000–2010

	Working at very high speed			Working to tight deadlines		
Country	2000	2005	2010	2000	2005	2010
Germany	3.53 (2.05)	4.08 (1.93)	3.94 (1.87)	3.86 (1.99)	3.91 (1.90)	3.86 (1.88)
France	3.34 (2.20)	3.24 (2.09)	3.45 (2.12)	3.54 (2.27)	3.53 (2.23)	3.65 (2.20)
Spain	2.83 (1.96)	3.48 (2.04)	3.32 (1.97)	2.84 (2.01)	3.33 (2.08)	3.24 (2.01)
Finland	3.99 (1.83)	4.25 (1.90)	3.89 (1.78)	4.00 (1.98)	4.18 (2.02)	3.97 (1.92)
United Kingdom	3.19 (2.26)	2.98 (2.08)	2.89 (2.10)	4.25 (2.38)	3.94 (2.29)	3.92 (2.26)

Data source: EWCS

Note: Means are presented in the first line; standard deviations are presented in parentheses in the second line

trajectories. We therefore also examined work intensification based on two nationally representative panel datasets. First, we used the G-SOEP to take a closer look at work intensification in Germany. As indicator for work intensity, we analyzed the item "Please think about the past four weeks. How often did you feel hounded or pressed for time during that period?" from the years 2002, 2004, 2006, and 2008. Respondents rated this item on a 5-point rating scale ranging from never to always. We found four distinct groups of work intensity trajectories: The first group was characterized by high and stable levels of work intensity; the second and the fourth groups were characterized by an increase in work intensity. The remaining group was characterized by a decrease in work intensity over time (see Fig. 3.1).

Over 50 % of the employees were classified into a high-level stability group. They reported relatively high levels of time pressure in 2002 which decreased subtly thereafter. Starting at a similar level of time pressure, a second group showed a strong decrease coming to a hold in 2006. Overall, 12 % of the employees were classified into this strong decrease group. A slight increase in time pressure was experienced by 26 % of the employees. Starting at relatively low levels (1.7), their time pressure rose to 2.0 in 2008. Finally, 7 % of the employees were classified into a strong increase group. This group experienced the strongest work intensification. Numerically, time pressure rose from 1.7 to 3.3 for those employees. As for the strong decrease group, the change in time pressure came to a hold in 2006 for employees belonging to the strong increase group. Thereafter, their level of time pressure remained fairly stable.

Employees belonging to the high-level stability group were younger, had more years of education, and were more likely to be female. By contrast, employees belonging to the slight increase group were older, less educated, and more likely to be male.

The findings obtained for Germany, a conservative welfare state, suggest that employees were not equally affected by work intensification. Rather, groups of workers exist that were actually confronted with less work intensity. In an attempt to test the generalizability of this finding, we also examined trajectories of work intensity using data from a liberal welfare state. Specifically, we used data from America collected biannually in the context of the Health and Retirement Study.

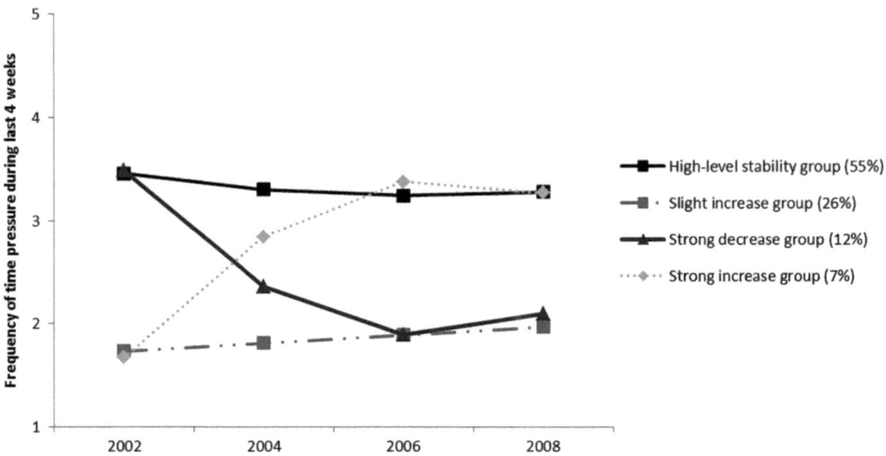

Fig. 3.1 Groups of work intensity trajectories (Data source: G-SOEP, $N = 24{,}239$)

In our analyses, we focused on the six most recent waves of data collection between 2000 and 2010. Among the items about work characteristics, one item was appropriate to measure work intensity, namely, "My job involves a lot of stress." At each measurement, respondents were asked to assess the item, using a 4-point rating scale ranging from strongly disagree to strongly agree. In order to compare trajectories of work intensity with frequency of ICT use, we also included the item "My job requires me to work with computers." in our analyses.

Among American employees, we found three work intensity trajectories (see Fig. 3.2, solid lines). The majority of respondents (53 %) were classified into a low-level stability group. Although these employees showed a slight decrease in work intensity between 2000 and 2004 followed by a slight increase from 2006 onwards, their work intensity oscillated around rather low levels. The second group consisted of 36 % of the respondents. The growth curve for this group was located on a high level and showed an inverted U-shape. Despite their rather high levels of work intensity in 2000, this group of employees experienced even an intensification of work until 2006, which came to a hold thereafter. A small number of employees (11 %) were classified into a strong decrease group, whose work intensity fell from 3.4 in 2000 to 2.0 in 2010.

Again, we were interested in differences between the three groups of work intensity trajectories. In addition to age, gender, and educational level, we investigated whether the three groups differ in their frequency of computer usage. As can be seen in Fig. 3.2, the trajectories of work intensity were somewhat related to the frequency of computer usage (dotted lines). Employees belonging to the low-level stability group reported less frequent use of computers at work than the other groups. They also were older and less educated. By contrast, employees classified into the slight increase trajectory on a high level of work intensity reported more frequent computer usage and were younger, higher educated, and more likely to be female.

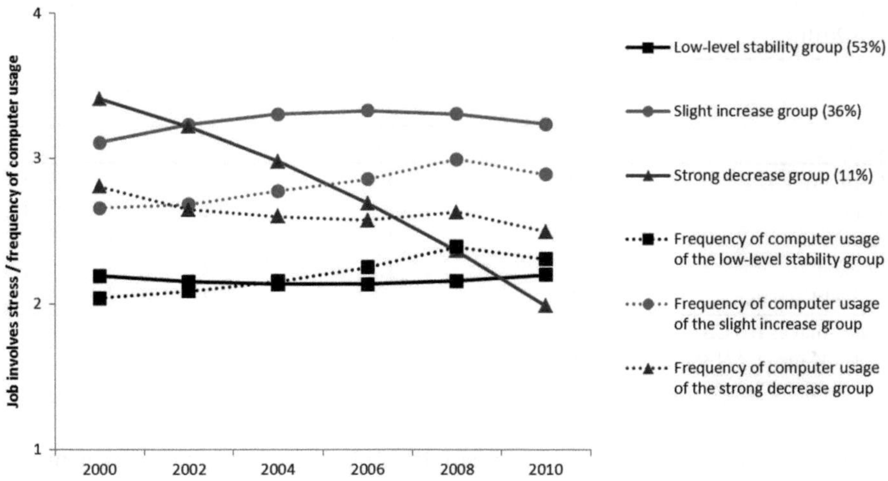

Fig. 3.2 Groups of work intensity trajectories (*solid lines*) and frequency of computer usage (*dotted lines*) (Data source: HRS, $N = 8{,}651$)

Taken together, the findings suggest that work intensification affects employees in modern Western societies, but they also suggest that this trend is far from being universal. First, work intensification varied by country with workers in conservative welfare states being the most affected ones. Second, work intensification varied by groups of employees. In Germany, workers experiencing work intensification were less educated, older, and more likely to be male. Moreover, the intensification started from a rather low level of time pressure. In America, the picture was rather different: Here, work intensification was experienced by workers with already high levels of work intensity. Moreover, those affected by work intensification were higher educated, younger, and more likely to be female. The HRS data also showed that the amount of computer use was related to work intensification, i.e., groups with more frequent computer use were more likely to be confronted with work intensification. Despite these differences, the work intensity trajectories found for German and American workers assumed comparable shapes. In both countries, most workers were polarized into two separate groups: a high intensity group on the one hand and a low intensity group on the other hand.

3.3.1.1 Changes in Job Insecurity

To investigate whether job insecurity had changed over the past years, we again looked at data from the EWCS first. In contrast to work intensity, job insecurity was only assessed in 2005 and 2010 using the following question: "I might lose my job in the next six months." Respondents were asked to answer the question on a five-point rating scale ranging from strongly disagree to strongly agree.

Table 3.2 Job insecurity in Germany, France, Spain, Finland, and the United Kingdom, 2005 and 2010

	Job insecurity			
	2005		2010	
Country	*M*	SD	*M*	SD
Germany	2.2	1.1	2.0	1.1
France	1.7	1.1	2.0	1.2
Spain	1.9	1.2	2.7	1.2
Finland	1.9	1.3	2.2	1.3
United Kingdom	1.7	0.9	2.0	1.1

Data source: EWCS
Note: *M* mean, *SD* standard deviation

Table 3.2 presents means and standard deviations for the job insecurity item. As can be seen, trends in job insecurity were similar among countries. In Spain, France, Finland, and the United Kingdom, the general trend pointed towards an increase in job insecurity. Only in Germany perceived job insecurity decreased from 2005 to 2010.

Next, we analyzed whether job insecurity varies according to employees' educational level. Based on the ISCO code, we again distinguished four skill levels: primary, secondary, and tertiary education and tertiary education with university degree. As for work intensification, employees with primary education experienced the strongest increase in job insecurity from 2005 to 2010. For this group of employees, the level of reported job insecurity rose from 2.1 in 2005 to 2.4 in 2010.

Again, we were interested in whether these general trends split up into more concrete change patterns. We therefore analyzed data from the G-SOEP and the HRS to obtain information on trajectories of job insecurity. The G-SOEP comprised the following question to measure job insecurity: "What is the chance that the following occupational changes occur within the next two years? That you lose your job." Respondents were asked to answer the question using a ten-point rating scale ranging from 0 to 100 %. Items from the years 2001, 2003, 2005, 2007, and 2009 were included in the analyses.

We identified six distinct groups of job insecurity trajectories (see Fig. 3.3). Nearly 80 % of the respondents experienced an increase in job insecurity in Germany between 2001 and 2009. About half of the sample (52 %) started at a very low level of perceived job insecurity but reported increasing chances of losing the job, indicating a slight increase trajectory from a low level. Additional 19 % of the respondents were classified into a slight increase trajectory from a mid-level. They differed from the first group by starting at a higher level of job insecurity. On average, they estimated the chance of losing their job with 23 % in 2001; by 2009, that estimation has risen to 27 %. A strong increase in job insecurity was experienced by 9 % of the respondents; this increase followed an inverted U-shape. Compared to the two slight increase trajectories, the members of this group also started at a rather low level of perceived job insecurity in 2001. They estimated the

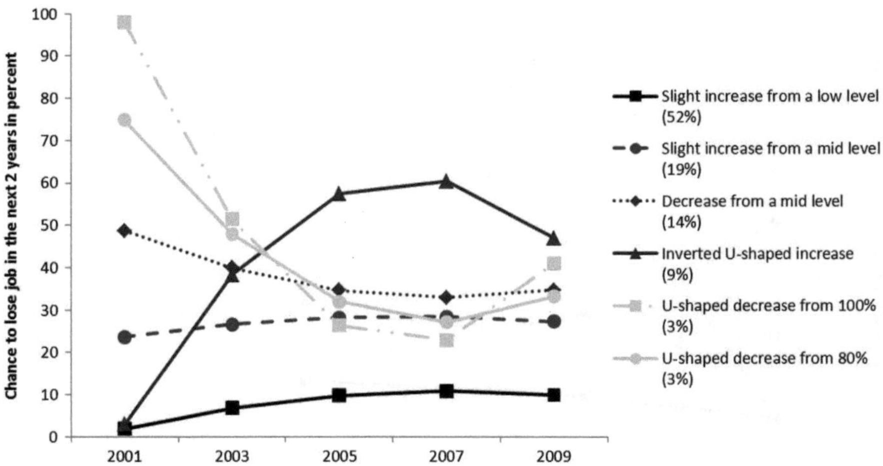

Fig. 3.3 Groups of job insecurity trajectories (Data source: G-SOEP)

chance of losing their job to be 3 %. By 2007, the perceived risk of a job loss had risen to 60 % and had fallen thereafter to 47 % in 2009. On average, the respondents classified into this inverted U-shaped increase trajectory reported the highest levels of perceived job insecurity in 2009. The remaining 20 % of the sample were classified into various decrease trajectories.

Employees belonging to the slight increase trajectory starting at very low levels of job insecurity in 2001 were older and better educated, as compared to the other groups. Those belonging to the inverted U-shaped increase trajectory were, on average, less educated and younger than members of the other groups.

As for changes in work intensity, we also examined data from the HRS, to assess the generalizability of the various job insecurity trajectories. The question to measure job insecurity enclosed in the HRS dataset had a similar wording to the item in the G-SOEP dataset. Specifically, respondents were asked to indicate the chances that they will lose their job during the next year. Again, the rating scale was in percent and ranged from 0 % (absolutely no chance) to 100 % (absolutely certain). We included data from 2000, 2002, 2004, 2006, and 2010 in the analysis. (Unfortunately, job insecurity was not measured in 2008.)

For employees in America, we found five groups of job insecurity trajectories (see Fig. 3.4). Apart from one exception, a similar pattern of change trajectories emerged as for employees in Germany. The majority of the American respondents (nearly 75 %) experienced an increase in job insecurity between 2000 and 2010. Again, this group split up into a slight increase trajectory from almost 0 %, including 64 % of the respondents, and an inverted U-shaped increase trajectory, including 10 % of the respondents. The various decrease trajectories cover 17 % of the sample: 11 % belonged to the decrease trajectory from about 50 % and 6 % belonged to the U-shaped decrease trajectory from almost 90 %. For a final group, consisting of 9 % of the respondents, job insecurity remained relatively stable during the past decade.

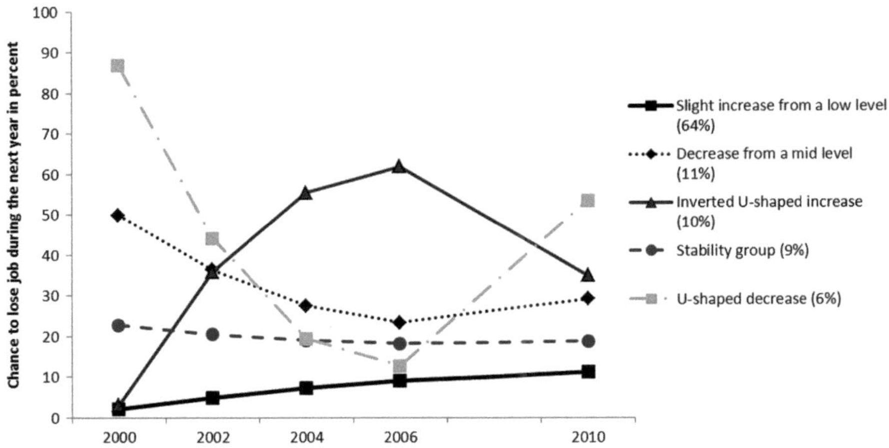

Fig. 3.4 Groups of job insecurity trajectories (Data source: HRS)

Members of the job insecurity trajectories differed with regard to educational level, but not with regard to age or gender. The frequency of computer usage correlated somewhat with group membership. Employees belonging to the slight increase trajectory were on average higher educated. By contrast, employees belonging to the inverted U-shaped increase trajectory were the least educated. Although the frequency of computer use rose in all groups from 2000 to 2010, employees with the strong (inverted U-shaped) increase in job insecurity reported less frequent computer usage than the other group members.

Taken together, the findings suggest that job insecurity has risen for most employees in Europe and America over the past decade. Although increases in the chance of a job loss ranged between rather low levels for a majority of employees, a non-negligible proportion of employees was confronted with a tremendous rise in perceived job insecurity. Thus, trends in job insecurity seem to be more universal than trends in work intensification. Despite some variation across countries, employees in liberal and conservative welfare states experienced similar changes in job insecurity over the last decade, as was shown by comparable patterns of change trajectories. As for work intensification, particular groups of workers were more likely to be affected by rising job insecurity. First, well-educated workers who have thus far been in rather stable employment relations perceived a slight increase in job insecurity. Second, strong increases in job insecurity were reported by workers with low educational levels and low frequencies of computer use.

3.4 Conclusion

Changes in work intensity and job insecurity in Europe and America were examined. Using data from the EWCS, we showed that trends in work intensity vary among European countries. Between 2000 and 2010, an intensification of work occurred in conservative welfare states (i.e., Germany, France, and Spain), but not in the United Kingdom or Finland. For the United Kingdom, we even observed a general decline in work intensity from 2000 to 2010. Concerning job insecurity, the EWCS data showed nearly identical increases across European countries. A rise in job insecurity from 2005 to 2010 was shown in social democratic (Finland), liberal (United Kingdom), and in most conservative welfare states (besides Germany).

Using data from two large-scale and nationally representative longitudinal datasets, namely, the G-SOEP and the HRS, we disentangled these general trends of work intensification and rising job insecurity into more specific change trajectories. For both work intensity and job insecurity, the modeling of change patterns resulted in distinct classes of trajectories, suggesting that employees differ in the extent to which they are confronted with changing working conditions. These change trajectories showed that nearly 35 % of German workers have experienced an increase in work intensity over the past decade. For the remaining 65 % of the workers, work intensity had remained nearly stable or had even declined from 2000 to 2010. The HRS data indicated that also about 35 % of American workers have experienced an increase in work intensity from 2006 onwards. Interestingly, different groups of workers were affected by work intensification in Germany and America. In Germany, workers affected by work intensification were less educated, older, and more likely to be male than workers who experienced no change or a decline in work intensity. In America, workers most affected by work intensification were higher educated, younger, and more likely to be female. Although these workers were already confronted with relatively high levels of work intensity in 2000, they even reported an intensification of work from 2000 to 2006. Interestingly, workers reporting high but stable levels of work intensity in Germany were also better educated, younger, and more likely to be female, as compared to workers belonging to the other groups of work intensity trajectories.

With regard to job insecurity, we found that the perceived risk to lose one's job in the near future has risen for a majority of employees in Germany and America. Although these increases ranged between rather low levels for most employees, a non-negligible proportion of employees (around 10 %) was confronted with a tremendous rise in perceived job insecurity. Slight increases on generally low levels of job insecurity were perceived by well-educated workers who have thus far been in rather stable employment relations. Strong increases in job insecurity were reported by less-educated workers.

Previous research based on the EWCS showed that intensity of work has increased from 1990 to 2000 (Paoli and Merllié 2005). The present study supplements this finding by showing that the trend towards an intensification of work holds on to the year 2010. Besides this general trend, we also found that changes in work intensity vary considerably across countries. Whereas workers in Germany, Spain, and France experienced an intensification of work, no such trend was observable for Finland and the United Kingdom. In Finland, levels of work intensity remained rather stable, and in the United Kingdom, we found a decline in the intensity of work from 2000 to 2010. In combining previous and our results, one may conclude that work intensification occurred earlier in liberal welfares and that this trend towards an intensification of work came to a hold in recent years. Conservative welfare states currently seem to catch up with liberal states, because work intensification has been more pronounced in Germany, Spain, and France over the last decade than in the United Kingdom.

With regard to changes in job insecurity, our findings are generally in support of previous evidence stating that workers in Europe and America are confronted with increasing risks of losing their job (Burchell et al. 2002; Erlinghagen 2007; Green 2003; OECD 1997). In addition to less-educated workers, in recent years also, highly educated workers perceive an increasing risk of losing their job in the near future. Thus, stable employment seems to become less certain (Blossfeld et al. 2005). This trend seems to lower the likelihood of linear upward mobility and may promote more patchy or protean careers (Briscoe et al. 2006; Hall 2004).

What do the observed trends tell us about the role of ICTs for work intensification and increased job insecurity? First of all, one has to keep in mind that ICTs are currently used in practically every workplace in the Western world, which is also confirmed by the HRS data. The rapid increase in the use of ICTs started in the mid-1980s in office workplaces and expanded to nearly all types of work in the last decade (see Chap. 2). Thus, one can expect that ICTs play at least a certain role in the observed changes in working conditions. As described by Hartmut Rosa (see Chap. 4), technological acceleration is one of the main triggers of social acceleration, which affects not only the world of work but practically every part of life in Western societies. In line with this argument, we found correlations between work intensification and the amount of computer use over time in the HRS data. These findings suggest that ICT usage is indeed associated with work intensification.

The analyses presented here also show that there are certain "risk groups" experiencing a stronger increase in work intensity compared with other groups. The most pronounced risk groups are workers with low educational levels. One may expect that this group has also less knowledge and experience with regard to computer use (see also Weber and Zink, Chap. 11). Workers having less experience and therefore less competence in ICT use also seem to be more affected by job insecurity, because they have less job opportunities as compared to a (younger) generation of well-educated "digital natives" (Prensky 2001).

All in all, one may conclude that a polarizing effect of ICT use (Korunka et al. 1995) still exists at least to some extent. Certain groups of workers (typically younger and better-educated employees; the "digital natives" generation) may benefit from their ICT competencies by having higher job security. On the other hand, elder and less-educated workers still do not seem to be able to take full advantage of the potentials of ICTs. Our results also suggest that women are no longer a risk group with regard to ICT usage. As compared to the early days of ICTs (see Korunka et al. 1995), women have rapidly catched up with regard to their ICT knowledge and competencies. But this development seems to come with a price, because female workers with high levels of computer usage were more likely to experience work intensification – at least in America.

Appendix

The EWCS is one activity of the European Foundation for the Improvement of Living and Working Conditions. The survey started in 1990/1991 and aims at gathering information about working conditions across different sectors and occupational levels in several European countries (ranging from 12 in 1990/1991 to 34 in 2010; Eurofond 2012). The EWCS is a trend dataset, which covers a random sample of employed and self-employed workers every 5 years. It is representative according to occupation, gender, age, sector, and company size (Paoli 1997). In 1991, 12,500 workers were interviewed; in 2010, 44,000 workers participated in the survey. Among other aspects, participants were asked about their working time, nature of work, work organization, and the impact of work on their health. For the present study, we used data from 2000, 2005, and 2010.

The G-SOEP has been initially conducted by the German Institute for Economic Research in 1984 and has been repeated annually since then. Every year, about 11,000 households participate in the study and provide information about, e.g., household composition, occupational biographies, employment, and earnings. For our analyses, we used data from 2001 to 2009 focusing on the work context (German Socio-Economic Panel, G-SOEP, 2010).

The HRS is a longitudinal panel study conducted by the Institute for Social Research (ISR) at the University of Michigan that collects data of about 26,000 Americans aged 50 years and older (Burkhauser and Gertler 1995). The panel was launched in 1992 and has been conducted biannually since then. Through interviews, data are – among other aspects – gathered on health, work, retirement, income, wealth, and family characteristics. In the present analyses, we focused on data from 2000 onwards.

References

Beck, U. (2009). *World at risk*. Cambridge: Polity Press.

Blossfeld, H.-P., Mills, M., Klijzing, E., & Kurz, K. (2005). *Globalization, uncertainty and youth in society*. London: Routledge.

Briscoe, J. P., Hall, D. T., & Frautschy DeMuth, R. L. (2006). Protean and boundary less careers: An empirical exploration. *Journal of Vocational Behavior, 69*, 30–47.

Burchell, B., Ladipo, D., & Wilkinson, F. (2002). *Job insecurity and work intensification*. London: Routledge.

Burkhauser, R. V., & Gertler, P. J. (1995). Introduction to special issue on the health and retirement survey/data quality and early results. *The Journal of Human Resources, 30* (Suppl.), 1–6.
Cascio, W. F. (1995). Whither industrial and organizational psychology in a changing world of work? *American Psychologist, 50*(11), 928–939.
Cascio, W. F. (2003). Changes in workers, work, and organizations. In W. C. Borman, D. R. Ilgen, & R. J. Klimoski (Eds.), *Handbook of psychology* (Industrial and organizational psychology, Vol. 12, pp. 401–422). Hoboken: Wiley.
Castells, M. (2000). *The rise of the network society*. Oxford: Wiley-Blackwell.
Chatzitheochari, S., & Arber, S. (2009). Lack of sleep, work and the long hours culture: Evidence from the UK time use survey. *Work, Employment and Society, 23*(1), 30–48.
Cheng, G. H. L., & Chan, D. K. S. (2008). Who suffers more from job insecurity? A meta-analytic review. *Applied Psychology: An International Review, 57*(2), 272–303.
Erlinghagen, M. (2007). Self-perceived job insecurity and social context: A multi-level analysis of 17 European countries. *European Sociological Review, 24*, 183–197.
Esping-Andersen, G. (1990). *The three worlds of welfare capitalism*. Cambridge: Polity Press.
Eurofond. (2012). *Fifth European Working Conditions Survey*. Luxembourg: Publications Office of the European Union.
German Social-Economic Panel (G-SOEP). (2010). *Data for years 1984–2009*, Version 26. SOEP.
Gottschalk, P., & Moffitt, R. (1999). Changes in job instability and insecurity using monthly survey data. *Journal of Labor Economics, 17*(4), 91–126.
Green, F. (2003). *The rise and decline of job insecurity* (Studies in economics 0305). Canterbury: Department of Economics, University of Kent.
Green, F. (2004). Why has work effort become more intense? *Industrial Relations, 43*, 709–741.
Green, F., & McIntosh, S. (2001). The intensification of work in Europe. *Labour Economics, 8*, 291–308.
Green, F., Felstead, A., & Burchell, B. (2000). Job insecurity and the difficulty of regaining employment: An empirical study of unemployment expectations. *Oxford Bulletin of Economics and Statistics, 62*, 855–883.
Hall, D. T. (2004). The protean career: A quarter-century journey. *Journal of Vocational Behavior, 65*, 1–13.
Jung, T., & Wickrama, K. A. S. (2008). An introduction to latent class growth analysis and growth mixture modeling. *Social and Personality Psychology Compass, 2*, 302–317.
Korunka, C., Weiss, A., Karetta, B., & Huemer, K. H. (1995). The effect of new technologies on job satisfaction and psychosomatic complaints. *Applied Psychology: An International Review, 44*(2), 123–142.
Muthén, B. O. (2004). Latent variable analysis: Growth mixture modeling and related techniques for longitudinal data. In D. Kaplan (Ed.), *Handbook of quantitative methodology for the social sciences* (pp. 345–368). Newbury Park: Sage.
OECD. (1997). Is job insecurity on the increase in OECD countries? In *OECD employment outlook July* (pp. 129–153). Paris: Organization for Economic Cooperation and Development.
Olsen, K. M., Kalleber, A. L., & Nesheim, T. (2010). Perceived job quality in the United States, Great Britain, Norway and West Germany, 1989–2005. *European Journal of Industrial Relations, 16*, 221–240.
Paoli, P. (1997). *Second European Survey on Working Conditions*. Dublin: European Foundation for the Improvement of Living and Working Conditions.
Paoli, P., & Merllié, D. (2005). *Eurofound. Ten years of working conditions in the European Union*. Luxembourg: European Foundation for the Improvement of Living and Working Conditions.
Prensky, M. (2001). Digital natives, digital immigrants. *On the Horizon, 9*, 1–6.
Roberts, K. (2007). Work-life balance – The sources of the contemporary problem and the probable outcomes. *Employee Relations, 29*(4), 334–351.
Smith, V. (1997). New forms of work organization. *Annual Review of Sociology, 23*, 315–339.

Sverke, M., Hellgren, J., & Näswall, K. (2002). No security: A meta-analysis and review of job insecurity and its consequences. *Journal of Occupational Health Psychology, 7*(3), 242–264.

Wang, M., & Bodner, T. E. (2007). Growth mixture modeling: Identifying and predicting unobserved subpopulations with longitudinal data. *Organizational Research Methods, 10*, 635–656.

Chapter 4
From Work-Life to Work-Age Balance? Acceleration, Alienation, and Appropriation at the Workplace

Hartmut Rosa

4.1 Introduction

A central, defining fact of modern societies is the fact that a modern society can only stabilize and reproduce itself dynamically. This means that it needs growth, acceleration, and (increasing rates of) innovation in order to maintain its structure, to keep the status quo. Most obviously, this is true for the economic sphere, where the absence of growth and innovation immediately results in decay and crisis, but it is also true for the realms of politics and the welfare state, and even for the production of science and the arts, etc. Moreover, the logic of increase and augmentation also is a strong cultural moment in modern societies: Social actors inevitably strive for an increase in wealth but also for an increase in the range of options and contacts. We can call this the escalatory logic of modernity. As I have tried to argue in my book *Social Acceleration: A New Theory of Modernity* (Rosa 2013), this results in an all-encompassing process of speedup that transforms the material, the social, and the mental worlds at ever higher rates. Since we can increase the number of goods we produce and consume (the average European or North American household today contains about 10,000 objects vs. a few hundred in 1900), the number of options for action, and the number of contacts almost indefinitely, whereas the time we can apply to all these goods, options, and contacts virtually remains the same (namely, 24 h a day or 365 days a year), the escalatory logic of modernity results in an ever-increasing time scarcity: Time cannot be increased, it can only be condensed or compressed, and this is what we all try to do in our lives.

In this chapter, I will first summarize the core elements (Sect. 4.2.1) and the driving motors of this ongoing process of social acceleration (Sect. 4.2.2), before

H. Rosa (✉)
Institute of Sociology, University of Jena, Jena, Germany
e-mail: Hartmut.rosa@uni-jena.de

C. Korunka and P. Hoonakker (eds.), *The Impact of ICT on Quality of Working Life*, DOI 10.1007/978-94-017-8854-0_4, © Springer Science+Business Media Dordrecht 2014

I then go on to identify some core consequences for the organization of the workplace and the work life (Sect. 4.2.3).

4.2 Social Acceleration

Even though the notion that in modern life "everything" seems to speed up incessantly has been quite widespread for at least two centuries (from Marx' and Engels' observation in the communist manifesto that "all that is solid melts into air" to Henry Adams' "law of acceleration" (2009) and James Gleick's best seller *Faster: The Acceleration of Just About Everything* (1999)), the concepts of speed and/or acceleration have virtually been absent from social theories about modernity so far. So what is dearly needed is a systematic theory and a sound concept of social acceleration.

The most obvious question such a theory has to pose is astonishingly difficult to answer: What is, in fact, accelerating in modern society? Surely, it can't be everything. The mere evidence of traffic jams and lengthening educational careers is enough to demonstrate that some processes even slow down.

In the following, I present an analytic framework that will allow a theoretically thorough and empirically justifiable (or at least contestable) definition of what it could mean for a society to accelerate and of the ways in which Western societies can be understood as acceleration societies.

Quite evidently, there is no single, universal pattern of acceleration that speeds up everything. To the contrary, some things slow down, while others stubbornly resist all attempts to make them go faster, like the common cold. Nevertheless, there are certainly many social phenomena to which the concept of acceleration can properly be applied. Athletes seem to be running and swimming faster and faster; fast food, speed dating, power naps, and drive-through funerals seem to testify our resolve to speed up the pace of everyday actions, computers compute at ever higher speeds, transport and communication need only a fraction of the time they took a century ago, people appear to sleep less (some scientists found that the average sleeping time decreased by 2 h since the nineteenth century and by 30 min since the 1970s (Garhammer 1999, p. 378)), and even our neighbors seem to move in and out of their flats more frequently.

But even if we can demonstrate that these changes are not accidental but follow a systematic pattern, is there anything these very different processes have in common such that they can be brought under the one concept of social acceleration? When looking more closely at this range of phenomena, it becomes apparent that we can separate them into three analytically as well as empirically distinct categories, namely, technological acceleration, the acceleration of social change, and the acceleration of the pace of life. In the following, I will first present these three categories of acceleration. In the next section, I will explore the connection between the different spheres of acceleration and the mechanisms or motors that lie behind them.

4.2.1 Forms of Social Acceleration

4.2.1.1 Technological Acceleration

The first, most obvious and most measurable form of acceleration is the intentional speeding up of goal-directed processes of transport, communication, and production that can be defined as technological acceleration. Obviously, the introduction of information and communication technologies (ICT) plays a crucial role in contemporary processes of this sort: These technologies not only help to vastly accelerate many processes of work and production but also increase the tempo of communication. Furthermore, in many ways, these technologies have replaced processes of (physical) transport. In addition, new forms of organization and administration which are intended to speed up operations also count as instances of technological acceleration in the sense defined here, i.e., as instances of intentional, goal-directed acceleration. Although it is not always easy to measure the average speed of these processes (which is far more important for the analysis of the social impact of acceleration than the maximum speeds), the general tendency in this realm is undeniable. Thus, the speed of communication is said to have increased by 107, the speed of personal transport by 102, and the speed of data processing by 1,010 (Geißler 1999, p. 89).

It is predominantly this aspect of acceleration that is at the center of Paul Virilio's "dromology," a narrative of historical acceleration which proceeds from the revolution in transport to that in transmission and finally to the impending "transplantation" revolution dawning in the emergent possibilities of biotechnology (Virilio 1997, pp. 9–15). The effects of technological acceleration on social reality are certainly tremendous. In particular, they completely transformed the "space-time regime" of society, i.e., the perception and organization of space and time in social life. Thus, the "natural" (i.e., anthropological) priority of space over time in human perception, which is rooted in our sense organs, and the effects of gravity allowing for an immediate distinction of "above" and "below," "in front of" and "behind," but not of "sooner" and "later," seem to have been inverted: In the age of globalization and the u-topicality of the Internet, time is increasingly conceived as compressing or even annihilating space (e.g., Harvey 1990, pp. 201–210). Space, it seems, virtually "contracts" by the speed of transport and communication. Thus, measured by the time it takes to cross the distance from, say, London to New York, space has shrunk from the preindustrial age of sailing ships to the time of jet planes to less than 1/60th of its original size, i.e., from about 3 weeks to about 8 h.

In this process, space in many respects loses its significance for orientation in the late modern world. Operations and developments are no longer located and actual locations such as hotels, banks, universities, or industrial compounds tend to become "non-lieux," i.e., places without history, identity, or relation (Augé 1992).[1]

[1] Harvey, however, referring to an inverse spatialization of time, cautions us to not dismiss space too quickly (Harvey 1990, pp. 272f).

4.2.1.2 Acceleration of Social Change

When novelists, scientists, journalists, and ordinary men and women since the eighteenth century have observed the dynamization of Western culture, society, or history, they were most often not so much concerned with the spectacular technological advancements, but rather, they appeared puzzled by the accelerated processes of social change that rendered social constellations and structures as well as patterns of action and orientation unstable and ephemeral. It is this increasing transformation of the patterns of social association, of forms of practice, and the substance of (practically relevant) knowledge that defines the second category of social acceleration, i.e., the acceleration of social change.

Whereas phenomena of the first category can be described as acceleration processes within society, the phenomena of this second category could be classified as accelerations of society itself. The underlying idea is that rates of change themselves are changing. Thus, attitudes and values as well as fashions and lifestyles; social relations and obligations as well as groups, classes, or milieus; and social languages as well as forms of practice and habits are said to change at ever-increasing rates.

However, empirically measuring the rates of social change remains a hard-to-meet challenge, not least because there is little agreement in sociology as to what the relevant indicators of change are and when alterations or variations actually constitute a genuine or "basic" social change. Therefore, I suggest that in order to develop a systematic sociology of social acceleration, we should make use of the concept of a "contraction of the present" (Gegenwartsschrumpfung) to gain a yardstick for the empirical measurement of the rates of change. This concept was developed by the German philosopher Hermann Lübbe who claims that Western societies experience an ongoing contraction of the present as a consequence of the accelerating rates of cultural and social innovation (Lübbe 2009). His measure is as simple as it is instructive: For Lübbe, the past is defined as that which no longer holds/is no longer valid, while the future denotes that which does not yet hold/is not yet valid. The present, then, is the time span for which (to use an idea developed by Reinhart Koselleck (2009)) the horizons of experience and expectation overlap. Only within these time spans of relative stability can we draw on past experiences to orient our actions and infer conclusions from the past with regard to the future. Only within these time spans we find some certainty of orientation, evaluation, and expectation. In other words, social acceleration is defined by an increase in the decay rates of the reliability of experiences and expectations and by the contraction of the time spans definable as the "present." Now, obviously, we can apply this measure of stability and change to social and cultural institutions and practices of all kinds: The present contracts in the political as well as the occupational, the technological as well as the aesthetic, and the normative as well as the scientific or cognitive dimensions, i.e., in cultural as well as in structural respects. As a rule of thumb test, the reader may simply consider the decay rates of his or her everyday practical knowledge: What are the time spans for which he or she can assume stability for things such as the addresses and phone numbers of friends or partners; the opening hours of shops and offices; the rates of insurances and telephone companies; and the popularity of TV stars, parties, and politicians, of jobs people hold, and of relationships they are engaged in?

But how could we verify this sense of contraction empirically? We can take as a starting point of reference those institutions that organize the processes of production and reproduction, since they appear to form the basic structures of society. For Western societies since the early modern period, these essentially include the family and the occupational system. In fact, most studies of social change focus on exactly these domains, along with political institutions and technology. I will later turn to the question of how technological and social change, and hence technological acceleration and the acceleration of social change, are interrelated. For the moment, I want to suggest that change in these two realms – family and work – has accelerated from an intergenerational pace in early modern society to a generational pace in "classical modernity" to an intragenerational pace in late modernity. Thus, the ideal-typical family structure in agrarian society tended to remain stable over centuries, with generational turnover leaving the basic structure intact. In classical modernity (roughly between 1850 and 1970), this structure was built to last for just a generation: It was organized around a couple and tended to disperse with their death. In late modernity, there is a growing tendency for family life cycles to last less than an individual life-span: Increasing rates of divorce and remarriage are the most obvious evidence for this (Laslett 1988, p. 33). Similarly, in the world of work, in pre- and early modern societies, the father's occupation was inherited by the son – again, potentially over many generations. In classical modernity, occupational structures tended to change with generations: Sons (and later on daughters, too) were free to choose their own profession, but they generally chose only once, i.e., for the whole of a lifetime. By contrast, in late modernity, occupations no longer extend over the whole of a work life; jobs change at a higher rate than generations. Thus, according to Richard Sennett, employees with higher education in the USA change their jobs about 11 times in the course of a lifetime (Sennett 1998). Consequently, as Daniel Cohen concludes, "whoever begins a career at Microsoft has not the slightest idea where it will end. Whoever started it at Ford or Renault could be well-nigh certain that it will finish in the same place."[2]

In this sense, to formulate the argument more generally, the stability of social institutions and practices could serve as a yardstick for the acceleration (or deceleration) of social change. In the work of authors like Peter Wagner, Zygmunt Bauman, Richard Sennett and Ulrich Beck, Anthony Giddens, and Scott Lash, theoretical as well as empirical support can be found for the thesis that institutional stability is generally on the decline in late modern societies (Bauman 2000; Beck et al. 1997; Wagner 1994).

[2] Quoted in Bauman (2000, p. 116).

4.2.1.3 Acceleration of the Pace of Life

Perhaps the most pressing and astonishing facet of social acceleration is the spectacular and epidemic "time famine" of modern (Western) societies. In modernity, social actors increasingly feel that they are running out of time, that they are short on time. It seems as if time was perceived like a raw material which is consumed like oil and which is, therefore, getting more and more scarce and expensive. This perception of time lies at the heart of a third type of acceleration in Western societies that is neither logically nor causally entailed by the first two. Quite to the contrary, at least at first glance, this time hunger appears to be totally paradoxical with respect to technological acceleration. This third category is the acceleration of the pace of (social) life, which has been postulated again and again in the process of modernity (e.g., by Georg Simmel (1978, pp. 470–512) or, more recently, by Robert Levine (1997)). It can be defined as an increase in the number of episodes of action or experience per unit of time, i.e., it is the consequence of the desire or felt need to do more things in less time. As such, it is the central focus of much of the discussion about cultural acceleration and the alleged need for deceleration.

But how could we measure the pace of life?[3] In my view, attempts to do so can follow a "subjective" or an "objective" approach, with the most promising route probably being a combination of the two. On the "subjective" side, an acceleration of the speed of life (as against the speed of life itself) is likely to have the observed effects on individuals' experience of time: It will cause people to consider time as scarce, to feel hurried and under time pressure and stress. Typically, people will feel that time goes by faster than before and they will complain that "everything" goes too fast; they will worry that they might not be able to keep up with the pace of social life. Hence, the fact that this complaint has accompanied modernity ever since the eighteenth century does not prove that the speed of life was high all the time – in fact, it does not help to determine the "speed of life" at all – but it does hint at its progressive acceleration. As we might expect, empirical studies indicate that in fact people in Western societies do feel under heavy time pressure and they do complain about the scarcity of time. These feelings seem to have increased over recent decades (Geißler 1999, p. 92; Garhammer 1999, pp. 448–455; Levine 1997, pp. 196f.), making plausible the argument that the "digital revolution" and the processes of globalization amount to yet another wave of social acceleration.

On the "objective" side, an acceleration of the "speed of life" can be measured in two ways. First, it should lead to a measurable contraction of the time spent on definable episodes or "units" of action like eating, sleeping, going for a walk,

[3] American sociologist Robert Levine and his team recently conducted a cross-cultural comparative empirical study in which three indicators for the speed of life were used: the speed of walking in inner cities, the time it takes to buy a stamp in a post office, and the exactness of public clocks. For a number of reasons I have discussed at length in Rosa (2013), this approach can at best serve as a very rough preliminary attempt. It certainly remains very unsatisfactory as an instrument in a thorough sociological analysis of the temporal structures of late modernity.

playing, talking to one's family, etc., since "acceleration" implies that we do more things in less time. This is a domain where time-use studies could prove of the highest importance. And in fact, some studies have found plenty of evidence for this: Thus, for example, there appears to be a clear tendency to eat faster, sleep less, and communicate less with our families than our ancestors did.[4] Nevertheless, one needs to be very careful with such results – first, because the data for longitudinal time-use studies is extremely limited; second, because we always find counter-instances (e.g., the time fathers spend with their children in at least some sections of Western societies is clearly increasing) without being able to adequately determine the significance of these findings; and third, because it is frequently unclear what drives the measured accelerations (e.g., that people on average sleep less today than previous generations did might simply be attributable to the fact that they grow older and don't work as hard physically).

The second way to "objectively" explore the acceleration of the pace of life consists in measuring the social tendency to "compress" actions and experiences, i.e., to do and experience more within a given period of time by reducing the pauses and intervals and/or by doing more things simultaneously, like cooking, watching TV, and making a phone call at the same time. The latter strategy, of course, is called "multitasking." This process of compression has been greatly enhanced and supported by the introduction of ICT: These technologies, for example, serve to work, to communicate, and to get information while traveling, and they enable us to seamlessly combine all sorts of activity. Actually, they allow us to speed up activities, to reduce pauses and intervals between activities, and to multitask at the same time.

Nevertheless, if we interpret the acceleration of "the pace of life" as a reaction to the felt time pressure, i.e., to a perceived scarcity of time, it is hard to see how it actually relates to technological acceleration. Technological acceleration can be defined as an increase in "output" per unit of time, i.e., in the number of kilometers covered per hour, or the data bytes transferred per minute, or the number of cars produced per day (see Fig. 4.1).

Therefore, technological acceleration necessarily entails a decrease in the time needed to carry out everyday processes and actions of production and reproduction, communication, and transport, given that the quantity of tasks and actions remains unchanged (Fig. 4.2).

Hence, technological acceleration should logically entail an increase in free time, which in turn would slow down the pace of life or at least eliminate or alleviate time famine. Since technological acceleration means that less time is needed to fulfill a task at hand, time should become abundant. If, quite to the contrary, in modern society time becomes more and more scarce, this is a paradoxical effect that calls for a sociological explanation.[5]

[4] For a synoptic discussion of the evidence, see Rosa (2013, chapter VI.1).

[5] For a very interesting economic explanation, see Lindner (1970).

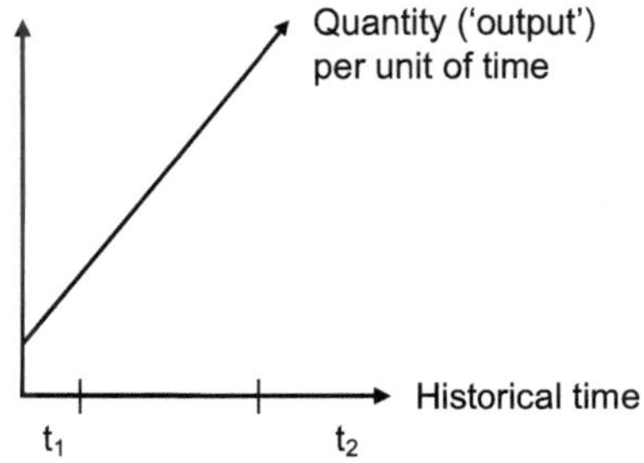

Fig. 4.1 Technological acceleration as an increase in quantity per unit of time. t_1 and t_2 variously might refer to 1800 and 1960 for the speed of transport as kilometers per hour, 1960 and 2000 for the operational speed of computers, etc.

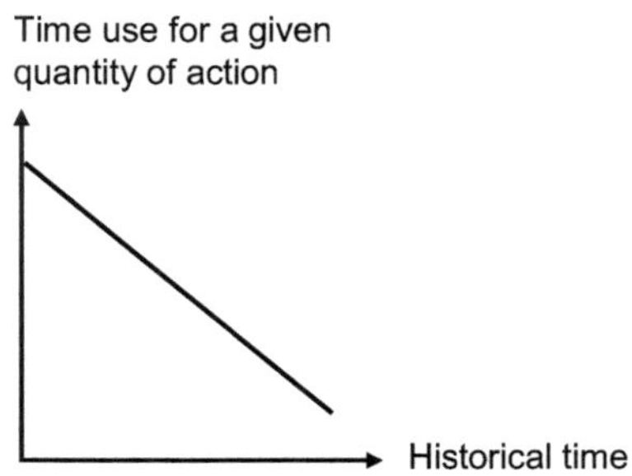

Fig. 4.2 Time resources needed for the execution of a certain quantity of action (e.g., the crossing of 10 km, the multiplication of a book, or the answering of 10 messages) in the age of technological acceleration (cf. Fig. 4.1)

We might start to find such an answer when we consider the preconditions for the expected time abundance or deceleration: As stated above, the time resources needed to fulfill the tasks of our everyday lives significantly shrink given that their quantity remains the same. But does it? We only need to contemplate the consequences the introduction of the email technology had for our time budget. It is quite accurate to assume that writing an email message is twice as fast as writing a conventional letter. Assume further that in 1990, we wrote and received on average ten letters per working day, for which we needed a total of 2 h of work. With the introduction of the new technology, we only need 1 h for our daily correspondence, given that the number of messages sent and received remains the same. Hence, we won 1 h of "free time" we can use for something else. Is this what happened? Surely not. In fact, if the number of messages we read and send doubled, then we need the same amount of time for getting done with our daily correspondence.[6] But empirical evidence suggests that by now, we read and write 40, 50, or even 70 email messages per day. Hence, we need much more time for communication than we needed before the World Wide Web was invented. And in fact, the same thing

[6] I leave aside at this point that this calculation is flawed, of course, for even if writing and sending an email message might take half as long as writing and sending a letter, thinking about and deliberating its content cannot be speed up at comparable rates. This might very well be a central explanation for why so many people report being completely overwhelmed and stressed out from the email business.

happened a century ago with the introduction of the car and, later on, with the invention of the washing machine: Of course, we would have gained a lot of free time resources if we crossed the same distances as before and did our washing as often as before – but we don't. We now drive or even fly hundreds of miles for work or pleasure, when before we might have covered only a circle of a few miles in all our life, and we change our clothing daily, when we only did so once a month (or less) a century ago.

Figure 4.3 shows this relationship between technological acceleration and quantitative growth rates quite clearly. It recurs with the history of more or less all technological inventions since the industrial age in an almost identical form: Growth rates exceed acceleration rates, and therefore, time is getting more and more scarce in the face of technological acceleration. Hence, we can define modern society as an "acceleration society" in the sense that it is characterized by an increase in the pace of life (or a shortage of time) despite impressive technological acceleration rates. How does this come about? In order to answer this, let us briefly examine the driving wheels of modern social acceleration in the next section.

4.2.2 *The Driving Wheels of Social Acceleration*

Modern society is defined by a most fateful combination of growth and acceleration. As I tried to show in the last paragraphs, and contrary to a widespread assumption, technology itself is not a cause of social acceleration. This can be seen from the email example discussed above: Nothing in this technology forces us, or even induces us, to read and write more messages per day, even though, quite obviously, technology is an enabling condition for the increase. But it can also be seen from historical evidence: As it appears, the technological revolutions of the industrial age as well as of digitalization were themselves driven by the time hunger of modern society, they were answers to the growing problem of time scarcity. Thus, long before the steam engine or the telegraph, let alone the railway and automobile were invented, people in early modernity attempted to speed up processes of transport, production, and communication. For example, they tried to do so by exchanging the horses before the horse carts more often or by using several messengers to deliver a piece of information instead of sending one who needed rest and sleep (cf. Koselleck 2009). Therefore, we have to look elsewhere to identify the motors of speed. In the following, I will present three answers to the question of how modernity got caught up in this relentless speedup process. These answers are analytically distinct even though they are, of course, empirically connected.

4.2.2.1 The Social Motor: Competition

When seeking for the mechanisms which drive and connect processes of acceleration and growth in modern society, there can be little doubt that the basic

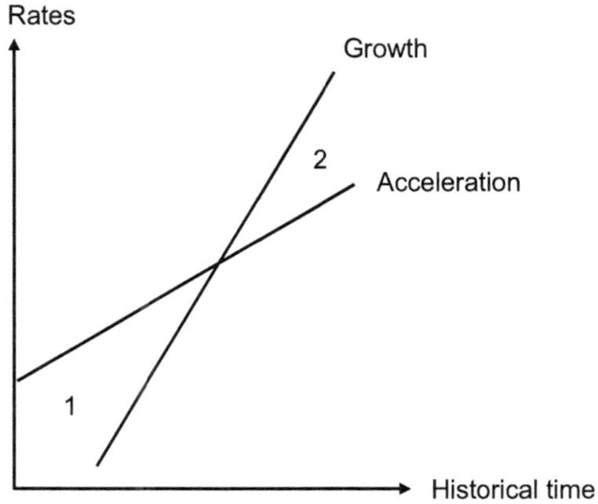

Fig. 4.3 "Free time" (1) and "time famine" (2) are consequences of the relationship between growth rates and acceleration rates. (1) depicts a decelerating and (2) an accelerating pace of life. If both rates are identical (at the intersection), the pace of life remains unchanged despite of technological acceleration. In "acceleration society," rates of growth systematically outweigh the rates of acceleration (2)

principles and the laws of profit pertaining in a capitalist economy play a major role here. The simple equation of time and money we find in Benjamin Franklin's famous dictum is true in many different ways. First, since working time is an essential factor of production, saving time is a simple and direct instrument for saving costs and gaining a competitive advantage. Secondly, the principles of credit and interest force investors to seek increasing speeds of returns and capital circulation which in turn accelerate not only production itself but also circulation and consumption. Finally, being temporally ahead of one's competitors with respect to innovations, both process and product related, is a necessary means of achieving some extra profits which are indispensable for keeping up the entrepreneur's competitiveness. Thus, social acceleration in general and technological acceleration in particular are logical consequences of a competitive capitalist market system.

However, in modern society, the principle of competition by far exceeds the (growth-oriented) economic sphere. In fact, it is the dominating mode of allocation in virtual all spheres of social life – from politics and science to art and social recognition – and therefore, as we know from Talcott Parsons (1951), a central defining principle of modernity. Since the determining or discriminating principle in competition is achievement, time and, moreover, the logic of acceleration are directly built in to the central mode of allocation in modernity: Achievement is defined as labor or work per time (power = work divided by time, as physics has it); hence, speeding up and saving time are directly linked to gaining competitive advantages – or, if everyone else tries to do the same, to keeping one's position. The social logic of competition is such that the competitors have to invest more and more energies into the preservation of their competitiveness, until keeping up the latter is no longer a means to lead an autonomous life according to self-defined ends, but the single overarching goal of social and individual life alike. This is confirmed in countless observations (and the repetitive and almost unanimous responses researchers get from interviewees in qualitative empirical studies) noting that we have to "dance faster and faster just to stay in place" (Conrad 1999, p. 6) or to "run as fast as we can in order to stay in the same place" (Robinson and Godbey 1999, p. 33). Folk wisdom always knew this in the warning that "the competitor never sleeps." The only significant realm of allocation that is not governed by the principle of competition are the distributional patterns and measures of the welfare regimes (see at length Nullmeier 2000). Hence, it is small wonder that people's sense of social acceleration sharpens right at a time when welfare policies are partially reduced and partially opened up to more competitive elements. Thus, I want to claim that the logic of competition is not the only, but the main driving force of social acceleration.

4.2.2.2 The Cultural Motor: Promise of Eternity

Nevertheless, social actors in modernity are not just the helpless victims of an acceleratory dynamic they cannot control. It is not just that they are forced to adapt to an acceleration game they have no stakes in. Quite to the contrary, I want to argue that the driving wheel of acceleration is also powered by a strong cultural promise: In secular modern society, acceleration serves as a functional equivalent for the (religious) promise of eternal life.

The reasoning behind this idea goes like this: Modern society is secular in the sense that in cultural terms, the central emphasis is placed on life before death. Whether or not people still hold religious beliefs, their aspirations, desires, and yearnings generally are directed toward the offers, options, and riches of this world. Now, the richness, fullness, or quality of a life, according to the dominant cultural logic of Western modernity, can be measured from the sum and the depth of experiences made in the course of a lifetime. Thus, in this conception of life, the good life is the fulfilled life, i.e., a life that is rich in experiences and developed capacities (Blumenberg 1986; Gronemeyer 1996). This idea no longer supposes a "higher life" waiting for us after death, but rather consists in realizing as many options as possible from the vast possibilities the world has to offer. To taste life in all its heights and depths and in its full complexity becomes a central aspiration of modern man.

But, as it turns out, the world unfortunately always seems to have more to offer than can be experienced in a single lifetime. The options on offer always outgrow those realizable in an individual's life, or, in Hans Blumenberg's terms, the perceived time of the world (Weltzeit) and the time of an individual life (Lebenszeit) dramatically diverge for individuals in the modern world (Blumenberg 1986). Acceleration of the pace of life therefore appears to be a natural solution to this problem: If we live "twice as fast," if we take only half the time to realize an action, goal, or experience, we can double "the sum" of experiences, and hence "of life," within our lifetime. Our share or "efficacy," i.e., the proportion of realized options to potentially realizable options, doubles. It follows that in this cultural logic, too, the dynamics of growth and acceleration are intricately interwoven.

Now, in this train of thought, if we keep increasing the speed of life, we could eventually live a multiplicity or even an infinity of lives within a single lifetime by realizing all the options that would define them. Acceleration thus serves as a strategy to erase the difference between the time of the world and the time of our life. The eudemonistic promise of modern acceleration therefore lies in the (unspoken) idea that the acceleration of "the pace of life" is our (i.e., modernity's) answer to the problem of finitude and death. Needless to say, this conception, unfortunately, in the end does not deliver its promise: Those very techniques which help us to save time have led to an explosion of world options. No matter how fast we become, our share of the world, i.e., the proportion of options realized and experiences made to those missed, does not rise, but falls incessantly. This, I daresay, is one of the tragedies of modern man: While he feels caught in a relentless hamster wheel, his hunger for life and world is not satisfied but frustrated on an increasing scale.

4.2.2.3 The Acceleration Cycle

Thus, we have identified two major "external" driving forces incessantly powering the acceleration wheel and setting it in motion in early modernity. It is complemented by the inherent logic of the division of labor, or functional differentiation, which first allows for and then calls for greater and greater speeds of social processing (Rosa 2013, chapter 7). However, in late modernity, social acceleration has turned into a self-propelling system which does not even need any external driving forces anymore. The three categories identified above – technological acceleration, the acceleration of social change, and the acceleration of the pace of life – have come to form an interlocking feedback system which incessantly drives itself. This, ultimately, is an inevitable consequence of the fact that modern societies can only stabilize dynamically, i.e., by following the logic of escalation.

As I tried to point out above, it is important to note that growth and acceleration are neither logically nor causally interconnected. Only the acceleration of steady processes logically entails a corresponding augmentation, whereas processes of transport, communication, or production are not by themselves steady: By accelerating them, one could normally expect a shortening of their duration. Therefore, I argued above, one would expect an inverse relationship between technological acceleration and the pace of life: Since the former sets free an abundance of time resources, people should have more time to freely dispose of.

Unfortunately, however, there is a way in which the acceleration of the pace of life and technological acceleration are positively interconnected: As I have argued at the outset, technological acceleration can be seen as a social answer to the problem of scarce time, i.e., to the acceleration of the "pace of life." When we examine the causal relations between the three spheres of social acceleration, a surprising feedback loop is revealed: Technological acceleration, which is frequently connected to the introduction of new technologies (like the steam engine, the railway, the automobile, the telegraph, the computer, or the Internet), almost inevitably brings about a whole range of changes in social practices, communication structures, and corresponding forms of life. For example, the Internet has not only increased the speed of communicative exchange and the "virtualization" of economic and productive processes, but it also established new occupational, economic, and communicative structures, opening up new patterns of social interaction and even new forms of social identity (cf. Turkle 1995). Hence, it is easy to see how and why technological acceleration is prone to go hand in hand with the acceleration of social change in the form of changing social structures and patterns, orientations, and evaluations of action. Furthermore, if the acceleration of social change entails a "contraction of the present" in the sense discussed above, this naturally leads to an acceleration of "the pace of life." The explanation for this is to be found in a phenomenon that is well known from the realm of capitalist production and might be called the "slippery slope phenomenon" of competitive society: The capitalist cannot pause and rest, stop the race, and secure his position, since he either goes up or goes down. There is no point of equilibrium, for standing still is equivalent to falling behind, as Marx as well as Weber pointed out.

Similarly, in a competitive society with accelerated rates of social change in all spheres of life, individuals always feel that they stand on "slippery slopes": Taking a prolonged break means becoming old-fashioned, outdated, anachronistic in one's experience and knowledge, in one's equipment and clothing as well as in one's orientations and even in one's language.[7] Quite obviously, the decay rates are particularly high in ICT world. If the reader seeks an illustration of this syndrome from his or her everyday life, he or she might simply think of their email accounts: After a long email session, we might reach the top of our account: All relevant messages read, all important messages answered. However, as soon as we turn to some other activity, we start falling back or going down again: At the end of the day, we are probably worse off in our account position than before. The account silently and incessantly fills up again, and we start to feel like Sisyphus. The same situation obtains with respect to soft- and hardware solutions on computers, smartphones, etc. No matter how up-to-date your equipment is today, you will receive notifications next week informing you that with respect to security, browsers, applications, etc., your ICT equipment is no longer top-notch. In this way, people feel pressed to keep up with the speed of change they experience in their social and technological world in order to avoid the loss of potentially valuable options and connections (Anschlussmöglichkeiten) and to keep up their competitive chances. This problem is aggravated by the fact that in a world of incessant change, it gets increasingly difficult to tell which options will eventually turn out to be valuable. Hence, accelerated social change will in turn lead to an accelerating "pace of life." And finally, as we saw at the outset, new forms of technological

[7] Thus, elderly people in Western society are frequently unable to understand the "technobabble" the young use when talking about their Game Boys, emails, iPads, Blue Rays, etc.

acceleration will be called for to speed up the processes of productive and everyday life. Thus, the "acceleration cycle" has turned into a closed, self-propelling system.

4.2.3 Acceleration at the Workplace

Now, obviously, this process of social acceleration has significant consequences for the organization of the workplace and for the everyday routines and experiences of the workers and employees as well as for their perspectives on their whole work life. In the remainder of this chapter, I will try to pinpoint some of the most significant effects.

4.2.3.1 The Undeniable Benefits of Speed

It goes without saying that the process of social and technological acceleration has had a host of very beneficial effects on working conditions. First of all, it has served to vastly increase the speed and ease with which goods (and sometimes services, too) are produced, and it just as much reduced the physical energy on the side of the workers needed to produce them. Furthermore, it just as much increased the range of products and features that can easily be realized in the production process. ICT has provided the most recent and perhaps most spectacular wave of acceleration here. The speedup of the innovation rates, moreover, resulted in an accelerated path of technological progress and in the production of economic wealth. Secondly, the acceleration of social change has (at least for a long time) vastly increased social mobility of workers and employees, allowing them to follow individual career paths. Thus, speed is an essential precondition for the pursuit of the modern normative goals of autonomy and authenticity. Nevertheless, in its late modern stages in particular, the need to still further increase the speed of production, innovation, and change comes at an increasing price.

4.2.3.2 Contraction of the Present: The Devaluation of Experience and Expertise

The acceleration of social change, as described in Sect. 4.2.2.1 above, leads to a progressive "contraction of the present." At the workplace, this means that there is a permanent change of colleagues and routines, machines and programs, rules and goals, products and clients. Thus, employees as well as employers feel that they have to "run faster and faster just to stay in place": They constantly are in danger of falling behind, becoming outdated in their knowledge and equipment, their capabilities and contacts. In the world of ICT, this problem appears to come in an aggravated form, for there is no other sector in society with higher rates of change. It is just a logical consequence of this state of affairs that experience and expertise are progressively devalued: It does not help to intimately know the routines and rules, the machines and technologies, the products and clients of yesterday. This is why for a long time, there was such a high priority on youth in many segments of the economy: Knowledge and expertise were seen as hindrances toward embracing the new rather than as advantages. By consequence, this also means that more or less all features of the workplace and the working conditions are under permanent revision, from suppliers and providers to the organizational structure of production and to the target markets and consumers: They need to be changed or replaced when they fail to deliver the highest benefits, but it might just as well be that suppliers or clients change their preferences and orientations on their own.

4.2.3.3 Lack of Appropriation and Identification

One obvious danger of this "dynamization" of the workplace is that workers and employees lack the time to really "appropriate" their workplace and their work. If, for example, computers and software programs we work with are exchanged at rates much faster than the time needed to really come to know and master them, a sense of "alienation" is unavoidable: While the machines and programs become smarter and faster by the year, the user is turned into a "cultural illiterate" with almost every innovation. Everyone is familiar with this constantly recurring situation: There is a new heater, but you cannot turn it on; a new electronic calendar, but you cannot open it; a new security system, but you cannot turn it off; a new format of data which you don't know how to read; a new set of rules which you never had the time to study; etc. In each instance, you have to start as a novice for something you once were an expert in (see at length Rosa 2010, pp. 83–98). In the end, people lose their intimate knowledge of their workplace and working conditions – but also of their colleagues and clients, which are exchanged just as quickly. Thus, a thorough form of alienation is the likely result of a workplace that is so dynamic that workers no longer even try to appropriate its features and conditions – they shift to a mode of "muddling through."

Biographically, the "contraction of the present" in the form of employment leads to a "natural" or rational shift away from identification with a particular job or employer: People no longer say I am a baker or a designer; rather, they say (right now) I work as a baker or for the past 3 years, I've been working as a designer (but no one knows what will come next). Almost all employment-related forms of identification tend to be preliminary now and come with a temporary marker.

4.2.3.4 Scarcity of Time: The Production of "Guilty Subjects"

The combined effect of growth and acceleration – the competitive, escalatory logic of modernity – systematically leads to a situation where the "to-do list" at every workplace grows longer and longer by the year and where workers and employees (and employers, too) feel they have to work harder and harder just to keep their position. We might also say that this is an inevitable by-product of an accelerating pace of life. Thus, many, if not most, workplaces systematically produce "guilty subjects" at the end of the day: No matter how hard they tried, they did not do enough. This is particularly true, of course, for employees who have some autonomy over their time and work schedules, but it also is a general tendency. The number of tasks that "really should be done now" always exceeds the capacity of the working. The email account still harbors unread or unanswered messages, the answering machine unreturned calls; there are machines and programs we yet again did not appropriate properly or did not clean and service enough, and there are colleagues and clients, superiors, or subordinates we did not pay enough attention to. And if we actually managed to satisfy them all, we are most likely guilty because we did not do the tax declaration and the banking, we did not care for our parents or kids, and we certainly did not do enough for our physical fitness and our mental relaxation. By consequence, more and more people report they find it hard to relax or "come down" or "turn off" in the evening or at the weekend. There is an overwhelming (and realistic) sense that the flows and fluids of the digital world – its challenges and opportunities – incessantly surround us and that whoever turns them off is in danger of being left behind.

4.2.3.5 The Hamster Wheel Effect: Burnout

Needless to say, the "guilty subject" that is alienated from his or her workplace and feels that he or she has to run faster and faster just to stay in place is eventually threatened by aggravated stress and even burnout. From my point of view, there is overwhelming evidence to conclude that "burnout" and other forms of pathological stress reaction do not result from the fact that people have to work hard or to run fast. Both, I believe, are quite natural for human beings, and we know from countless testimonies that both can actually give a lot of pleasure and satisfaction. Thus, if there is a significant increase in pathological psychic or psychosomatic reactions to working conditions, this, in my view, is due to two factors. (1) First, what I have described as a lack of appropriation, or as alienation, can be reinterpreted as a lack of "resonance." Burnout is a realistic possibility if we "lose touch" with both our colleagues and our clients, patients, or customers. If we fail to establish and maintain a responsive, resonating relationship not only to them but also to our physical workplace, to the tools and instruments we work with, to the goals and purposes of our work. Thus, it is not chance that many who suffer from burnout do report a lack of resonance in the form of a lack of gratification and recognition: Their efforts went more or less unnoticed and, in any case, unacknowledged. Thus, they feel they work in dead, deaf, non-resonating surroundings. Addiction to screens seems to be a symptom of this: It is as if the signals coming in from the digital world are the only "respondents" in an otherwise silent world. Quite obviously, relationships of resonance (with people, tasks, and spaces) are time-consuming to establish as well as to maintain. It is one thing to exchange data or information with a colleague or client, quite another thing to establish a relationship. Unfortunately, most employers think the latter is a waste of time. (2) Secondly, and maybe even more importantly, running fast or working hard does become a problem when there is no goal toward which we are running or working. As I said before, running somewhere seems to be quite a natural activity for human beings. But in late modern work life, there is an overwhelming impression that we have to run uphill just in order to not slip down the drain – i.e., to stay in place. This, culturally, is a most significant difference: For two centuries, the modern process of acceleration was connected to the perception of individual as well as collective progress. Now, for the first time in modern history, parents in Western societies no longer work hard to enable their kids to have a better life – they do so in order to spare them a much harder life. Thus, individually as well as collectively, we are no longer running toward a goal, we are running away (in panic) from the abyss that is at our heels. One clear symptom of this is the impression that there is never time to pause and celebrate any success or achievement: Burnout, so it seems, becomes a likely (albeit involuntary) "exit option" if our efforts and achievements are never met with gratification, security, recognition, and rest, but with the immediate sense of progressive devaluation.

A paradigmatic example of the combined effect of these two conditions can, perhaps, be studied from the events at France Télécom between March 2008 and March 2010 (Ugettho 2010): Led by the slogan "Time to move," the company introduced a rapid series of permanent reforms, requiring 7,000 top executives to change their workplace after at most 3 years. In this way, it actually sought to avoid the building of "resonating" relationships, which were thought to be hindrances to further reforms, and to establish a process of permanent change. As a result, at least 41 employees committed suicide during that period, while many more tried. In the end, the company was sued by French authorities for involuntary manslaughter.

4.2.3.6 From Work-Life to Work-Age Balance

Needless to say, so far, only a minority of workers and employees react with pathological symptoms to the acceleratory pressures of late modern work life. One quite promising and successful "coping strategy," so it appears, is the private reintroduction of a clear finish or target line for the rat race. While it becomes almost impossible for many or even most employees (and in particular IT workers) to maintain a healthy or sound work-life balance under the working condition identified so far – they feel that their work life sucks up all their energies, and even their recreational activities serve only one purpose, i.e., the maintenance or improvement of their competitiveness – they nevertheless hope they might succeed in keeping the balance: "Life" in the sense of autonomously defined activities free from the imperatives of the economic sphere for them begins once they are ready to retire, once they reach their pension age. This, I think, is the main reason why there is such fierce and strong resistance against all attempts to raise the retirement age. The 'life' employees lose during their working-years they hope to get back afterwards; they simply postpone the "life part" of the lost work-life balance. Of course, with increasing life-spans, prospects are that they will still be healthy and strong enough to then, at last, reap the fruits of all the running and laboring they did not have time to enjoy before. This shift from the synchronic work-life balance to a new, diachronic "work-age" balance, in my view, needs to be taken into account in all further discussions of the work-life balance and of the adequate retirement age.

References

Adams, H. (2009). The law of acceleration. In H. Rosa & W. Scheuerman (Eds.), *High-speed society. Social acceleration, power and modernity* (pp. 33–40). University Park: Pennsylvania State University Press.

Augé, M. (1992). *Non-lieux. Introduction à une anthropologie de la surmodernité*. Paris: Verso.

Bauman, Z. (2000). *Liquid modernity*. Cambridge: Polity Press.

Beck, U., Giddens, A., & Lash, S. (1997). *Reflexive modernization: Politics, tradition and aesthetics in the modern social order*. Cambridge: Polity Press.

Blumenberg, H. (1986). *Lebenszeit und Weltzeit*. Frankfurt am Main: Suhrkamp.

Conrad, P. (1999). *Modern times and modern places. How life and art were transformed in a century of revolution, innovation and radical change*. New York: Alfred A. Knopf.

Garhammer, M. (1999). *Wie Europäer ihre Zeit nutzen. Zeitstrukturen und Zeitkulturen im Zeichen der Globalisierung*. Berlin: Edition Sigma.

Geißler, K. (1999). *Vom Tempo der Welt. Am Ende der Uhrzeit*. Freiburg im Breisgau: Herder.

Gleick, J. (1999). *Faster. The acceleration of just about everything*. New York: Pantheon Books.

Gronemeyer, M. (1996). *Das Leben als letzte Gelegenheit. Sicherheitsbedürfnisse und Zeitknappheit* (2nd ed.). Darmstadt: Wissenschaftliche Buchgesellschaft.

Harvey, D. (1990). *The condition of postmodernity. An enquiry into the origins of cultural change*. Cambridge, MA/Oxford: Blackwell.

Koselleck, R. (2009). Is there an acceleration of history? In H. Rosa & W. Scheuerman (Eds.), *High-speed society. Social acceleration, power and modernity* (pp. 113–134). University Park: Pennsylvania State University.

Laslett, P. (1988). Social structural time: An attempt at classifying types of social change by their characteristic paces. In M. Young & T. Schuller (Eds.), *The rhythms of society* (pp. 17–36). London/New York: Routledge.

Levine, R. (1997). *A geography of time: The temporal misadventures of a social psychologist, or how every culture keeps time just a little bit differently*. New York: Basic Books.

Lindner, S. B. (1970). *The harried leisure class*. New York: Columbia University Press.

Lübbe, H. (2009). The contraction of the present. In H. Rosa & W. Scheuerman (Eds.), *High-speed society. Social acceleration, power and modernity* (pp. 159–178). University Park: Pennsylvania State University.

Nullmeier, F. (2000). *Politische Theorie des Wohlfahrtsstaats*. Frankfurt am Main/New York: Campus.

Parsons, T. (1951). *The social system*. New York: Free Press.

Robinson, J., & Godbey, G. (1999). *Time for life. The surprising ways American use their time* (2nd ed.). University Park: Pennsylvania State University Press.

Rosa, H. (2010). *Alienation and acceleration. Towards a critical theory of late-modern temporality*. Aarhus/Malmö: NSU Press.

Rosa, H. (2013). *Social acceleration: A new theory of modernity*. New York: Columbia University Press.

Sennett, R. (1998). *The corrosion of character. The personal consequences of work in the new capitalism*. New York/London: Norton & Company.

Simmel, G. (1978). *The philosophy of money* (D. Frisby, Ed.). London: Routledge.

Turkle, S. (1995). *Life on the screen: Identity in the age of the Internet*. New York: Simon & Schuster.

Ugettho, P. (2010). *Wave of employee suicides swept France Telécom*. www.eurofound.europa.eu/eiro/2009/11/articles/fr0911029i.htm

Virilio, P. (1997). *Open sky*. London/New York: Verso.

Wagner, P. (1994). *A sociology of modernity: Liberty and discipline*. London: Routledge.

Chapter 5
Time and Work Pressure in Today's Working World

Jörn Hurtienne, Ulrike Stilijanow, and Gisa Junghanns

5.1 The Importance of Time and Work Pressure

Time and work pressure has become increasingly predominant in today's world of work. The European Working Conditions Survey (1991–2010) shows that work intensity – for instance, working at high speed or working to tight deadlines – has increased over the last two decades and seems to have stabilised at a high level since 2005. In 2010, two thirds of the workforce in the EU stated that they have to work to tight deadlines at least for a quarter of their working time (Table 5.1).

Breaking down the results according to type of occupation reveals that highly skilled workers more often report that they work to tight deadlines than low-skill workers. The development over time also differs between the groups. In contrast to a general stabilisation, the high-skilled clerical workers show a substantial increase between 2000 and 2010 (Table 5.2).

Data from other sources corroborate these findings. In the representative ESENER Study (European Survey of Enterprises on New and Emerging Risks), conducted in 31 European countries, management representatives and health and safety representatives were asked about psychosocial risk factors in their establishments. More than half of the management representatives named 'time pressure' as a concern, followed by 'having to deal with difficult customers, patients, pupils, etc.' (Table 5.3). Health and safety officers also indicated most frequently time pressure as a relevant concern in their organisation.

These numbers show that in the EU, time and work pressure is a growing and persistent phenomenon that has been identified not only by the workers themselves

J. Hurtienne (✉)
Psychological Ergonomics, Julius-Maximilians-Universität Würzburg, Würzburg, Germany
e-mail: joern.hurtienne@uni-wuerzburg.de

U. Stilijanow • G. Junghanns
Mental Workload, Occupational Health Management, Federal Institute for Occupational Health and Safety, Berlin, Germany
e-mail: stilijanow.ulrike@baua.bund.de; junghanns.gisa@baua.bund.de

C. Korunka and P. Hoonakker (eds.), *The Impact of ICT on Quality of Working Life*,
DOI 10.1007/978-94-017-8854-0_5, © Springer Science+Business Media Dordrecht 2014

Table 5.1 Percentage of the workforce working to tight deadlines for at least a quarter of their working time, EC12, EU15 and EU27, 1991–2010

Year	EC12	EU15	EU27
2010	63.2	63.6	62.0
2005	61.8	62.4	61.8
2000	58.6	59.2	59.0
1995	54.9	55.9	n/a
1991	49.6	n/a	n/a

Eurofound (2010)

Table 5.2 Percentage of the workforce working to tight deadlines for at least a quarter of their working time, EU27, type of vocation

Year	Low-skilled manual	High-skilled manual	Low-skilled clerical	High-skilled clerical
2000	58.8	67.1	54.0	60.8
2010	60.9	68.1	57.5	67.1

Source: Eurofound Online Survey mapping tool; http://www.eurofound.europa.eu/surveys/smt/ewcs/ewcs2010_14_03.htm

Table 5.3 Concern about psychosocial risk factors (percentage of organisations in the EU)

'Several factors can contribute to stress, violence and harassment at work; they concern the way work is organised and are often referred to as 'psychosocial risks'. Please tell me whether any of the following psychosocial risks are a concern in your establishment' (multiple responses possible)	Management representatives ($N = 28.649$)	Health and safety representatives ($N = 7.226$)
Time pressure	52.2	58.5
Having to deal with difficult customers, patients, pupils, etc.	49.7	46.7
Poor communication between management and employees	28.0	32.9
Job insecurity	26.8	30.3
Poor cooperation between colleagues	25.7	22.6
Long or irregular working hours	21.9	27.7
Problems in supervisor-employee relationships	20.4	26.2
Lack of employee control in organising their work	20.7	21.4
An unclear human resources policy	14.8	22.8
Discrimination (e.g. due to gender, age or ethnicity)	6.9	7.3

Source: ESENER survey 2009; http://osha.europa.eu/sub/esener/en/front-page

but also by management and by health and safety officers. As more than half of the workforce is affected by time and work pressure, it seems worthwhile to have a closer look at how time and work pressure can be treated theoretically, how it comes about, what strategies people have developed to cope with time and work pressure and what possibilities exist for work redesign.

5.2 Time and Work Pressure in Current Theory

Time and work pressure is already a component in many theories of stress and well-being at work. The Job-Demands-Control model by Karasek (1979), for example, has been very successful in describing the origins of work-related stress, using a combination of two factors: job demands and decision latitude (control). According to this theory, high job demands can be buffered if the worker enjoys a high level of control. High-demand, high-control jobs thus are called 'active jobs' where people do not suffer from increased stress at work. In contrast, high-demand low-control jobs are 'stressful jobs' as decision latitude cannot buffer the high demands. Time and work pressure, according to the model, is a component of the job demands. Therefore, the amount of control available to the worker influences the negative consequences of time and work pressure experienced by the worker.

Action Regulation theory (e.g. Hacker 2003) describes how actions are regulated by a hierarchy of goals, subgoals and operations that translate into visible actions. According to the theory, stress at work results when action regulation is frustrated. Such frustrations or hindrances create additional workload by creating the need for repeated actions, restarts, diversions or additional demands on concentration. If time constraints exist, this extra workload causes time pressure. Time pressure puts excessive demands on action regulation capabilities, has adverse effects on concentration and attention, increases the probability of risky behaviour and in the long term leads to negative health outcomes (Greiner and Leitner 1989; Zapf 1993).

The Effort-Reward Imbalance model (Siegrist 1996) claims that if great effort is spent on work and if that effort is not recognised with an equal level of job rewards (e.g. money, esteem, career opportunities), then negative emotions and sustained stress responses are likely to ensue. Here, time and work pressure puts off the balance between efforts and rewards as it increases the necessary effort without necessarily increasing the rewards. The model also assumes that a motivational variable is contributing to a sustained imbalance between efforts and rewards, namely, overcommitment at work. Overcommitment at work shows as excessive work-related commitment and may be a contributing factor when time and work pressure results in negative health consequences.

In conclusion, current theories do explain how time and work pressure may influence the way in which stress is experienced at work and what moderating and mediating variables need to be taken into account. Among these variables are job design variables (decision latitude), motivational variables (rewards) and personal variables (overcommitment). Time and work pressure does not per se have positive or negative consequences for the experience of stress; this will instead depend on interaction with other variables. A notable gap in current theoretical models is that although time and work pressure is an important precondition for stress, these theories do not explain how time and work pressure comes about and what strategies are available to deal with it on the individual and organisational level.

5.3 Defining Time and Work Pressure

Work intensity, *workload* and *work effort* are terms related to the concept of time and work pressure. Just how these concepts are related can be explored using an analytic approach.

Following Trägner (2006), *work intensity* may be defined as the relation between the quantity of work, the quality of work and the available time to accomplish the work. Work intensity thus can be measured by asking: How much do the workers have to do? What is the desired quality of the result? And how fast do they have to work? Thus, not a single measure, but the interplay of these three factors determines work intensity.

An important distinction needs to be made between work intensity that is *anticipated* and work intensity that is *realised*. Anticipated work intensity ('What I have to do') may be set by the company as norms, targets and objectives for the work (e.g. to deliver a given number of products of a defined quality within a specified period of time). The realised work intensity ('What I have done'), however, may differ from the anticipated work intensity when solving unforeseen problems, working on additional tasks or being influenced by exceptionally low or high worker motivation.

Note that the difference between anticipated and realised work intensity is not only one of looking forwards or backwards in time. Anticipated work intensity may only contain the countable, already known and explicit while realised work intensity may also acknowledge all the invisible and often less acknowledged work people have to do, e.g. to coordinate their activities with others, maintain social networks or appease customers. The difference between anticipated and realised work intensity may also be used to distinguish the terms workload and work effort. Then, the term *workload* refers to anticipated work intensity. The term *work effort* mostly refers to realised work intensity (e.g. as used by Burke et al. 2009, 2010; Green 2001, 2004).

Time and work pressure then results from a misfit between the three components determining work intensity: quantity, work quality and time (Fig. 5.1). More specifically, time and work pressure can be defined as the subjectively perceived misfit between the amount of work to do, the quality of the work required and the time available to finish the work. The perceived misfit depends on the situation, the individual abilities, the working conditions and the company culture. This subjective definition of time and work pressure recognises that the same objective relationship between the amount of work, quality of work and time can differ on a subjective level when judged by people with differing work experience, motivations and interests and within differing company cultures.

Perceiving time and work pressure may have positive or negative effects, e.g. it may be perceived as activating or stressing. Short- and long-term effects need to be considered and it is possible that positive short-term effects may lead to negative long-term effects.

Fig. 5.1 The subjective misfit between the three components – quantity of work, quality of results and time available – defines the perceived time and work pressure

The terms *time pressure* and *work pressure* might be differentiated according to the most salient component of work intensity. If the time is short, e.g. due to an approaching deadline, then this results in time pressure. If quality and quantity of the work is in the foreground, we would speak about work pressure. However, we do prefer to use the compound term *time and work pressure*, because in many areas (e.g. knowledge work), time pressure cannot be readily separated from the quality and quantity of work to do.

Each of the three corners of the triangle in Fig. 5.1 may be predetermined by management or may be determined by the workers. The greater their latitude and control over their work, the more it is possible for them to increase or decrease the amount of work, the time available to finish the job and the quality achieved. Therefore, if workers perceive time and work pressure as a misfit between these corners, they may develop coping strategies that address one or several of the corners. The amount of work can be reduced by delegating tasks or subtasks to others, by trying to multitask or by dropping tasks or task steps. The quality of the work can be lowered by reducing the amount of effort per task. To influence the time component, workers may work faster, extend their working hours or reduce the number and length of breaks between work units.

Expressed in a linear order, anticipated work intensity (or workload) may lead to time and work pressure that determines the realised work intensity (work effort). This rather formal analysis may give some hints at how to define, measure and influence time and work pressure. It is, however, still too coarse to show how time and work pressure is caused under the specific circumstances of today's world of work and which strategies people have developed to influence the amount of time and work pressure they experience and to counteract its negative effects. In the following comments, we therefore open the discussion by looking at recent work in industrial sociology and work psychology. The aim is to identify the driving forces behind increasing time and work pressure, especially in relation to the introduction of information and communication technology (ICT) and issues of acceleration. We will also have a quick look at strategies that workers have adopted to cope with increasing time and work pressure. We find that many findings are of qualitative nature and the research on the topic has only just started. Still, it is possible to draw some conclusions on how to approach work redesign in the future.

5.4 Origins of Time and Work Pressure in a Changing World of Work

Interviews with experts and screening the literature have let us identify four larger trends that influence how time and work pressure comes about and how it is viewed in today's working life (Junghanns et al. 2011). First, there is increased competition between companies and – increasingly – between different groups of workers. Second, workers' performance is increasingly being measured by the outcomes of their work instead of merely being based on the time they put in to achieve these results – a phenomenon we discuss under the heading subjectification of work. Third, the increasing availability of and reliance on information and communication technology (computerisation) has influenced work patterns in a way that also increases time and work pressure. Fourth, an overarching trend in society towards acceleration eventually forms an environment that makes it difficult to evade time and work pressure.

The following sections discuss each of these four trends in greater depth. Although they interact and form a contingent web of influences on workers' time and work pressure, we discuss each of the four trends separately. While computerisation and acceleration directly relate to the issues discussed in this book, the other two (competition and subjectification) are needed in order to understand the framework in which these two trends operate and affect workers' time and work pressure. Although many of these trends may also contribute to better working conditions, greater motivation and sometimes less time and work pressure (e.g. Buch and Andersen 2009), we primarily focus on developments with negative consequences. More than these four trends could be thought of, but to us they seemed the most pervasive and characteristic of today's changing world of work.

5.4.1 Competition

Competition, i.e. the struggle among companies to capture larger portions of the market, has become more aggressive. Economic globalisation, the opening of markets around the world, means that the number of competitors has been increasing, the pressure to produce more cost-efficiently has become greater and market conditions have become more volatile. The more companies there are in the market, the more likely that a better service or product will emerge, perhaps at some distant location, at a better price for the customer. Companies are forced to produce more efficiently and streamline their structures. Their reaction to this is a constant adjustment of their processes and structures to meet the requirements of the market. Strategies to keep ahead of the competition include offshoring (relocating business processes to other and cheaper countries), site closures or downsizing.

Information and communication technology, in the eyes of the management, plays a major role in remaining competitive. While the promise of introducing ICT often is a streamlining of business processes, reduced costs of data processing and a higher transparency of business processes and financial outcomes, there also is a literature discussing the 'productivity paradox of IT', i.e. the finding that investments in ICT do not show in revenue statistics (Brödner 2002; Brynjolfsson 2003). Enterprise resource planning systems like SAP software, for example, are often implemented with the intention to implement the industry's one best way. Ironically, implementing standard ICT systems is at best a strategy to avoid falling behind rather than realising a competitive advantage, because competitors are highly likely to use the same system (Hurtienne et al. 2009). Still, the company-wide introduction of ICT systems is often a major trigger for reorganising the company's structure and business processes (e.g. as prescribed by the one best way implemented in the software).

Reorganisations often go hand in hand with staffing cuts and these very often mean that the same amount of work has to be done by fewer people. Efficiency enhancements frequently mean that work processes are being speeded up, in the employees view. Quality standards are rising to meet the customers' increasing demands, generating even more work. These changes, occurring either singly or in combination, can create higher time and work pressure for workers by directly affecting the amount of work to be done. But these changes also introduce extra work that is required to adjust to ever-changing company policies, new organisational structures, ICT systems, tasks and work processes. In addition, a feeling of insecurity spreads among the workforce: Will my qualifications, skills and knowledge still be adequate after reorganisation? Whom will I be working with next year? Might I even lose my job? A permanent feeling of job insecurity may lead to employees taking on more work and raise the threshold on how much time and work pressure is tolerated (cf. Valenduc et al. 2009).

Due to these reorganisation activities, competition between companies may become competition between groups of workers with different statuses. The standard employment contract (i.e. full time, permanent employment) is gradually being replaced by fixed-term and part-time work or by employment via temporary employment agencies. The classic career goals for permanent staff are reduced to 'keeping my job' while temporary staff aim to 'get permanent employment' in the same company. Increased competition between groups of workers by inducing fears of precarisation increases the amount of tolerated (or even self-induced) work pressure, thereby enhancing the likeliness of negative health outcomes (Brinkmann 2011; Kieselbach et al. 2009; Kratzer and Nies 2009; Menz et al. 2011; Peters 2011).

Organisational and occupational case studies highlight an increasing importance of market constraints for the organisation of work. The general trend can be summarised as 'closer to markets, closer to customers, and faster' (Valenduc et al. 2009, p. 37). In a number of organisational case studies in 14 European countries, Valenduc et al. (2009) find that market pressure is salient for all business functions across the value chain. However, different occupational groups are

Table 5.4 Company variables and their effects on time pressure and workload of employees as rated by the members of works councils of 1,674 German companies

Effects of... on...	Time pressure	Workload
Increasing customer orientation	Large	Large
Restructuring	Medium	Large
Management by objectives	Medium	Medium
Profit centre	Low	Medium
Project work	Low	Low
Intensified controlling	Low	Low
Good order situation	None	None

Adapted from Ahlers (2009)

affected differently. For some (e.g. researchers and designers), market pressure is perceived as new or having become more systemic. For others, especially in manufacturing occupations, the main manifestation of market pressure is a speeding-up of just-in-time processes. Again in others (e.g. in software engineering and front-office public service occupations), customer-centred strategies have been starting to drive the reorganisation of business processes (Valenduc et al. 2009).

The effects of changes in the organisational structure and processes on time and work pressure are illustrated by a study by Ahlers (2009, 2011). Table 5.4 shows that while a full order book does not influence time pressure and workload measures to any great extent, competition-related strategies like the introduction of profit centres, management by objectives, restructuring and an increased focus on customer orientation have a much stronger effect on time pressure and workload for employees in Germany.

5.4.2 *Subjectification of Work*

Subjectification of work (German *Subjektivierung von Arbeit*) is a concept originating in the German-speaking sociology of work. The term, on the one hand, refers to the ever-increasing tendency for workers to bring to bear their personal views, aspirations and subjective standards in their work. On the other hand, it means a shift in how management envisages the relation between working abilities and the person. In contrast to Taylorism, which officially excluded workers' subjectivity, managers now often aim at fully utilising the 'whole person' by demanding, to an ever larger extent, that workers bring to the work process their subjective capacities, i.e. their ingenuity, experience, judgements, tacit skills, etc. (Huws 2008). Subjectification of work is linked to a discussion of concepts of the *intrapreneur* (Pinchot 1985), the *entreployee* (German: *Arbeitskraftunternehmer*, Pongratz and Voß 2003) or the *entrepreneurial self* (Bröckling 2007).

In practical terms, and of interest here, subjectification means that companies have begun loading the uncertainties of the market onto the individual worker. This often is referred to as *indirect control* or *indirect management* (Peters 2011).

Instead of, as in classical management, to assess and control how much effort workers put into solving a task, with indirect control only the output of the work is specified and monitored, not the actual doing. One application of this is *management by objectives*. The employee's performance towards predefined standards is measured continuously and compared against these standards. A consequence of this management style is employees' enhanced responsibility for how they go about their work and how they achieve the results.

Empirical data illustrate the effects of management by objectives on different aspects of time and work pressure (Ahlers 2011, Fig. 5.2). In their sample of 1,700 companies, about half employed management by objectives (53 %). In these companies works council members are more likely to report greater time pressure, a larger workload and longer working hours. They also indicate that employees are more likely to undermine measures for health and well-being that are already in place, that employees do not feel that work time can be planned and that employees are more likely to engage in presenteeism (i.e. employees attending work when actually sick).

Although management by objectives also has positive effects by enhancing employees' decision latitude and control of how and when they do their work, there are several implications of this management style that can lead to higher time and work pressure. The role of ICT in this is ambivalent, however. It may support workers in coping with the demands but it may also hinder them doing their work.

First, targets are mostly set quantitatively as monetary *key performance indicators* (KPI), leaving other (qualitative) factors, e.g. the quality of customer service, disregarded. This may lead to situations where the KPI targets that have been set are in conflict with other job objectives that are not measured (e.g. delivering excellent customer service that meets clients' needs). If all these various targets are still to be achieved, employees need to increase their efforts, thus increasing time and work pressure. ICT acts as medium in which KPIs are set, communicated and measured. Although this may render KPIs and the progress towards fulfilling them transparent to the worker, the danger is that these KPIs become predominant and other objectives of the work become underemphasised. As enterprise resource planning software acts as the main information tool for managerial decisions, non-quantified objectives of the work can hardly influence these decisions.

Second, the targets are often deliberately set to be very *ambitious*, so as to enhance worker motivation and performance (often with a reference to the Goal-Setting theory by Locke and Latham 1990). Very often, however, employees cannot realistically meet these targets, because they lack the necessary resources (e.g. time, equipment, qualifications). If there is no possibility to revise targets, efforts to achieve overambitious targets lead to increased time and work pressure. Targets are often set via ICT. Although the functionality of the system may not allow for the revision of targets, revising via other channels (e.g. by calling face-to-face meetings) may not be legitimate and therefore not done. In addition, by allowing for comparisons between workers, a subtle form of peer pressure can be created via ICT. For example, when on-screen statistics show that the majority of co-workers

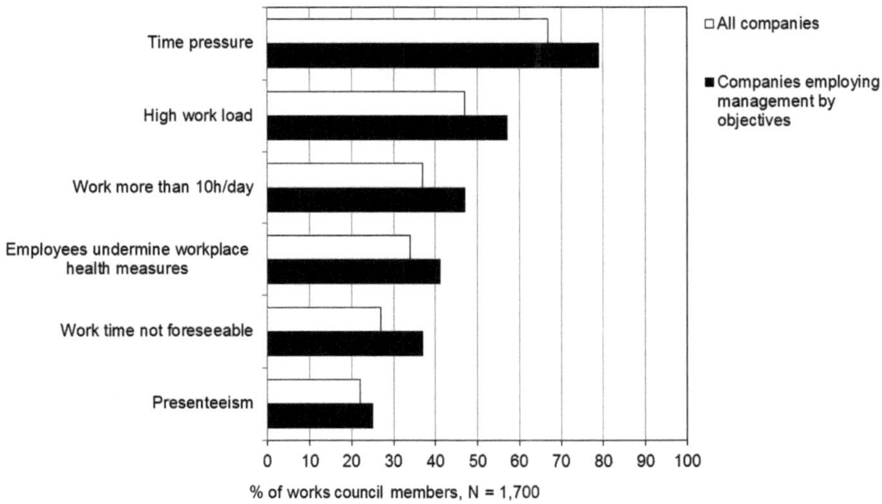

Fig. 5.2 Aspects related to time and work pressure in companies employing management by objectives compared to all companies in the sample ($N = 1{,}700$, Data from Ahlers 2011)

have already accepted overambitious targets, it will be difficult to not accept these targets oneself.

Third, the work is not only influenced by the targets set by management. Increasing *demands voiced by others* (customers, colleagues and network partners) can increase the amount of work and quality required. Customers may have additional requirements, colleagues depend on one's work outcomes and personal networks need to be nurtured (Kratzer and Nies 2009) – all adding to the amount of work to do. Demands of others are often mediated by ICT: ticketing systems and e-mail. Usually, ICT lowers the threshold for others to create new tasks for the workers (see below).

Fourth, monitoring workers' performance often means that performance measurement, documentation and reporting are shifted to the employees. This also adds to the amount of work they have to do. These *additional controlling tasks* are likely to be mediated by ICT. Very often this increases the amount of manual data entry. Sometimes, ICT systems measure KPIs like total output per day automatically. If these numbers are fed back to the workers, this may enhance transparency. But also new areas of conflict may arise, e.g. regarding worker surveillance.

Fifth, increased worker autonomy creates additional *tasks associated with self-organisation and coordinating with others*, finding a balance between work and life, etc. These additional tasks require time but are very often invisible, because they are not part of the measurement and reporting system. Depending on the degree of autonomy of the workers, ICT may provide the means to solve these tasks more easily. E-mail and intranets, knowledge management applications as well as mobile communication devices may help with staying connected and self-organised. More often than not, however, new software introduces new functionalities, new complexity and more demands on learning its usage, thus creating extra workload.

Sixth, performance targets, especially if financial, tend to be increased periodically. This means that if employees meet their targets today, they will *face increased standards tomorrow*. This may lead to a feeling of 'permanent insufficiency' that increases stress and undermines one's sense of accomplishment (Dunkel et al. 2010). ICT can play a role in this if performance targets are increased automatically, say by 10 % for all employees. Automatic increases may be coupled to external market data making the whole process anonymous and seemingly 'objective' so that not even management can be held personally responsible for the extra workload.

Seventh, the direct coupling of employees' performance targets to the company's market performance also increases the *unpredictability* of future performance targets. ICT may help with making the market more transparent and predictable. Such functionality, however, mostly remains accessible to management and not to the ordinary employee.

Eighth, as these new management techniques generate new work requirements and tasks, they create *new demand for skills and qualifications*, beyond the core skills of each vocation (e.g. in areas such as marketing, communication, public relations, teamwork, project management, customer relationships, e-skills). The responsibility for acquiring such extended skills is often shifted to the individual worker – through self-training or on-the-job training – again adding to a workload which is already high (Valenduc et al. 2009). Although e-learning may help and make it easier to distribute knowledge and engage in learning, ICT in itself also creates new demands for learning.

Looking at the implications of the subjectification of work, another theory might be able to explain the origins of time and work pressure on a more general level. It is the *theory of conflicting work requirements* (Moldaschl 2010, Fig. 5.3). According to this model, stressful working conditions are created when there are conflicts between goals (tasks, informal expectations), rules (regulations, business processes) and resources (time, knowledge, tools). Time and work pressure occurs when there are conflicts between resources (time) and objectives (quantity and quality of work) or between resources (time) and regulations (administrative rules for documentation). But we also find typical conflicts between the personal goal to act professionally and the company's objective to fulfil financial targets. An insurance agent, for example, is given the target to sell policies generating profits of ten thousands of euros per month, even though he knows that most of these policies are not needed by his clients. This undermines his feelings of serving the customer well. Another potential conflict is that between the goal of fulfilling company-set performance standards (often coupled to individual earnings) and the goal of maintaining one's own health and welfare (Kratzer and Dunkel 2011). By working long hours at high speed and reducing the time for rejuvenation, employees put their health and well-being at risk – should this working pattern persist over longer periods of time. Another conflict is opening up between an

Fig. 5.3 The model of conflicting work requirements (Adapted from Moldaschl 2010)

increased nominal autonomy for workers and a simultaneous increase in the amount of rules and regulations. Salespeople, for example, might be allowed to sell their customers' products only in standardised bundles instead of custom-tailored packages. Thus their possibility to control the outcomes of their work is reduced and can only be regained by creating time-intense workarounds.

Finally, the discussion so far should have shown that ICT as a tool and thus as a resource for work is not fully utilised. It is often used as a conveyor of objectives and rules and regulations. Its main value is for management supporting indirect control and enhancing the transparency of the company. Its value as a resource for workers, however, is not fully utilised. In the context of time and work pressure, ICT might be used to facilitate (self-)scheduling and organising work as well as cooperation and coordination. The means to achieve this are available with techniques of *user-centred design* and *usability management* (ISO 2010; Hurtienne et al. 2009). The next section on computerisation looks more specifically at how ICT itself may contribute to increasing time and work pressure.

The main challenge for workers, however, is to see the negative consequences of indirect control as a structural problem instead of a personal insufficiency. Today, for most employees, these conflicts need to be resolved intrapersonally. Employees are motivated to want these goals simultaneously – to be a good entreployee, to be a good servant to the customer and to maintain their health and well-being. If they are unable to resolve these conflicts, employees often feel they are deficient and incapable of reaching the targets they are responsible for. As a consequence they put even more effort into showing what they can do. If employees could see these conflicts as a structural problem in which companies deliberately set unrealistically high-performance targets, they might have discovered one mechanism that expand their workload and their time and work pressure and they might take the steps necessary to counteract this (Kratzer and Nies 2009; Menz et al. 2011; Peters 2011).

5.4.3 Computerisation

Computerisation here stands for the increasing availability and reliance on information and communication technology (ICT) in everyday work. In Germany, for example, 58 % of the population say they cannot imagine life without the Internet, and about half (51 %) cannot imagine life without their mobile phone. Similarly, in their jobs, 58 % say they cannot forgo using their mobile phones at all (or at most for some hours) without getting into trouble; 36 % say this about their e-mail accounts (Huth 2011).

Information and communication technologies, on the one hand, are used to leverage the efficiency of work by making cooperation easier, providing faster and more accurate access to information and automatising repetitive working procedures. Users can work wherever necessary and share information with colleagues in real time. On the other hand, ICT can have negative effects that contribute to increased time and work pressure. One of the most widely discussed topics is *information overload*. About a third of the respondents in the study by Huth (2011) say they often feel flooded by information (another third say 'sometimes', a third 'never'). Time and work pressure is caused by having to sift through too much available information. New information is being produced at an increasing rate while copying and distributing information has become easier. In addition to its sheer amount, the information available may be contradictory and inaccurate, requiring time for evaluation. Apart from the Internet, where information just sits and waits to be used, e-mail is a major source of information overload, because information is pushed to the user, often requiring immediate attention; people struggle to keep up with the stream of incoming messages. As well as filtering out unsolicited commercial messages (spam), users also have to contend with a growing mass of e-mail attachments in the form of lengthy reports, presentations and media files. The problem becomes one of managing the e-mail inbox by sorting out unwanted e-mail from informative e-mail and from e-mail that needs to be acted upon.

A second consequence of increasing ICT use is that the technology enables employees to become *constantly available* to their bosses, colleagues and clients, thus extending time and work pressure into time periods that are actually meant for recreation and rejuvenation. Companies increasingly expect that their employees be available whenever needed, although they are not formally on standby service. This may also include nights, weekends and holidays. In the above study (Huth 2011), about 29 % say that they are always available outside of regular working hours, 37 % restrict this to evenings, but 8 % each are also available at weekends and in their holidays. Only 12 % say that they are never available outside of working hours. As a consequence the boundaries between work and life are blurring. A side effect of being constantly connected is that people may become compulsive about feeling connected and that they feel forced to respond instantly to work-related communication (Tarafdar et al. 2011; Rosa 2005).

Third, constant availability via phone or e-mail goes along with *frequent interruptions* of ongoing work and leads to multitasking (Tarafdar et al. 2011). This, of course, is detrimental to work that requires long periods of concentration like programming, writing reports, etc. Interruptions may result in tasks that are never finished. After an interruption it is necessary to return one's undivided attention to the original task at hand, and this requires additional time and mental resources.

Fourth, apart from lowering the threshold for the dissemination of information, modern ICT can also *lower the threshold for assigning new work tasks.* One example is the boss who assigns new tasks via the enterprise resource planning system instead of communicating personally. But it may also be the client who informally adds a new requirement to the ticketing system, because he can easily write an e-mail without going through a formal process of approval. The software engineer is likely to respond to the requirement because she later will be evaluated by this customer. Thus, the number of 'grey' assignments for workers is rising. These tasks are rarely official, but if not acted upon, they might harm the evaluation of the work unit or the individual employee who chooses not to respond to them. In combination with constant availability, these processes lower the ability of employees to plan their work and to stick to an assigned schedule. They do require that workers develop skills in scheduling tasks for themselves and that they renegotiate assignments with others, again activities that require additional time.

Fifth, if the *usability* of ICT is low, employees will spend unnecessary time entering and searching for data, formatting reports and trying to learn obscure functionalities; they will spend endless time recovering from errors (cf. Marcus 2005; Brodbeck et al. 1993). Computer crashes, downtime, network instabilities and idiosyncratic software not only waste time and effort but also frustrate users and, if they take the situation personally, can even enrage them (Brinks 2005). Our own research shows that negative ergonomic quality of software enhances worker's irritation and even the level of psychosomatic complaints (Hurtienne and Prümper 2003).

Sixth, one of the main reasons for introducing ICT systems is the *standardisation* of working tasks. Enterprise resource planning software like SAP software is often sold with the promise that implementing the software also implements the 'best practices' of the industry involved. However, companies usually refrain from customising the software to their specific needs and thus work with a one-size-fits-all solution that is often too complex to allow for efficient usage (cf. Hurtienne et al. 2009). This – aggravated by centralised decision-making about performance targets – introduces imperfect standardisation that actually keeps employees from being able to fully exploit the autonomy they purportedly gained through a management-by-objectives approach. The combination of overly ambitious targets and restricted autonomy through standardisation facilitated by ICT use is a very explosive mixture regarding workers' time and work pressure and its stressful consequences (Menz et al. 2011).

Seventh, enterprise resource planning systems are often sold with the promise to have real-time access to all relevant process variables in the company. What is not said, however, is that someone must *provide all the data* that gives management the ability to achieve a 'transparent company'. This promise often means additional work for employees on the shop floor, who must enter data into the system that are not germane to the job at hand and only add to their workload.

Eighth, ICT use also changes how teams work together (cf. the notion of *virtual teams*). ICT contributes to a shrinking world; communication is possible across great distances and work teams become distributed over large spatial areas, often spanning several continents. This may add problems of cooperation and coordination due to different working styles, languages and work rhythms. So, for example, it was found that virtual teams located in different time zones were more strongly affected than teams spread across similar distances within the same time zone, because the former spent more time maintaining their communications (Cummings 2011). ICT also may impoverish communication by reducing the amount of small talk in a virtual meeting. This 'chatter' is necessary to keep up a team spirit, to gauge the general mood and stress level, to smooth out potential conflicts and to grease the wheels of cooperation.

In summary it must be said that ICT does not directly cause information overload, constant availability, assignment of new tasks, standardisation, etc. Instead it works as facilitator and accelerator of behavioural tendencies that were observed before. Sometimes this facilitation and acceleration effect crosses a threshold and then a new quality is added to the experience of time and work pressure by employees.

5.4.4 Acceleration

In his theory of social acceleration, Hartmut Rosa (2003, 2005) differentiates between technological acceleration (e.g. the acceleration of transport, communication and production), acceleration of social change (e.g. of institutions, habits, fashions and lifestyles) and the acceleration of the pace of work and life (i.e. the time needed for activities, the feeling of being hurried and of time and work pressure). ICT in this case would be part of technological acceleration. From this, however, it does not follow that increased use of ICT would result in more time and work pressure. Paradoxically, technology use has been connected with saving time, because technology enables us to do things quicker than before. The same for ICT. A letter that took several days before can now be sent instantly using e-mail. Thus, the speed of communication is said to have increased by a factor of 10^7, and the speed of data processing by 10^6 (Rosa 2003). If everything can be done faster, then how can an increase in time pressure be possible at all?

Rosa suggests that time pressure is a phenomenon where growth rates overtake acceleration rates. Although we can do things faster, the number of things to do grows even more, in the result making it difficult to keep pace. And so – even though competition in a global market, subjectification of work and increased use of ICT contribute to a faster working life – they also facilitate the accretion of more and more work.

As an example, the ever-changing nature of the World Wide Web opens up new communication channels that allow for a fast distribution of information. In the past, information about a new product could be posted to the press and it may have secured the attention of the target group. With the advent of the Internet, the same information now needs to be put on a website, might be part of an e-mail newsletter, and gets announced on social media platforms like Twitter and Facebook. Although essentially the same content, it needs to be tailored to the specific media channels, thus introducing more work than before. On a more trivial note, if the introduction of new ICT accelerates business processes, this often goes along with staffing cuts. The result is that the amount of work to do per person increases and the impact of each additional colleague missing (e.g. due to illness) on time and work pressure is higher than before.

The consequences of social acceleration are also indirect. What – under conditions of low-speed change – remained one-off or occasional tasks are now permanently on the agenda and thus increasing time and work pressure. The rapid sequence of technological and organisational changes, for example, requires more effort by the employees to adjust to ever-changing circumstances. Changes might occur through 'permanent restructuring' of organisations to meet market needs. They might occur through technological change but also due to changing requirements of customers and clients. The consequences are that work is less foreseeable; employees are less able to schedule and plan their upcoming tasks. On a larger scale, their employment situation is no longer predictable.

Constant change leads to a decrease in resources. Skills and qualifications rapidly become outdated, previous routines are not applicable, and the time available is too short to establish a new routine. As a consequence, experience and expertise is devalued and there is increasing need for permanent learning and familiarising oneself with new styles of work, new colleagues, etc. All these activities require time and acceleration devalues the time previously invested. Hence acceleration-related time and work pressure is one of the major stressors of modern working life (cf. Kubicek et al. 2013; Ulferts et al. 2013, for first empirical results on Rosa's theory).

5.4.5 *Interim Conclusion*

The above trends, loosely knitted together, show the main trends in today's world of changing work. Although our focus was on how these trends affect time and work pressure today, it also is possible that these enhance possibilities for coping. Management by objectives, for example, can provide greater autonomy that allows for a better and more flexible scheduling of work (Kratzer and Nies 2009). The use of ICT, and especially mobile phones, may change social practices; it may make it possible to cope with and coordinate during times of high work density (instead of just producing these; Wajcman 2008). Of course these four factors are not distinct.

They work together and depend on one another in producing time and work pressure.

Finally, by looking at competition, subjectification, computerisation and acceleration, the 'ordinary' causes of time and work pressure should not be forgotten. Classic problems in the regulation of work activity remain valid: all kinds of interruptions, inadequate equipment, lack of information, social conflicts with supervisors, colleagues and clients, etc. These also contribute to increasing time and work pressure, as do personality variables like skills and knowledge, commitment, tolerance for stress, ambition, etc.

In summary one can say that many causing factors of time and work pressure are known. Empirical research is scarce, however, on the way in which conditions and actors work together to produce concrete instances of time and work pressure, on how employees evaluate the time and work pressure they experience, on how they deal with that pressure and cope with increased demands and on which individual and organisational strategies can prevent the negative consequences of time and work pressure. The remainder of this chapter will briefly look at the issues of coping and work design and hint at further research that is necessary to better understand and address these issues.

5.5 Coping Styles and Work Redesign: First Approaches

If time and work pressure is too high or too long lasting to be sustainable any more: what are typical coping strategies under the circumstances discussed so far? Kratzer and Dunkel (2011), under the heading 'work and health in conflict', discuss defensive and active coping techniques. A defensive style would be characterised by renouncing career progression, enhanced status or higher pay in order to escape from higher demands. Often people reduce their working time to minimise their exposure to pressure at work. Others move to a different employer in the hope of finding a better work environment there. Some withdraw into a niche where they hope to be less affected; others diminish their commitment to work. The more committed are more likely to postpone a solution to a later time. Instead they modify their perception of the situation or even deny negative consequences of time and work pressure (especially with regard to their health and well-being).

People who actively cope with pressure will proactively seek rejuvenation during their time away from work. They exercise, work in the garden, foster social relationships and pay more attention to their nutrition. They try to work more efficiently and be better time managers. They put up rules for themselves and others. They hone their skills, read books and attend seminars. Others tend to over-engage and overcommit to work, ending up in what Peters (2011) describes as 'interested self-harming'.

Although these coping styles have been shown to exist, little is known about the circumstances in which they are possible and effective and what their specific benefits, drawbacks and side-effects might be. Most importantly, these coping strategies remain at the individual level while the problems are more of an organisational and structural nature. A large number of self-help books on time management and self-management are available that address individual coping strategies. Similarly, a number of companies offer training and coaching to their employees to cope with time and work pressure. But their perspective is still on the individual coping styles, e.g. more effective and efficient work habits as well as better nutrition and exercise. Although these strategies may be helpful in coping with the strain resulting from time and work pressure, they do not address the underlying problems that are structural, organisational, cultural and social. For example, it may help to go for a run after a stressful day but the underlying causes of work-related stress are not addressed.

Adhering to traditional occupational psychology (Gniza 1994; Hacker 1998), we believe that changing the circumstances or conditions under which work is carried out is more effective than trying to change workers' behaviour by individual strategies alone. Traditional work design concepts like job enrichment, job enlargement or job rotation are not applicable anymore, because jobs today are already enriched, enlarged and offer multiple challenges to workers. Under today's conditions of greater autonomy and highly individualised work conditions, the main task becomes to enable employees to change their own working conditions and redesign their work themselves.

Although further research remains necessary, any work redesign that addresses the problems of time and work pressure needs to observe some basic rules. Due to the complex and subjectivised nature of the work today, work design needs to be done bottom-up, should get employees involved and should not be a process that is top-down controlled by management or external consultants. Work design should be understood as a continuous process, not as a one-off project. An appropriate tool to work design therefore is the workshop in which problems are discussed in teams and changes to the working conditions can be decided. The continuous process ensures a revision of the strategies and enables to change procedures when general conditions change. One major aspect of such workshops is to agree on new rules and regulations to balance work demands and workers' health.

Examples of work redesign strategies as the result of a number of workshops involving IT knowledge workers are provided by Gerlmaier (2010). The strategies developed to change working conditions, by way of example, suggest:

- Limiting to a maximum of two the number of projects in which an employee is involved at any given time
- Agreeing on blocks of 'quiet time' permitting interruption-free work on tasks that require high levels of concentration
- Segregating the times in which project work is done from periods reserved for answering customer inquiries
- Making stress and psychic well-being a regular topic in weekly group meetings
- Optimising technical reporting and documentation systems to reduce time spent on administrative duties

Although these are recommendations that go far beyond the usual company offerings on the individual level, the implementation of these ideas is not widespread and there is no empirical data available yet on their effectiveness.

While the suggested approaches focus on the levels of workgroups and project teams, it remains less clear how to address changes in employees' working conditions in the higher levels of management. First, due to a high-performance culture among managers, they may not see time and work pressure as something that needs to be addressed at all. Second, and more importantly, however, since they are far removed from the operational level of business, they are not competent enough to understand what resources and tools are needed to help employees cope with their jobs. Third, it is highly unlikely that upper management is undoing the processes of flexibilisation, subjectification, computerisation and acceleration, because they currently seem to be the only solution to the many problems businesses face in today's globalised and competitive markets. Thus, if the problem is recognised at all, it is delegated to Health and Safety or Corporate Health Management departments that again come up with individualised solutions.

Because it is difficult to address work redesign beyond the operational level, sociologists tend to suggest collective actions. Trade unions and works councils should on the political level get involved with changing working conditions. Again, this appears difficult, because the problems with time and work pressure seem highly individualistic and subjectivised and do not (yet) lend themselves to collective action. Similarly, individual circumstances seem to evade policy making and health and safety legislation. It is known that employees feel, for example, even more time pressured when faced with – in their eyes restrictive – working time regulations (Kratzer and Dunkel 2011; Menz et al. 2011).

To conclude, from the above trends, some suggestions for further strategies include:

- To supply employees with the appropriate resources to meet ambitious targets
- To reduce the amount of administrative duties, documentation and reporting
- To acknowledge and support the large amount of invisible work employees are engaged in
- To reduce the density and speed of communication, especially via ICT systems
- To simplify complex process chains
- To support self-education and training
- To sensitise and to provide room for reflection on how to improve unsatisfying working conditions

5.6 Conclusion and Outlook

Time and work pressure is an important topic in today's world of work. Many people are affected and the consequences can be grim. Current theoretical models, however, say little about how time and work pressure comes into being, under what circumstances its consequences are positive or detrimental to health and what to do about it. Although it is easy to derive simple analytical models that can describe the main contributors to time and work pressure (i.e. large amounts of work to do, at high quality, with insufficient time), empirical research undertaken by sociologists shows that the picture has many more facets and is not as easy to understand as the simple triangle model in Fig. 5.1 suggests. This chapter has reviewed four major trends that contribute to the predominance of time and work pressure in today's world of work. We have identified a complex web of influences that can be described with the keywords of competition, subjectification, computerisation and acceleration. We briefly looked at how people cope with the increasing demands resulting from these trends and have looked at first attempts to derive techniques and methods for work redesign.

The central thesis is that acceleration and information technology do influence the quality of working life, but this must be seen against a background of larger trends involving competition and subjectification of work. Therefore, measures derived to enhance the quality of working life need to take the larger picture into account in order to be successful and sustainable. It is not technological or social acceleration per se that needs to be observed and monitored, but instead the interaction of these developments, how people go on with their lives and the changing values, activities and relationships that develop in interaction with these trends. Or as Judy Wajcman (2008, p. 67) puts it, 'We need to ask whether there is evidence that people are collectively finding ways to appropriate, adapt and actively shape the use of digital technologies to take more control of time rather than being victims of uncontrollable instantaneous time'.

Our approach to further research, therefore, is coping oriented. What are the strategies and coping mechanisms developed by organisations, teams and individuals as a reaction to time and work pressure? What strategies for prevention and coping are deemed useful? What are the organisational and cultural conditions that influence whether these strategies and coping mechanisms are realised? Thus, we combine the individual level of analysis with the organisational and team-related levels. Strategies for work design, so is our belief, need to address the interactions between these levels and cannot be focussed on one of these areas alone.

Finally, although strongly involved in the creation of time and work pressure, technology is not the culprit. ICT may facilitate human behaviour that increases time and work pressure, e.g. by enhancing workload, allowing a blurring between work and leisure, posing new learning challenges, etc. But in the end, ICT may also facilitate coping with time and work pressure by supporting the 'micro-coordination of everyday life, allowing for tighter and more efficient 'real time' planning of activities [...] They may offer positive forms of temporal control, enabling more people to have not only more time but time of their choice' (Wajcman 2008, p. 71). While we did not focus on these effects in this chapter, this promises a fruitful area of further exploration.

Further research will help to develop sustainable approaches to dealing with time and work pressure. Although individual strategies are en vogue at present, they often cannot be effective because of organisational or cultural restrictions.

We believe that novel approaches to work design need to take account of individual, team-related and organisational options for influencing time and work pressure and to consider the interactions among those options.

Acknowledgements This research was conducted within the research cluster 'Work Intensity/ Time and Work Pressure in Qualified Service Work' of the German Federal Institute for Occupational Health and Safety in Berlin, Germany. We would like to thank our expert interviewees for their contributions to our understanding of time and work pressure in today's world of work.

References

Ahlers, E. (2009). *WSI/PARGEMA Betriebsrätebefragung 2008/09 zu Arbeitsbedingungen und Gesundheit im Betrieb* [WSI/PARGEMA survey of works councils about working conditions and occupational health] [PowerPoint slides]. http://www.pargema.de/files/pargema_10_ahlers_1.pdf

Ahlers, E. (2011). *Belastungen am Arbeitsplatz und betrieblicher Gesundheitsschutz vor dem Hintergrund des demografischen Wandels* [Stress at the work place and occupational health in relation to demographical change] (WSI-Discussion Paper Nr. 175). Düsseldorf: Wirtschafts- und Sozialwissenschaftliches Institut in der Hans-Böckler-Stiftung.

Brinkmann, U. (2011). *Die unsichtbare Faust des Marktes: Betriebliche Kontrolle und Koordination im Finanzmarktkapitalismus* [The invisible fist of the market. Organisational control and coordination in financial market capitalism]. Berlin: Edition Sigma.

Brinks, M. (2005). *Aggression gegen Computer: Eine wissenschaftliche Untersuchung eines alltäglichen Phänomens* [Aggression against computers. A scientific investigation of a daily phenomenon]. Stuttgart: Ibidem.

Bröckling, U. (2007). *Das unternehmerische Selbst. Soziologie einer Subjektivierungsform* [The entrepreneurial self. Sociology of a form of subjectification]. Frankfurt am Main: Suhrkamp.

Brodbeck, F. C., Zapf, D., Prümper, J., & Frese, M. (1993). Error handling in office work with computers: A field study. *Journal of Occupational and Organizational Psychology, 60*(4), 303–317.

Brödner, P. (2002). Über den notorisch unproduktiven Umgang mit Computersystemen [About the notoriously unproductive use of computer systems]. Reports of the Faculty IV. Technical University Berlin. *Elektrotechnik und Informatik, 25*, 48–51.

Brynjolfsson, E. (2003, July). The IT productivity gap. *Optimize Magazine,* 21.

Buch, A., & Andersen, V. (2009, July 13–15). *Knowledge work and stress – Between strain and enthusiasm.* Paper presented at CMS6 Conference – Stream 17 – The Meaning of Work, Warwick Business School, Coventry, UK. http://www.videnogstress.dk/

Burke, R. J., Koyuncu, M., Fiksenbaum, L., & Acar, F. T. (2009). Work hours, intensity, satisfactions and psychological well-being among Turkish manufacturing managers. *Europe's Journal of Psychology, 5*(2), 12–30.

Burke, R. J., Singh, P., & Fiksenbaum, L. (2010). Work intensity: Potential antecedents and consequences. *Personnel Review, 39*(3), 347–360. doi:10.1108/00483481011030539.

Cummings, J. N. (2011). Geography is alive and well in virtual teams. *Communications of the ACM, 54*(8), 24–26.

Dunkel, W., Kratzer, N., & Menz, W. (2010). "Permanentes Ungenügen" und "Veränderung in Permanenz" – Belastungen durch neue Steuerungsformen ["Permanent insufficiency" and "permanent change" – Stress through new forms of control]. *WSI Mitteilungen, 63*(7), 357–364.

Eurofound. (2010). *Changes over time - First findings from the fifth European Working Conditions Survey*. Retrieved from http://www.eurofound.europa.eu/pubdocs/2010/74/en/3/EF1074EN.pdf

Gerlmaier, A. (2010). Innovationsarbeit alternsgerecht gestalten [Designing innovation work for ageing]. *Wirtschaftspsychologie, 12*(3), 38–48.

Gniza, E. (1994). Bedeutung und Ergiebigkeit von Unfalluntersuchungen [Importance and productiveness of investigations of accidents]. *Arbeitsschutz aktuell, 5*, 4–7.

Green, F. (2001). It's been a hard day's night: The concentration and intensification of work in late twentieth century Britain. *British Journal of Industrial Relations, 39*(1), 53–80.

Green, F. (2004). Why has work effort become more intense? *Industrial Relations: A Journal of Economy and Society, 43*(4), 709–741.

Greiner, B., & Leitner, K. (1989). Assessment of job stress: The RHIA-instrument. In K. Landau & W. Rohmert (Eds.), *Recent developments in job analysis*. Proceedings of the international symposium on job analysis (pp. 53–66), University of Hohenheim. London: Taylor & Francis.

Hacker, W. (1998). *Allgemeine Arbeitspsychologie: Psychische Regulation von Arbeitstätigkeiten* [General work psychology. Psychological regulation of work activities]. Berlin/Stuttgart: Hans Huber.

Hacker, W. (2003). Action regulation theory: A practical tool for the design of modern work processes? *European Journal of Work and Organizational Psychology, 12*(2), 105–130.

Hurtienne, J., & Prümper, J. (2003). Stress in the office: The influence of software-ergonomic quality. In D. Harris, V. Duffy, M. Smith, & C. Stephanidis (Eds.), *Human-centred computing: Cognitive, social, and ergonomic aspects* (pp. 63–67). Mahwah/London: Lawrence Erlbaum Associates.

Hurtienne, J., Prümper, J., & Rötting, M. (2009). When enterprise resource planning needs software ergonomics: Some typical scenarios. In *Proceedings of the 17th World Congress on Ergonomics (IEA 2009)* [CD-ROM]. Beijing: IEA.

Huth, N. (2011). *Connected worlds*. Presentation held at the symposium "Permanent online!? Betriebliche Herausforderungen der Erreichbarkeitsökonomie". Evangelische Akademie, Tutzing.

Huws, U. (Ed.). (2008). *The globalisation glossary: A researcher's guide to understanding work organisation restructuring in a knowledge-based society*. Leuven: Katholieke Universiteit Leuven, Higher Institute of Labour Studies. http://www.worksproject.be/documents/Glossary_DRUK.pdf

ISO. (2010). *EN ISO 9241 Ergonomics of human-system interaction – Part 210: Human-centred design process for interactive systems*. Berlin: Beuth.

Junghanns, G., Hurtienne, J., & Stilijanow, U. (2011). Arbeitsintensität/Zeit- und Leistungsdruck bei Dienstleistungstätigkeiten – Entstehungszusammenhänge und Gestaltungsmöglichkeiten im Bereich der Arbeitsorganisation [Work intensity, time and work pressure in service work – Origins and possibilities for work design with regard to work organisation]. In F. W. Nerdinger & S. Curth (Eds.), *Arbeit – Organisation – Wirtschaft. Wissenschaft für die Praxis. 7. Tagung der Fachgruppe Arbeits-, Organisations- und Wirtschaftspsychologie der Deutschen Gesellschaft für Psychologie* (p. 10). Rostock: Universität Rostock.

Karasek, R. A. (1979). Job demands, job latitude, and mental strain: Implications for job redesign. *Administrative Science Quarterly, 24*, 285–308.

Kieselbach, T., Rogovsky, N., Sahler, B., Thomson, G., Triomphe, C. E., Widerszal-Bazyl, M., Armgarth, E., et al. (2009). *Health in restructuring: Innovative approaches and policy recommendations*. München/Mering: Rainer Hampp.

Kratzer, N., & Dunkel, W. (2011). Arbeit und Gesundheit im Konflikt [Work and health in conflict]. In N. Kratzer, W. Dunkel, K. Becker, & S. Hinrichs (Eds.), *Arbeit und Gesundheit im Konflikt – Analysen und Ansätze für ein partizipatives Gesundheitsmanagement* (pp. 13–34). Berlin: Edition Sigma.

Kratzer, N., & Nies, S. (2009). *Neue Leistungspolitik bei Angestellten* [New performance policy for white collar workers]. Berlin: Edition Sigma.

Kubicek, B., Korunka, C., & Ulferts, H. (2013). Acceleration in the care of older adults: New demands as predictors of employee burnout and engagement. *Journal of Advanced Nursing, 69* (7), 1525–1538. doi:10.1111/jan.12011

Locke, E. A., & Latham, G. P. (1990). *A theory of goal setting and task performance*. Englewood Cliffs: Prentice-Hall.

Marcus, A. (2005). User interface design's return on investment: Examples and statistics. In R. G. Bias & D. J. Mayhew (Eds.), *Cost-justifying usability. An update for the internet age* (pp. 17–39). Amsterdam: Morgan Kaufmann.

Menz, W., Dunkel, W., & Kratzer, N. (2011). Leistung und Leiden. Neue Steuerungsformen von Leistung und ihre Belastungswirkungen [Performance and suffering. New forms of performance control and their effects on stress]. In N. Kratzer, W. Dunkel, K. Becker, & S. Hinrichs (Eds.), *Arbeit und Gesundheit im Konflikt – Analysen und Ansätze für ein partizipatives Gesundheitsmanagement* (pp. 143–198). Berlin: Edition Sigma.

Moldaschl, M. (2010). Widersprüchliche Arbeitsanforderungen. Ein nichtlinearer Ansatz zur Analyse von Belastung und Bewältigung in der Arbeit [Conflicting work requirements. A non-linear approach to analysing stress and coping at work]. In G. Faller (Ed.), *Lehrbuch Betriebliche Gesundheitsförderung* (pp. 82–94). Bern/Zürich: Huber.

Peters, K. (2011). Indirekte Steuerung und interessierte Selbstgefährdung [Indirect control and interested self-harming]. In N. Kratzer, W. Dunkel, K. Becker, & S. Hinrichs (Eds.), *Arbeit und Gesundheit im Konflikt – Analysen und Ansätze für ein partizipatives Gesundheitsmanagement* (pp. 105–122). Berlin: Edition Sigma.

Pinchot, G. (1985). *Intrapreneuring: Why you don't have to leave the corporation to become an entrepreneur*. New York: Harper & Row.

Pongratz, H. J., & Voß, G. (2003). *Arbeitskraftunternehmer. Erwerbsorientierungen in entgrenzten Arbeitsformen* [Entreployee. Employment orientation in boundaryless work]. Berlin: Edition Sigma.

Rosa, H. (2003). Social acceleration: Ethical and political consequences of a desynchronized high-speed society. *Constellations. An International Journal of Critical and Democratic Theory, 10*, 3–52.

Rosa, H. (2005). *Beschleunigung: Die Veränderung der Zeitstrukturen in der Moderne* [Acceleration. Changing time structures in modernity]. Frankfurt am Main: Suhrkamp.

Siegrist, J. (1996). Adverse health effects of high-effort/low-reward conditions. *Journal of Occupational Health Psychology, 1*, 27–41.

Tarafdar, M., Tu, Q., Ragu-Nathan, T. S., & Ragu-Nathan, B. S. (2011). Crossing to the dark side: Examining creators, outcomes, and inhibitors of technostress. *Communications of the ACM, 54* (9), 113–120.

Trägner, U. (2006). *Arbeitszeitschutzrechtliche Bewertung der Intensität von Arbeitsleistungen unter besonderer Berücksichtigung der Rechtsprechung des Europäischen Gerichtshofes zum Bereitschaftsdienst* [Evaluation of work intensity with regard to working time legislation in particular with respect to the jurisdiction of the European Court of Justice regarding on-call duty]. Konstanz: Hartung-Gorre.

Ulferts, H., Korunka, C., & Kubicek, B. (2013). Acceleration in working life: An empirical test of a sociological framework. *Time & Society, 22*(2), 161–185. doi:10.1177/0961463X12471006

Valenduc, G., Vendramin, P., Pedaci, M., & Piersanti, M. (2009). *Changing careers and trajectories how individuals cope with organisational change and restructuring*. Leuven: Katholieke Universiteit Leuven, Higher Institute of Labour Studies. http://worksproject.be/Works_pdf/WP12%20publiek/13_D12.5%20Thematic%20Report_New%20career_DRUK.pdf

Wajcman, J. (2008). Life in the fast lane? Towards a sociology of technology and time. *The British Journal of Sociology, 59*(1), 59–77.

Zapf, D. (1993). Stress-oriented analysis of computerized office work. *European Work and Organisational Psychologist, 3*(2), 85–100.

Chapter 6
Technostress: The Dark Side of Technologies

Marisa Salanova, Susana Llorens, and Mercedes Ventura

6.1 Conceptualizing Technostress Experiences

Internet, Wi-Fi, teleworking, e-conomy, and the information society are all familiar concepts nowadays. Technologies have become part of our private and public lives. In the workplace, these technologies have been introduced in most socioeconomic sectors, as well as in all functional areas of modern organizations. Data from European surveys reveal that 74 % of workers in European countries use technologies in their daily work and 93 % use the Internet in different facets of their lives (see Llorens et al. 2011). However, although organizations recognize the benefits of using technologies to increase business competitiveness and promote economic prosperity, the use of those technologies can also produce serious disadvantages, like technostress, as a job stressor in the workplace.

The concept of technostress was first coined in 1984 by Craig Brod (1984) in his book *Technostress: The Human Cost of the Computer Revolution*. Technostress was defined as a modern disease of adaptation caused by an inability to cope with new computer technologies in a healthy way. For Brod the technostress is a form of adaptation disorder. Since the original concept of technostress was put forward, different definitions have been developed that include psychological, physical, or behavioral strain responses to technostressors. For example, Wang et al. (2008, p. 3004) defined technostress as a "reflection of one's discomposure, fear, tenseness, and anxiety when one is learning and using computer technology directly or

M. Salanova (✉) • S. Llorens
WONT (Work & Organization NeTwork) Research Team, Department of Social Psychology, Universitat Jaume I, Castelló de la Plana, Castellón, Spain
e-mail: Marisa.Salanova@uji.es; llorgum@uji.es

M. Ventura
WONT (Work & Organization NeTwork) Research Team, Department of Education, Universitat Jaume I, Castelló de la Plana, Castellón, Spain
e-mail: mventura@uji.es

C. Korunka and P. Hoonakker (eds.), *The Impact of ICT on Quality of Working Life*,
DOI 10.1007/978-94-017-8854-0_6, © Springer Science+Business Media Dordrecht 2014

indirectly, that ultimately ends in psychological and emotional repulsion and prevents one from further learning or using computer technology."

Based on workplace contexts, Salanova and colleagues (Salanova et al. 2007, 2013) proposed a more operational definition of the technostress experience in the workplace. They defined technostress at work as a negative psychological state associated with the use (and abuse) of technology as well as the threat of technology use in the future. Moreover, technostress is related to a mismatch among demands and resources related to technology in the workplace. This experience is related to negative psychological experiences such as feelings of anxiety, mental fatigue, skepticism, inefficacy beliefs, and addiction to technology. The novelty of this definition is that (1) technostress is seen as a negative psychological experience; (2) technostress does not occur as a result of the negative impact of technology per se, but depends on the relationship between demands and resources; (3) technostress is extended to the use of technology in general (e.g., computers, tablets, smartphones, videogames, e-mail, social networks); and (4) two different technostress experiences should be differentiated: technostrain and technoaddiction.

6.1.1 Technostrain: Feeling Anxious with Technologies

Technostrain could be considered a negative psychological experience composed of (1) high levels of anxiety and fatigue (affective dimension), (2) skepticism (attitudinal dimension), and (3) inefficacy (cognitive dimension) related to the use of technology (Salanova et al. 2013). As shown by the results of a review of "technostress" from 1982 to 2012 in the PsycINFO database, around 90 % of the publications are specifically related to technostrain experiences (521 articles). This provides evidence that technostrain is the most traditional type of technostress experience.

According to previous research, the technostrain experience is commonly determined by high levels of anxiety, that is, by high physiological activation, tension, and discomfort with regard to technologies. Experiencing anxiety includes the fear of hitting a wrong key and losing information, doubts about using computers for fear of making a mistake, and finding computers intimidating (cf. Ragu-Nathan et al. 2008).

Secondly, users also feel lower levels of psychological activation, i.e., mental fatigue. One of the special experiences of fatigue is information fatigue syndrome (IFS), which derives from the current requirements of the information society and from dealing with information overload (Lewis 1996). The consequences of IFS are related to poor decision-making, difficulty in memorizing and remembering, and reduced attention span.

The third component in the technostrain experience is skepticism, which refers to the attitudinal dimension of the syndrome. The term skepticism is based on studies conducted on job burnout, specifically on the burnout dimension of "cynicism." Skepticism, as a dimension of technostrain, is defined as the display of indifferent, detached, and distant attitudes toward the use of technology. More specifically it is a feeling of cognitive distancing that consists in developing indifference or a cynical attitude when users are exhausted and discouraged due to the use of technology (Schaufeli and Salanova 2007).

The last dimension of technostrain is inefficacy beliefs about the right use of technology. Previous research has shown that technology-related self-efficacy influences the choice of whether to use technologies or not, the expenditure on effort and persistence, and the performance achieved with the use of technology (Bandura 1997). In fact, technology self-efficacy has proven its role in enhancing motivation in the use of technology and moderating the levels of job burnout (Salanova et al. 2000) and anxiety related to technology use (Henderson et al. 1995).

This multidimensional model of technostrain was tested in a sample of 1,072 ICT users ($N = 675$ non-intensive ICT users and $N = 397$ intensive ICT users) (Salanova et al. 2013). Results from multigroup confirmatory factor analyses among non-intensive and intensive ICT users showed, as expected, the four-factor structure of technostrain in both samples.

6.1.2 Technoaddiction: Being Abusive with Technologies

According to the World Health Organization (WHO) (Arias et al. 2012; Kessler and Ustun 2008), the abuse of technology has increased and one out of four people is suffering from addiction to technologies in one way or another in 2008. The concept of technoaddiction is based on the literature on workaholism, i.e., the tendency to work excessively hard in a compulsive way (Libano et al. 2010). Workaholism and technoaddiction might go together, as there is a connection between working excessively and the use of technology (Porter and Kakabadse 2006).

Technoaddiction is defined "as a specific technostress experience due to an uncontrollable compulsion to use technology 'everywhere and anytime' and to use them for long periods of time in an excessive way" (Salanova et al. 2007, p. 2). People experience technoaddiction when using technology not for pleasure or satisfaction but from an internal impulse through which they feel compelled to use it and keep up to date with the last technological advances. In fact, they become psychologically dependent on the technology and, consequently, technology becomes the only relevant thing in their lives. This psychological dependence results in an individual's inability to live without technology, without their mobile phone, without checking their e-mail all day long, without being connected to the Internet anytime and anywhere, without their social networks, and so forth.

To sum up, recent research shows that technoaddiction is characterized by (1) "compulsion" in the use of technology, i.e., the person is obsessed with technology and persistently and frequently thinks about/uses it; (2) "excessive use" of technology, i.e., they tend to allocate exceptionally large amounts of time to using technology; (3) they feel anxious when they are not using it; and (4) fatigue related to using technology in excess (see Llorens et al. 2011; Salanova et al. 2013).

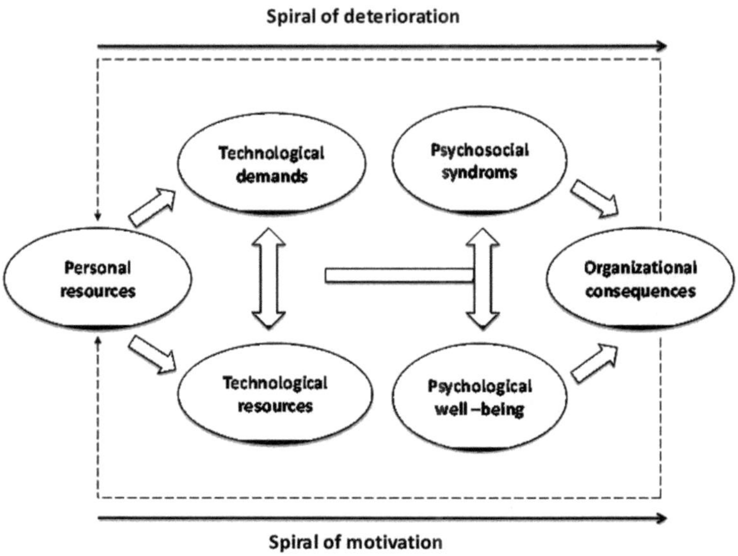

Fig. 6.1 Spiral Model of Occupational Health (SMOH)

6.2 Predictors and Consequences of Technostress

Several theoretical models in Occupational Health Psychology may be useful to understand the process of technostress (e.g., Lazarus and Folkman 1984), but we explain the antecedents and consequences of technostress based on the Spiral Model of Occupational Health (SMOH; Salanova et al. 2007, 2009). Generally speaking, the SMOH Model displays the following characteristics (see Fig. 6.1):

1. According to WHO, health is a state of complete physical, psychological, and social well-being, and not just the mere absence of illness.
2. The model is grounded in Positive Occupational Health Psychology (POHP), since it tests psychosocial health in a holistic, comprehensive way that encompasses not only the assessment of psychosocial distress (e.g., technostress) but also well-being (e.g., technoflow).
3. The technostress experience is explained by a negative spiral of deterioration (i.e., a vicious spiral) which is determined by low personal resources (specifically, low technology self-efficacy). These resources enhance the perception of high technological demands and low technological resources, which in turn gives rise to psychosocial syndromes (e.g., technostrain), negative organizational consequences (e.g., low performance), and so on.

Based on the key dimensions of the SMOH Model, the main determinants of technostress (technological demands and lack of technological and personal resources), as well as their consequences, are described below.

6.2.1 Technological Demands and Technostress

Technological demands are defined as "those physical and/or psychological, social and organizational aspects related to technology that require a sustained physical and/or psychological effort from the worker, and which are associated to certain physiological and/or psychological costs" (Llorens et al. 2011, p. 53). Based on the SMOH Model, we can distinguish four types of technological demands, which are detailed below.

First, technological demands at the task level are the ones closest to users, since they are associated with the tasks that users employ technology to perform. The main technological demands are (1) quantitative overload, the degree to which a technology user perceives there is an excess of work generated as a result of the use of technology or network outages (Salanova et al. 2013; Yang and Carayon 1995); (2) mental qualitative overload, the extent to which work with technologies requires excessive attentional demands such as concentration, precision, or multitasking to solve problems in order to prevent or correct errors (Salanova et al. 2007); (3) ergonomic qualitative overload, the extent to which technology causes ergonomic workload, in terms of awkward postures and repetitive movements that can lead to psychosomatic complaints, such as itchy eyes or carpal tunnel syndrome (Tarafdar et al. 2007); (4) continuous pace of technology, the extent to which the user perceives that the time required to perform one or more tasks using technology is less than the time available to do them (Korunka et al. 1995); (5) role ambiguity, the degree to which tasks performed with technologies are vague, unclear, and ill-defined (Salanova et al. 2013); and (6) routine, the degree to which tasks performed with technology are boring, repetitive, monotonous, unchallenging, and not motivating.

Second, technological demands at the social level refer to the relationship people establish with other people at the workplace because of the use of technology. These relationships can be developed with co-workers but also with people outside the organizations (e.g., external clients). The most important social demand is role conflict, i.e., when the technology user perceives a conflict between the use of new and traditional technology, as well as when the user belongs to multiple virtual teams whose modus operandi is completely different (Tarafdar et al. 2007). Social isolation due to the use of virtual relations with colleagues and clients could be another social technostressor. Finally, in the study by Salanova et al. (2013), it was showed that emotional overload and mobbing were also predictors of technostrain at work.

Third, technological demands at the organizational level are those which are related to the maintenance of competitive advantage and to "staying" alive in the labor market: (1) job insecurity, when users perceive that their job is at risk because technologies will replace them or, otherwise, because of "technological unemployment"; (2) organizational culture, the organizational pyramid structure and innovative structure show higher levels of technostress because of the lack of employees' participation in decision-making and higher levels of international competitiveness (Wang et al. 2008); (3) technological obstacles such as lack of training regarding ICT (Salanova et al. 2013); and (4) the technology implementation approach: if the implementation is focused on "technology," it will produce technostress, whereas if the implementation is focused on the "end user," it will produce well-being (Salanova et al. 2007).

Finally, technological demands at the extra-organizational level are mainly related to work-family conflict. These are basically produced when there is a conflict between working and personal life which comes about when technologies invade our private live; that is, people need to be connected to answer their e-mail, thus reducing the time available to enjoy life with their family at the weekend, for example.

6.2.2 (Lack of) Technological Resources and Technostress

Other key factors in the development of the technostress experience are the lack of technological resources. Generally, they are defined as "those physical, structural, social and organizational aspects of work with technologies that are functional in achieving goals, reduce the technological demands, and stimulate growing and personal development" (Llorens et al. 2011, p. 53). Again, technological resources can be differentiated into three levels that are detailed below.

First, the main technological resources at the task level are (1) autonomy (the degree of control, responsibilities, and challenges related to work with technologies (Jackson et al. 1993; Salanova et al. 2013)); (2) participation in the process of implementing technologies at work; (3) variety of tasks, (novelty and change in the work environment caused by technology, in terms of the activities and skills that need to be carried out (intrinsic variety) and changes in the environment (extrinsic variety)); and finally, (4) clarity in the task, which refers to the degree to which the role and tasks to be carried out by the technology users are well defined.

Second, technological resources at the social level refer to (1) social networks and trust, which is understood as the contacts within the work context that allow technology users to relate with one another inside as well as outside the organizations in order to avoid the isolation brought out by the use of technology (Zorn 2002); (2) social support climate (personal relationships among technology users and stakeholders (co-workers or supervisors) in which empathy, trust, and instrumental support are exchanged (Salanova et al. 2013)); (3) transformational leadership was also good negative predictor of technostrain (Salanova et al. 2013); and (4) feedback, the degree to which the technology user has clear and direct information about the effectiveness of their performance provided by their supervisor, colleagues, and customers themselves (Salanova and Schaufeli 2000).

Third, technological resources at the organizational level are related to healthy practices in human resource development. The presence of these organizational resources promotes the acceptance and use of technology and the development of positive psychosocial consequences on technology users. These resources are the following: (1) technology-implementing policies focused on the final user, that is, when the user has responsibility for and control over the work instead of technology (Salanova et al. 2007); (2) promoting high-quality training actions for technology in changing contexts (e.g., training workshops related to the new technologies) (Salanova and Llorens 2008); and (3) implementing strategies to balance work-personal life, by means of flexible schedules (e.g., by teleworking), providing benefits and assistance for the care of relatives, and giving advice and training as well as social or extralegal benefits (Salanova et al. 2013).

In addition, we should also mention the extra-organizational resources, which can serve as facilitators of technological change. The main resource at this level is private-work life support from friends and family (e.g., one's own partner). This support makes it possible to combine personal and technological demands and acts as a buffer for the technostress experience (Poelmans et al. 2005).

6.2.3 (Lack of) Personal Resources and Technostress

According to the SMOH Model, personal resources are the key elements to coping with technological demands and low technological resources. There are basically three main personal resources in technostress: (1) coping strategies, (2) assessment of past experience with technologies, and (3) technology self-efficacy.

First, coping strategies (focusing on the problem and on emotion) refer to cognitive and behavioral efforts that are made to control the specific external and/or internal demands that are evaluated as exceeding the individual's resources (Lazarus and Folkman 1984). Research has shown two main coping strategies to deal with technostress: (1) focused on the problem, behaviors to change the situation which enhances technostress (e.g., look for information, attend training courses), and (2) focused on emotions, behaviors to change the emotion felt by the technology users although the problematic situation persists and is accepted (e.g., to see the positive side of technological change) (see Llorens et al. 2011, for more details).

Second, assessment of past experience constitutes another personal resource to cope with technostress. Research has shown that the experience of technology has no direct relationship with technostress, but its (negative) effect depends on (1) the technological resources available to the user and (2) the assessment of past experiences with technology (Chua et al. 1999), that is, by the value, significance, and relevance of the past experience with each person's use of technology. Such users, who assessed the experience of technology in a negative way, will experience technostress (Korunka and Vitouch 1999).

Finally, the most relevant personal resource in coping with technostress is specific self-efficacy regarding technology. Based on the Social Cognitive Theory (Bandura 1997), this refers to the belief in one's capabilities to use technology successfully (Salanova et al. 2000). Research has shown that self-efficacy in technology enhances (1) the desire, effort, and persistence to do activities in which technology is used; (2) positive emotions related to the use of technology (e.g., satisfaction); and (3) thoughts about success in the use of technology. On the other hand, people with low levels of self-efficacy in technology tend to exaggerate the magnitude of their shortcomings and difficulties in using the technology, which can lead to burnout.

6.2.4 Consequences of Technostress

In addition to the antecedents, there is also empirical evidence regarding the consequences of technostress. Basically, we can classify the main consequences of technostress into four categories, based on the review performed by Llorens et al. (2011): (1) physiological, (2) psychosocial, (3) organizational, and (4) societal consequences.

Regarding the physiological consequences, research has shown that the use/abuse of technology may generate psychosomatic problems in users, such as sleep problems, headaches, musculoskeletal pain, carpal tunnel syndrome, depression symptoms, increased levels of adrenaline and noradrenaline, higher blood pressure and heart rate, and increases in skin conductance. Especially in technoaddiction, sleep deprivation due to the long hours spent using technologies could enhance fatigue, immune system problems, and health deterioration in general (e.g., Thomee et al. 2007).

At the psychological level, technostress may be responsible for anxiety, job dissatisfaction, and a decrease in the levels of work engagement. As a consequence of the technostress experience over a long time, the user could also experience burnout, mainly as a general state of mental exhaustion due to the use of technology. This negative experience leads to an increase in the user's skeptical attitudes toward the usefulness of technologies, which finally enhance the belief that they are not very competent in the performance of their professional duties (Llorens et al. 2007).

Technostress could also generate organizational consequences such as absenteeism and low performance. This reduction in performance could be triggered by the nonuse, misuse, or abuse of technology at work, as well as due to the pervasiveness of technology in human life. In fact, in order to remain up to date in technologies, users have to dedicate long hours of their own personal time to the matter. Other consequences of technostress are represented by low levels of commitment and a low level of intention to remain in the organization (Salanova and Schaufeli 2000).

Finally, technostress may also show its consequences at the societal level. The abuse of technology can significantly reduce the user's social activities. Social networks are also deteriorated, since the user becomes more irritable, with mood changes, and neglects both their working life (e.g., poor communication with peers) and their personal life (e.g., poor relationship with their partner, which can lead to divorce). In addition, the technology addict spends so much time using technology that societal and financial problems are evident (Douglas et al. 2008).

6.3 Assessing Technostress: The RED Technostress Questionnaire

Policies on Occupational Health Psychology should begin by conducting an accurate assessment of the psychosocial factors deriving from technology use and the technostress experience. Basically, testing the technostress experience seeks to accomplish three main objectives: (1) to identify and test the psychosocial risks due to the use/abuse of technology as a part of the evaluation process, (2) to propose suitable measures to eliminate or mitigate the psychosocial risks from technology, and (3) to improve the security and psychosocial health of technology users and their quality of life.

Despite the great variety of instruments in the form of interviews and checklists that may be used for such purposes, self-report questionnaires are the key tools. One of the most operative, comprehensive, and scientific questionnaires is the RED Technostress (see Llorens et al. 2011; Salanova et al. 2007, 2013).

Its main characteristics are the following: (1) it is based on theoretical models, such as the Spiral Model of Occupational Health; (2) it is reliability and validity have been demonstrated in research; (3) it is easy to complete and correct (20 min); (4) it diagnoses the phenomenon of the technostress experience (technostrain and technoaddiction), as well as its antecedents and consequences; and (5) it can be completed using the traditional paper format or the online version (www.wont.uji.es). In its online version, the user receives immediate feedback about his/her results in comparison to a baseline value (Llorens et al. 2011; Salanova et al. 2013; Salanova and Schaufeli 2000).

In the studies conducted in Spain with the RED Technostress questionnaire, (1) the samples were made up of individuals from a variety of fields ($N = 1{,}790$ ICT users) (21 % technical and qualified professionals, 8 % supervisors, 5 % managers, 4 % blue-collar workers, 27 % secondary school teachers, 22 % university lecturers, and 13 % university students); (2) 63 % commonly used ICT (e.g., computers, tablets, PDAs) as just another tool in their work, and 37 % (mainly women) used computers in an intensive way; and the results also showed that (3) technology workers perceived more technological resources and personal resources than technological demands and more positive experiences (e.g., Llorens et al. 2006, 2007; Rodríguez et al. 2008; Salanova and Llorens 2009; Salanova et al. 2003, 2010, 2013) (see Tables 6.1 and 6.2).

Table 6.1 Percentage of technological demands and resources and personal resources perceived by ITC users

Technological demands	Technological and personal resources
60 % emotional overload	74 % positive appraisal of exposure to ICT
57 % work overload	78 % mental competences
60 % technology obstacles	74 % autonomy
39 % role ambiguity	70 % efficacy beliefs related to technology
12 % mobbing	66 % social support
	64 % transformational leadership
	60 % technology facilitators

Table 6.2 Percentage of positive and negative experience perceived by ICT users

Positive experience	Negative experience
84 % enthusiasm	39 % anxiety
81 % satisfaction	34 % burnout
78 % comfort	
78 % organizational commitment	
66 % engagement	
37 % task performance	

6.4 Strategies for Technostress Prevention and Intervention

The intervention process is defined as "... such specific actions to eliminate/reduce sources of stress, their responses or their effects, and optimize health factors and their consequences" (Salanova et al. 2009, p. 50).

Despite the relevance of protecting and promoting employees' (and in our case technology users') well-being, the psychosocial intervention processes remain an ongoing issue in current research, as does their implementation in real organizations. Linking research and professional practice (Research to Practice – R2P) is a challenge for the occupational health psychologist. Based on Salanova et al.'s classification (2009), technostress interventions could be distinguished by (1) the focus (technology users and technical system) and (2) the objective of the intervention (primary, secondary, and tertiary intervention). Below we explain the main prevention-intervention strategies on technostress (for a review, see Llorens et al. 2011; Salanova et al. 2007).

6.4.1 Prevention Strategies on Technostress

Prevention strategies are aimed at healthy individuals (groups) who are not under risk conditions. They are of a general nature oriented toward all technology users and are proactive and very effective (Lamontagne et al. 2007), their aim being to prevent harm. The main prevention strategies in technostress are classified taking into account: (1) the end users, (2) the organization, and (3) the technological system. These strategies are shown below.

6.4.1.1 Prevention Strategies Focused on the Final User

Survey feedback. This is a strategy based on bidirectional communication between facilitators and participants. It has two objectives: (1) to know more about technostress and (2) to establish improvement strategies that are under the technology users' control.

Technostress workshop. This consists in a work meeting (with practical exercises) to solve technostress in a group of users. This strategy seeks (1) to draw the study of technostress closer to the participants through their own self-diagnosis, (2) to teach them how to apply these processes to their own situation, (3) to become more familiar with diagnostic measures of technostress, and (4) to learn how to discriminate prevention and intervention strategies that are useful for them.

6.4.1.2 Prevention Strategies Focused on the Social System

Information and Communication. This is easy to apply and very beneficial for users. It consists in giving information to users, supervisors, and indeed everybody that could be involved in the changes due to the technology. The main objective is to inform them about (1) the changes in the organization as a consequence of the technology implementation and (2) the results obtained from the technostress diagnosis. This is a good strategy to avoid rumors, resistance to change, boycotts, and the development of negative attitudes toward the use of technology.

Job Redesign. This strategy involves enriching those jobs in which technology should be implemented. Its objective is to promote (1) the development of technology users at the individual, social, and professional levels and (2) the perception of technology as a resource in order to cope with the environment. It implies three types of specific strategies: (1) enriching jobs (i.e., giving more autonomy), (2) clarifying the role (i.e., giving feedback about the job with technologies), and (3) improvement of the ergonomic aspects of technology (i.e., use of ergonomic keyboards).

Participation in Decision-Making. Users of technology can participate in (1) the implementation of technology, (2) the selection of the specific characteristics of the technology, (3) the evaluation of technostress, and (4) the selection of the prevention-intervention strategies to be implemented. The benefits to be gained from participating are the following: (1) it provides a feeling of "gratitude" because the user perceives that his/her opinion is taken into account, (2) it involves a greater commitment to decisions, (3) it reduces the stressful effects of changing technology (technostress experience), (4) it increases the levels of psychological attachment to technology, and (5) it increases the likelihood of technology acceptance.

6.4.1.3 Prevention Strategies Focused on the Technological System

Prevention strategies can also be aimed at changing the system through the technology design. According to research, technology will succeed when three basic criteria are met: (1) the technology design is ergonomic (e.g., use of wireless connections, widescreen displays, ergonomic keyboards) and avoids the appearance of physical problems in users (eye problems, headaches, back pain); (2) it is "usable" and functional in order to ensure the use of technology; and (3) it is friendly, simple, and easy to use successfully, both for experts and for other less proficient users.

6.4.2 Secondary Intervention Strategies on Technostress

Secondary intervention strategies are carried out in individuals and groups that are under risk conditions, with the aim of minimizing or eliminating the risk. These strategies (1) are applied when the first symptoms of psychosocial and/or organizational damage are starting to manifest; (2) are only applied to those users or groups in which a symptom is detected; and (3) have an active agent, i.e., the user, whose role is crucial in the implementation of these strategies (Lamontagne et al. 2007). These strategies are shown below.

6.4.2.1 Secondary Intervention Strategies Focused on the Social System: The User

Tutoring and coaching. The aim of this strategy is to support the user in the development of specific skills in technological innovations. The coach should help the technology user to establish goals, objectives, and work planning and should offer advice to help in the development of their employability. This strategy requires a transformational leader to guide technology users and to help them solve problems, but it also gives rise to questions and even the expression of positive emotions that can spread to other employees.

6.4.2.2 Secondary Intervention Strategies Focused on the Social System: The Organization

Team Building and Team Development. This involves the creation of stable work teams through a series of activities and exercises (e.g., testing prototypes, outdoor training). These strategies allow technology users to identify themselves with the team goals and objectives by promoting group cohesion and effectiveness. The creation of these groups is even more important in these technological contexts where the groups have the power to solve any problems generated as a result of the use/abuse of technology.

6.4.2.3 Secondary Intervention Strategies Focused on the Technical System

Replacement Technologies. This strategy is related to changing technology that has become obsolete, useless, barely usable, "unfriendly," or ergonomically stressful. The decision to replace technologies could be determined as a result of the team building and team development strategy, outlined earlier.

6.4.3 Tertiary Intervention Strategies on Technostress

Finally, tertiary intervention strategies are carried out in individuals and groups who are sick, where technostress has appeared with the full range of all its symptoms. Its aim is to reduce the severity or disability associated with technostress by trying to help people recover. These strategies are (1) therapeutic and attempt to recover and rehabilitate workers and groups that have suffered from technostress and (2) reactive, since they are applied once all the damage has been done. This last objective is the reintegration and/or rehabilitation of users who have suffered technostress in their workplace. These strategies are as follows.

6.4.3.1 Tertiary Intervention Strategies Focused on the Social System: The User

Counseling and psychotherapy. Briefly, both are related to psychosocial treatment, and obviously the user should be sent to an expert. The aim is to make the user aware that he/she has a psychological problem, to eliminate negative reactions, to increase confidence as well as positive attitudes toward technology, and to help him/her regain control over the use of technology. In general, these strategies imply that users actively learn to take responsibility for their behavior and to realize the situation is under control. To be successful, these strategies should be controlled and guided by a specialist, but they also involve working with the group (especially peers, tutor, supervisor, and even the family), which has to receive and reintegrate the technology user.

6.4.3.2 Tertiary Intervention Strategies Focused on the Social System: The Organization

This last strategy is focused on promoting the institutionalization of prevention services in order to promote the overall health of employees. The aim of this strategy is to ensure the care and the overall well-being of workers, and by extension technology users, in the organization. It involves the assessment of future and proactive needs and organizational changes derived from the culture of creativity and innovation in the organization. It also involves planning and monitoring the implementation of prevention-intervention measures to deal with technostress. Generally, this strategy reveals the relevance of integrating prevention within the company, which should be seen as a priority in organizations.

6.5 Concluding Remarks

Despite the relevance of technology nowadays, psychological consequences such as technostress could be experienced in non-intensive as well as intensive technology users. In order to facilitate the interventions, it is relevant to diagnose it in a correct way. For this reason, it is important to conceptualize technostress as an umbrella attending to both typologies of technostress, i.e., technostrain and technoaddiction experiences. Furthermore, we must distinguish among the experience of technostress (technostrain and technoaddiction) and their predictors and consequences. To achieve this objective, the Spiral Model of Occupational Health and specifically the RED Technostress questionnaire are a scientific and operative way to explain and measure the technostress experience. According to this, technostress could be assessed attending to three fundamental "ingredients": technological demands, technological resources, and personal resources. In particular, (the lack of) specific self-efficacy with technology has been shown to be a key element in the determination of technostress. Also the model and the questionnaire establish the main consequences of technostrain. These consequences should be oriented to capture not only the idiosyncratic character of the phenomenon (physiological and psychological) but also the organizational and societal problems derived from technostress. If the evaluation and diagnosis of technostress are important, also the strategies for preventing and intervening are a key subject. From a practical point of view, it is recommended to select the better strategy attending to the objective (prevention, secondary, and tertiary interventions) and the focus (on the users of technology, the organization, and the technical system) of the intervention. At this point, we have to highlight the need to combine the strategies in order to intervene in technostress in a suitable way.

In sum, in this chapter, we have shown that technology has the power to make our lives easier, but sometimes it fails to do so. Thus, the dark side of technologies has reared its head in the form of technostress. We really would like to encourage researchers, practitioners, organizations, governments, and society in general to establish mechanisms that make it possible to turn technology into our ally. Nevertheless, more research is needed in order to better understand the mechanisms underlying technostress, as well as ways to prevent it in today's organizations and societies.

Acknowledgments This research was supported by a grant from the Spanish Ministry of Economy and Competitiveness (#PSI2011-22400).

References

Arias, O., Gallego, V., Rodríguez, M. J., & Pozo, M. A. (2012). Adicción a las nuevas tecnología [Addiction to new technologies]. *Revista de Psicología de las Adicciones, 1*, 2–6.

Bandura, A. (1997). *Self-efficacy: The exercise of control*. New York: Freeman.

Brod, C. (1984). *Technostress: The human cost of the computer revolution*. Reading: Addison-Wesley.

Chua, S. L., Chen, D. T., & Wong, A. F. L. (1999). Computer anxiety and its correlates: A meta-analysis. *Computers in Human Behavior, 15*, 609–623. doi:10.1016/S0747-5632(99)00039-4.

Douglas, A. C., Mills, J. E., Niang, M., Stepchenkova, S., Byun, S., Ruffini, C., Lee, S. K., Loutfi, J., Lee, J. K., Atallah, M., & Blanton, M. (2008). Internet addiction: Meta-synthesis of qualitative research for the decade 1996–2006. *Computers in Human Behavior, 24*, 3027–3044. doi:10.1016/j.chb.2008.05.009.

Henderson, R. D., Deane, F. P., & Ward, M. J. (1995). Occupational differences in computer-related anxiety: Implications for the implementation of a computerized patient management information system. *Behaviour & Information Technology, 14*, 23–31. doi:10.1080/01449299508914622.

Jackson, P. R., Wall, T. D., Martin, R., & Davis, K. (1993). New measures of job control, cognitive demand and production responsibility. *Journal of Applied Psychology, 78*, 753–762. doi:10.1037/0021-9010.78.5.753.

Kessler, R. C., & Ustun, T. B. (2008). *The WHO world mental health disorders*. New York: Cambridge University Press.

Korunka, C., & Vitouch, O. (1999). Effects of the implementation of information technology on employees' strain and job satisfaction: A context-dependent approach. *Work and Stress, 13*, 341–363. doi:10.1080/02678379950019798.

Korunka, C., Weiss, A., Huemer, K. H., & Karetta, B. (1995). The effect of new technologies on job satisfaction and psychosomatic complaints. *Applied Psychology: An International Review, 44*, 123–142. doi:10.1111/j.1464-0597.1995.tb01070.x.

Lamontagne, A. D., Keegel, T., Louie, A. M., Ostry, A., & Landsbergis, P. A. (2007). A systematic review of the job stress intervention evaluation literature. *International Journal of Occupational and Environmental Health, 13*, 258–280.

Lazarus, R. S., & Folkman, S. (1984). *Stress, appraisal and coping*. New York: Springer.

Lewis, D. (1996). *Dying for information?* London: Reuters Business Information.

Líbano, M., Llorens, S., Salanova, M., & Schaufeli, W. B. (2010). Validity of a brief workaholism scale. *Psicothema, 22*, 143–150.

Llorens, S., Bakker, A. B., Schaufeli, W. B., & Salanova, M. (2006). Testing the robustness of the 'Job Demands-Resources' model. *International Journal of Stress Management, 13*, 378–391. doi:10.1037/1072-5245.13.3.378.

Llorens, S., Salanova, M., & Ventura, M. (2007). Efectos del tecnoestrés en las creencias de eficacia y el burnout docente: un estudio longitudinal [Effects of technostress on efficacy beliefs and teacher burnout: A longitudinal study]. *Revista de Orientación Educacional, 2*, 47–65.

Llorens, S., Salanova, M., & Ventura, M. (2011). *Guías de intervención: Tecnoestrés* [Intervention guidelines: Technostress]. Madrid: Síntesis.

Poelmans, S., O'Driscoll, M., & Beham, B. (2005). An overview of international research on the Work-Family interface. In S. A. Poelmans (Ed.), *Work and family. An international research perspective*. Mahwah: Lawrence Erlbaum Associates.

Porter, G., & Kakabadse, N. K. (2006). HRM perspective on addiction to technology and work. *Journal of Management Development, 25*, 535–560. doi:10.1108/02621710610670119.

Ragu-Nathan, B., Tarafdar, M., Ragu-Nathan, S., & Tu, Q. (2008). The consequences of technostress for end users in organizations: Conceptual development and empirical validation. *Information Systems Research, 19*, 417–433. doi:10.1287/isre.1070.0165.

Rodriguez, A. M., Schauefli, W. B., Salanova, M., & Cifre, E. (2008). Flow experience among information and communication technology users. *Psychological Reports, 102*, 29–39. doi:10.2466/pr0.102.1.29-39.

Salanova, M., & Llorens, S. (2008). *Desarrollo de recursos humanos a través del aprendizaje para el cambio* [Human resource development through learning for change]. Madrid: Parthenon.

Salanova, M., & Llorens, S. (2009). Exposure to information and communication technology and its relationship to work engagement. *C&T, Ciencia & Trabajo, 32*, 55–63.

Salanova, M., & Schaufeli, W. B. (2000). Exposure to information technology and its relation to burnout. *Behaviour and Information Technology, 19*, 385–392. doi:10.1080/014492900750000081.

Salanova, M., Grau, R., Cifre, E., & Llorens, S. (2000). Computer training, frequency of use and burnout: The moderating role of computer self-efficacy. *Computers in Human Behavior, 16*, 575–590. doi:10.1016/S0747-5632(00)00028-5.

Salanova, M., Llorens, S., Cifre, E., Martínez, I., & Schaufeli, W. B. (2003). Perceived collective efficacy, subjective well-being and task performance among electronic work groups: An experimental study. *Small Group Research, 34*, 43–73. doi:10.1177/1046496402239577.

Salanova, M., Llorens, S., Cifre, E., & Nogareda, C. (2007). Tecnoestrés: concepto, medida e intervención psicosocial [Technostress: Concept, measurement and psychosocial intervention]. *Nota técnica de prevención, 730, 21ª Serie*. Madrid: Instituto Nacional de Seguridad e Higiene en el Trabajo.

Salanova, M., Martínez, I., Cifre, E., & Llorens, S. (2009). La salud ocupacional desde la perspectiva psicosocial: aspectos teóricos y conceptuales [Occupational health from a psychosocial perspective: Theoretical and conceptual characteristics]. In M. Salanova (Ed.), *Psicología de la salud ocupacional* [Occupational health psychology] (pp. 27–62). Madrid: Editorial Síntesis.

Salanova, M., Llorens, S., & Schaufeli, W. B. (2010). Yes, I can, I feel good, and I just do it! On gain cycles and spirals of efficacy beliefs, affect, and engagement. *Applied Psychology: An International Review, 60*, 255–285. doi:10.1111/j.1464-0597.2010.00435.x.

Salanova, M., Llorens, S., & Cifre, E. (2013). The dark face of technologies: About the concept and measurement of technostress experience. *International Journal of Psychology, 48*, 422–433. doi:10.1080/00207594.2013.680460.

Schaufeli, W. B., & Salanova, M. (2007). Efficacy or inefficacy, that's the question: Burnout and engagement, and their relationships with efficacy beliefs. *Anxiety, Coping & Stress, 20*, 177–196. doi:10.1080/10615800701217878.

Tarafdar, M., Tu, Q., Ragu-Nathan, B., & Ragu-Nathan, T. S. (2007). The impact of technostress on role stress and productivity. *Journal of Management Information Systems, 24*, 301–328. doi:10.2753/MIS0742-1222240109.

Thomee, S., Eklof, M., Gustafsson, E., Nilsson, R., & Hagber, G. M. (2007). Prevalence of perceived stress, symptoms of depression and sleep disturbances in relation to information and communication technology (ICT) use among young adults – An explorative prospective study. *Computers in Human Behavior, 23*, 1300–1321. doi:10.1016/j.chb.2004.12.007.

Wang, K., Shu, Q., & Tu, Q. (2008). Technostress under different organizational environments: An empirical investigation. *Computers in Human Behavior, 24*, 3002–3013. doi:10.1016/j.chb.2008.05.007.

Yang, C., & Carayon, P. (1995). Effect of job demands and social support on worker- stress: A study of VDT users. *Behaviour & Information Technology, 14*, 32–40. doi:10.1080/01449299508914623.

Zorn, T. E. (2002). The emotionality of information and communications technology implementation. *Journal of Communication Management, 7*, 160–171. doi:10.1108/13632540310807296.

Chapter 7
The Balance Concept Revisited: Finding Balance to Reduce Stress in a Frantic World of IT

Pascale Carayon and Michael J. Smith

It is inevitable that everyone will be stressed at some time. Stress has many causes, some related to an individual's personality and psychological mood, some to personal social interactions, others to the larger social environment, and many to the demands on the person's energy, mental and emotional capabilities, resources, and motivation. The effects of stress on individuals, groups, and societies can be immediate as well as long term. At the individual level, the effects are systemic including psychological and physiological responses that can affect motivation, mood, behavior, mental health, physical health, and spiritual health. At the group level, stress affects the social environment and interaction, organizational climate, and relationships within the larger society in which the organization operates. At the level of society, stress affects social interaction, social climate, the image and confidence of a society, the expectations for the future, and the moral and spiritual fiber.

In the United States, the American Psychological Association has been conducting annual and spot surveys using the Harris Polls for several years to follow the level of experienced stress in the population and specific groups (American Psychological Association 2012). Over the last several decades, the information from these polls has indicated that the level of individual and group stress of Americans has been steadily increasing. Major sources of stress identified in the surveys were the time pressures in people's lives and work, particularly as

P. Carayon (✉)
Center for Quality and Productivity Improvement (CQPI), University of Wisconsin–Madison, Madison, WI, USA

Department of Industrial and Systems Engineering, University of Wisconsin–Madison, Madison, WI, USA
e-mail: carayon@engr.wisc.edu

M.J. Smith
Department of Industrial and Systems Engineering, University of Wisconsin–Madison, Madison, WI, USA
e-mail: mjsmith@cae.wisc.edu

C. Korunka and P. Hoonakker (eds.), *The Impact of ICT on Quality of Working Life*,
DOI 10.1007/978-94-017-8854-0_7, © Springer Science+Business Media Dordrecht 2014

influenced by the increased demands at work and home. The amount of time a person has to think, organize, and plan has been diminishing over the years due to immediate and future demands on the person's available time to do so many things. This has led to feelings of a loss of control over how people lead their lives.

As information technology (IT) has progressed over the last three decades, the opportunity to be constantly in contact with individuals, groups, and media has increased at a fast pace. At any time on any day, billions of people are connected to the Internet, cloud, or cell tower through IT. Many spend their entire day (until they sleep, if ever) tied to an IT device. They are tethered to a device that can provide needed information and services but can also make demands on them at any time. In some ways, this connectivity can diminish the amount of control that they have over their time and lives and can add to the demands that are already placed on them by their families, work, recreation, and general living. The potential that such connectivity has for creating stress on an individual or group is high. On the other hand, this connectivity may allow individuals to share information with others and build a network of resources. This is a paradox of IT as it can provide benefits as well as problems for individuals, groups, and society. This paradox and other emerging conflicts related to IT are described below.

7.1 Overview of Job Stress

Fifty years of research on job stress has shown that there are critical features of job design that affect the level of job stress in individuals and groups (Quick et al. 2012). Of particular importance are the amounts of demands that are put on people and work groups in comparison to the resources they have to meet the demands, the extent of control that people and groups have over the level of the demands and how they are met, and the extent of social support available to people and groups when they are put under high demands (Caplan et al. 1975; Harrison 1978; Karasek and Theorell 1990). In addition, time pressure has been shown to exacerbate the effects of the level of the demands. If we extrapolate the findings of the research on job stress to the broader area of the influences of IT on people's lives, we can see parallel issues regarding high demands, low control, and time pressures.

Much has been written about how to reduce job stress. Approaches have dealt with prevention information and services from national agencies, improving organizational culture and climate, redesigning jobs and/or family life to decrease the demands and increase individual and group control, enhancing opportunities for social support at work and within families and groups, individual therapies for reducing the psychological and physiological effects of stress, and combinations of these approaches (Quick et al. 2012). There have been successes and failures for each of the approaches and various combinations, but lessons have been learned from their results that can be useful in mitigating the potential impact of IT on stress.

One lesson is the importance of developing "balance" among the various potential sources of stress from society, organizations, technology, and environmental factors that influence life and job demands, time pressure, and the control over life and job tasks (Carayon 2009; Smith and Carayon-Sainfort 1989; Smith and Carayon 2001). A second lesson is the importance for individuals to find ways to "balance" the external demands and time pressures with the internal psychological and physiological reactions to them. In this chapter, we will discuss the concept of "balance" and provide examples of how "balance" can be disturbed. We will discuss possible ways to achieve better "balance" to prevent stress or to respond when stress occurs due to the demands, time pressures, and loss of control from interaction with IT.

The "Balance model" we will discuss developed over 30 years from ideas and research at NIOSH and the University of Wisconsin-Madison. Early ideas came from a comprehensive examination of the occupational stress and the human factors literatures. One of the ideas that emerged was the belief that various sources of occupational stress were related and influenced each other in positive and negative ways (Smith 1981; Smith et al. 1981). Later ideas examined the work system and the interdependence of various aspects of work on stress and safety (Smith 1987; Smith and Beringer 1987). In 1989, we develop a more complete concept of the work system and described how various elements interacted to increase or mitigate stress and health outcomes (Smith and Carayon-Sainfort 1989). This model was further developed in 1995 to examine how new technologies influenced the work system, stress, and "balance" (Smith and Carayon 1995, 1996). The "Balance model" was later described in relation to a variety of occupation stress concepts (Kalimo et al. 1997). Carayon and Smith (2000) examined the "balance concept" in regard to the larger macroergonomic view of work systems. Recent expansions of the balance model include (1) impact of the work system on other outcomes besides stress (e.g., performance) (Carayon 2009), (2) incorporation of the work system in the SEIPS (Systems Engineering Initiative for Patient Safety) model of work system and patient safety (Carayon et al. 2006a), and design of work system at multiple levels (Karsh and Brown 2010; Karsh et al. 2006).

It is clear that we live in a time of great stress, tension, and time compression. This forces us to think of the concept of "balance" in a larger context of sources of stress and safety. At this writing, we see a world of international wars, uprisings, famine, and disease; economic decline, increasing poverty, and homelessness; job loss, high unemployment, and housing foreclosures; and an ever-increasing pace of living with little or no time for ourselves. Superimposed on this stressful external environment is an increased time pressure due the rapid development and deployment of information technologies that allow us to be continuously wired and connected to the web and each other. There is hardly time to catch our breath and very little if any time to tune out and be alone with our own thoughts and activities. These technologies are great wonders that have given us unheard-of access to information and people far and near, and they have enriched our lives. Yet, these technologies have brought additional stress to already stressful lives. Many of these sources of stress will be examined in other chapters in this book, but we will summarize some of the critical stressors that are influenced by information technologies. We will discuss how the stressors due to the rapid increase in the use of information technologies disrupt the balance of our lives and lead to stress. Then we will discuss improving balance that will reduce stress and its health problems.

7.1.1 Historical Review of Job Stress

The great scientist, physician, and educator Hans Selye wrote *The Stress of Life* in 1956 (Selye 1956). In this landmark book, he described his journey of discovery to find a fundamental biological process that led to nonspecific responses of the body to external irritants that later were defined as stressors. In his journey, he found that the body's responses were consistent over a wide spectrum of stressors, and when stressors and their resultant stress were chronic, the resultant bodily responses could lead to very serious health effects. As he traveled his journey, he found that psychological stressors were as significant as chemical and physical agents in producing the bodily responses. In 1974, Selye wrote *Stress Without Distress* in which he proposed that while chronic stress could lead to serious health consequences, it could also be used as a positive process to motivate and energize a person (Selye 1974). He further proposed that a proper psychological perspective, value system, and following guidelines regarding personal behavior would lead to a life without distress. Selye's fundamental contribution to our understanding of stress and disease led to the understanding that chronic exposures to stressors can produce biological effects that are maladaptive and can lead to sickness. He believed that a proper psychological attitude and behavior could mitigate the biological effects of exposure to stressors by turning stress into a positive influence.

In the United States, prior to Selye's work, early psychologists and physiologists developed theories about the relationships between biochemical responses and emotions (James 1890, 1913; Cannon 1915, 1927, 1931, 1932; Lange and James 1922). Cannon (1915, 1927, 1931, 1932) defined a theory of "homeostasis" wherein the internal body strived to achieve a balance. From these early scientists and theorists came the recognition that emotion and physiology were intertwined. Mason (1959, 1971, 1975a, b) provided a description of the process of stress physiology and psychology. Later, psychologists (Lazarus 1974; McGrath 1976; Schachter and Singer 1962) added a process of cognitive assessment in determining emotions and responses to stressors.

In a parallel area of physiology, Grandjean (1968, 1970) described the process of human fatigue. He illustrated that the same brain pathway and centers related to emotions and stress responses were central to the process of fatigue and sleep. He emphasized the importance of psychological states in the perception of fatigue. He proposed a theory of fatigue where daily sources of environmental loads accumulated into a combined load that increased fatigue. Through recovery processes such as rest and sleep, recovery from fatigue occurred and balance was restored. If daily recovery was not achieved, then chronic fatigue could occur with attendant negative health effects.

This brief historical review of job stress highlights the systemic effects of stress on both physical and mental health, the interactions between psychological and physiological processes of stress, and the importance of psychological, physical, behavioral, and emotional resources in determining individual stress reactions.

7.1.2 Balance Theory of Job Stress and Work System

We developed the Balance model of occupational stress control based on the theories from these predecessors (Smith and Carayon-Sainfort 1989; Smith and Carayon 1995; Carayon and Smith 2000). The general idea was there were stressors in the work environment that had the potential to lead to stress responses, and by providing a better balance in job design, the effects of these stressors could be reduced or eliminated. A major concept was using the positive aspects of jobs to negate the effects of the negative aspects of jobs that could not be changed.

The Job Strain model (Karasek and Theorell 1990) and the Effort-Reward model (Siegrist 1996) are probably the two most popular models of job stress. The recent Job Demands-Resources (JD-R) model integrates the concepts of work engagement and burnout into a comprehensive model of work-related well-being (Bakker et al. 2003a, b; Demerouti et al. 2001; Schaufeli and Bakker 2004). All three models incorporate ideas of balance in work. According to the Job Strain model (Karasek 1979; Karasek and Theorell 1990), a mismatch between job demands and job decision latitude can produce negative health consequences: high-strain jobs are characterized by high demands and low job control. The Job Strain model was later extended to include social support (Johnson 1989). A job, therefore, lacks balance and produces strain if demands are high, decision latitude is low, and social support is low. According to the Effort-Reward model, stress outcomes are the result of an imbalance between the effort of workers and the rewards they receive from performing their job (Siegrist 1996, 2009; Siegrist and Wahrendorf 2009). According to the JD-R model (Bakker et al. 2003a, b; Demerouti et al. 2001; Schaufeli and Bakker 2004), job demands are characteristics of the job that require sustained physical or psychological effort or skills. Job resources are job characteristics that help workers achieve their work goals, that buffer or reduce job demands and stress consequences, and that promote individual growth, learning, and development. The interaction between job demands and resources influences stress and health. For instance, job resources can buffer the impact of job demands on stress (House 1981). The Job Strain model, the Effort-Reward model, and the JD-R model proposed concepts of stress that incorporate the idea of balance; however, the models are limited in their ability to capture all of the work system elements that can contribute to balance (or lack of balance). The balance theory and the associated work system model provide a more systematic framework for describing and assessing work and its impact on stress and for producing realistic, feasible solutions for work redesign.

The work system as shown in Fig. 7.1 is a network of interactions between the following elements: individual, tasks, tools and technologies, physical environment, and organizational conditions (Carayon and Smith 2000; Smith and Carayon-Sainfort 1989). Each system element can have characteristics that produce stress. For instance, the task may be characterized as requiring high workload and providing little opportunity for task control. The environment may be characterized by the presence of numerous physical stressors. On the other hand, the system elements may have a lot of "pluses" that help to reduce or mitigate stress. For instance, the organizational element may be characterized by numerous on-the-job opportunities for socialization, which could buffer the effects of stressful work conditions. The work system can therefore be described as a series of "pluses" and "minuses." It is also important to understand the system interactions and how the pluses can help in balancing and compensating for the minuses in the work system. This concept of balance in the work system is central to the balance theory (Smith and Carayon-Sainfort 1989).

Our approach was based on our own research in factories and offices where changes in work processes occurred that led to stress among employees. In some instances, we studied the impact of the changes when they occurred, and in others we redesigned the work processes and jobs to achieve what we believed would be a better balance. Much of this research examined the introduction of computerization to offices or new automation to factories. We used well-established survey instruments so that we could compare our findings with those from prior studies in the literature to see if computerization had different effects on job design than changes in factories. While we found many of the same stressors as prior studies, the levels of somatic health complaints and emotional distress in our studies of workers undergoing computerization were higher even though the physical loads of the work were much lower (Smith et al. 1992). We realized that psychological aspects of the work were as essential for achieving good balance as the physical ergonomic design aspects (Carayon et al. 1999). Thus, our Balance model incorporated the entire system of work elements for examining balance in jobs (Smith and Carayon-Sainfort 1989; Smith and Carayon 2001) and organizations (Carayon and Smith 2000).

7.2 Contribution of Information Technology to Job Stress

Today, IT has so proliferated in all aspects of our lives in much of the world that we find a need to expand our conceptualization of the workplace-based Balance model to incorporate elements from the broader environment and technologies to discuss the idea of balance. IT is only one component of the work system (Carayon and Haims 2001); it interacts with the individual who uses the technology to perform

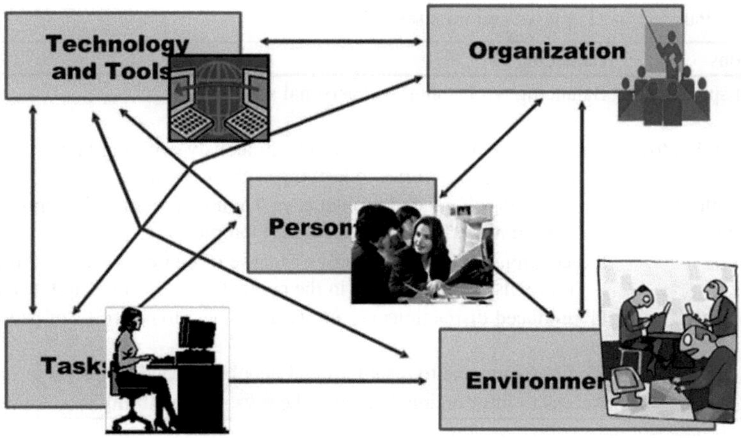

Fig. 7.1 Model of the work system (Carayon and Smith 2000; Smith and Carayon-Sainfort 1989)

tasks in a specific environment. The organizational conditions of IT implementation and use also influence the users.

Interaction with IT occurs from various sources (levels of interaction) such as international and national media, local media, social media, family, organizations, work, school, church, friends, other persons, advertisers, and other sources. The level of interaction influences the amount of control a person or group has over the source. For example, a news headline on a personal communication device can be ignored, while a text message from a spouse cannot (or should not). On the other hand, if a headline indicates that the company a person works for has been sold, the communication cannot be ignored and may start a whole series of further communications with coworkers, friends, and family. Thus, each level of communication has the potential to put increased demands and stress on the recipient.

IT can lead to stress by intensifying work either because of its direct impact on work tasks and operations or because of the poor IT design and implementation strategies (Eason 2001; Carayon 2007). Technological changes have largely contributed to the work intensification that has occurred in the past decade (Green 2004). Both managers and employee representatives cite changes in technology as having the largest impact on employees. IT can be used to connect workers anytime and anywhere; this constant connectivity to the workplace can heighten work pressures (Harris et al. 2011). The impact of technological changes on work intensification is also related to the many changes in work organization that occur simultaneously; as indicated above, technology is only one aspect of a larger work system, and when new technology is implemented, other work system elements are affected (see Fig. 7.1). IT may produce efficiency gains; some tasks can be performed more quickly. However, time savings are often used to increase performance expectations. Hancock and Drury (2011) frame this issue in the form of a question: "Humans as means or ends?" Who benefits from IT? When IT produces efficiency gains, how is work reorganized, and does the new work organization

Table 7.1 Paradox of IT: pluses and minuses

Dimensions	Balancing IT
Different spheres of life	Balancing work sphere vs. personal sphere
Evolving technology	Dealing with demands related to continuously evolving IT vs. developing and applying abilities to keep up with evolving IT
Dealing with IT problems	Experiencing IT-related problems vs. having access to IT support and opportunities to fix or deal with IT problems
Expectations	Expectations for quick responses because of continuous access to IT vs. realistic expectations in the context of constraints and demands
Communication with others	IT-produced distractions vs. ability to connect to networks of people
Privacy	Ability to connect to resources and people vs. need for privacy
Access	Access to information from anywhere vs. no possibility to get away

benefit workers? This discussion highlights the paradox of IT that can produce both benefits and problems from a human factor and ergonomic viewpoint. Table 7.1 describes various paradoxes of IT on a range of dimensions.

IT poses unique challenges in the balance between different spheres of life. For instance, IT can be used for telecommuting, therefore reducing the need for workers to commute between their home and the workplace and allowing workers additional time with family and friends. This impact of this benefit may be limited if work-life balance is negatively affected because workers are unable to create clear boundaries between the work sphere and the personal sphere. Telecommuters may also experience isolation and are more likely to be passed over for promotion (Morganson et al. 2010). This is related to another paradox of IT as it provides increased opportunities to communicate via the Internet while possibly isolating people (Kraut et al. 2002).

The relentless and continuous changes in IT pose unique challenges because workers have to constantly learn new skills and knowledge (Smith and Carayon 1995; Tarafdar et al. 2007). Transitioning from one technology to the next requires that workers forget certain skills and knowledge, continue to use other skills and knowledge, and develop new skills and knowledge. This concomitant process of mental model maintenance and mental model building associated with continuous learning of IT (Zhang and Xu 2011) may affect worker stress.

IT changes expectations for performance. Continuous connection to IT can provide easy and timely access to resources and support; this is especially important because of the increased dependence on the technology for production and service delivery. However, expectations for quick response may actually conflict with increase in demand (Tarafdar et al. 2007). This leads to another paradox, i.e., efficient access to information from any location versus the constant connection.

7.3 Balancing IT

Achieving "balance" can occur in different ways at each level of IT interaction. We will discuss ways of examining "balance" at the levels of society, organization, and individual. We approach this with the understanding that IT provides advantages of easy connectivity to others and information, access to huge storehouses of knowledge, and benefits to performance, productivity, and quality of products. Yet IT also poses the potential burdens of immediate and constant contact, continuous monitoring of activities and performance, and time pressures. IT also changes the ways in which people interact socially and psychologically. Thus, our ideas about balance try to capture both the positives and negatives of IT in regard to job stress (see Table 7.1).

7.3.1 Society-Level Interventions

Dealing with the potential stressors of IT through government action is a confounded and complex situation. It is confounded because protecting the rights of the individual users may introduce potential harm to society, such as when IT is used by terrorists and repressive governments. The complexity comes from the multitude of IT interfaces and the sources of information of unequal validity and quality, business market forces, historical and emerging social processes, and political processes.

Some areas where governments might affect the potential stressors due to IT are through policies, laws and regulations on privacy, social media regulation, intrusions on personal time, influences on personal control over IT, the use of IT for "bullying," and the development of preventive and palliative stress reduction services using IT. These are just a few examples of areas where government action might be possible, and there are likely to be many more. The point to make is government has a role in the application, uses, and abuses of IT that could lead to group and personal stress. What the specific role of government will be will depend on the existing and new laws and regulations, societal needs, group needs, personal needs, and the nature of current and new technologies. We will provide a few examples of potential issues.

Invasion of privacy is a recognized stressor related to personal anxiety, fear, anger, aggression, and psychological distress (Carayon 1993). Let's assume that Mr. X works for a large corporation that practices ongoing surveillance of employees' Facebook pages, work email accounts, employee web surfing on workplace IT devices, and external news services. Should the government compel an employer to inform (warn) employees about this practice? Would knowing about this practice create more employee stress than not knowing? Is taking action against employees after discovering behavior displeasing to the employer fair without warning them about monitoring? Should the government define the type of information and information sources that the employer can examine? Should the government define labor regulations about the types of actions that employers can and cannot take against employees engaged in displeasing behaviors? What if the employer is the government looking for potential terrorists among its employees?

We do not have any immediate answers when looking at the issue of employee monitoring or other government roles related to IT information gathering about individuals and their behavior. We can only point out the complexity of these issues and suggest that government has a role to play if as yet undefined. That role will be defined by forces beyond our knowledge and expertise such as societal needs and pressures, the nature and structure of government, the powers assigned to/by government through laws and regulations, and politics.

One area where government may be able to help reduce job stress due to IT is when employers require employees to be continuously connected and available for contact by the employer. Labor laws and/or regulations can be developed to provide employees with defined periods of "breaks" from employer intrusions on their time. Decades of research and organization design and management practice tell us that time pressures, work overload, overtime work, continuous monitoring of status and performance, and inadequate rest away from work are significant stressors with physical and psychological stress consequences (Kalimo et al. 1997). Regulations can be established to provide adequate "technology breaks" when employees are away from work, with contingencies for specific emergency jobs.

Another area where government can make a contribution would be in promoting the development of IT resources and technologies to provide information about job stress and job stress reduction methods. In addition, government can promote and fund research on new methods for stress reduction using IT resources (http://www.cdc.gov/niosh/topics/stress/).

7.3.2 Company-Level Interventions

Various aspects of how an organization operates have been shown to affect job stress, for example, corporate culture and climate, monitoring employees' performance, uses of IT to keep "in touch" 24 h/day, family friendly policies, employee training, and employee competence building (Kalimo et al. 1997).

Companies see IT as a productivity and quality improvement tool/process. Huge investments in IT are made with the expectations that there will be bottom-line returns. Many studies have found that a lack of training or poor training about the purposes of new IT and the technical aspects of how to use IT have led to difficult implementation, underachievement of desired improvements, employee stress, employee turnover, and labor strife (Carayon et al. 2006b; Korunka and Vitouch 1999). However, when IT is usable and useful, was developed with worker input and participation, and is implemented with sufficient organizational support, it is more likely to be accepted and used (Mahmood et al. 2000) and to enhance satisfaction and reduce stress (Smith and Carayon 1995). Consideration for physical, cognitive, and organizational ergonomic aspects in the IT design cycle is important to produce benefits for both workers and the company (Boivie et al. 2003; Sandblat et al. 2003).

Corporate culture and policies can be tools for achieving expected improvements from IT and for reducing employee stress and labor strife. One type of company culture defined as "healthy and productive organizations" has a good record for achieving positive business results and a happier, healthier, and less stressed workforce (Murphy and Cooper 2000; Sauter et al. 1996). This culture emphasizes employee participation and involvement, adequate employee training and skill development, positive supervision, adequate resources to carry out work activities, and resources to help employees having problems (Carayon et al. 2012).

Good ergonomics is good economics (Derjani-Bayeh and Smith 1999; Government Accounting Office 1997; Hendrick 1996, 2008; Smith and Derjani-Bayeh 2003). There is a substantial literature that demonstrates having work designed for proper workload, task requirements, and physical demands leads to better productivity and quality and less stress. Companies should use established and valid industrial and systems engineering methods to define task requirements and workload when introducing new technologies. While this is common in manufacturing industries, it is uncommon in IT applications. In addition, research and practice have shown that good ergonomic characteristics of IT and workstations lead to better performance and less physical and psychological stress. Improving employee physical comfort through good physical ergonomics can have benefits in balancing some of the negative consequences of psychosocial problems such as workload and work pressure. Smith and Taveira (2011) and Smith and Carayon (2012) have provided guidance for proper ergonomics in IT applications.

The use of social media for bullying has emerged as a significant concern for school-age children, college students, and workers. Throughout the world, there have been examples of where such bullying has led to suicide and retaliation. Companies can establish policies and rules that deal with the use of IT for bullying coworkers and/or their families. Companies can also provide ways for employees who have suffered from bullying to get assistance such as counseling and reputation remediation.

7.3.3 Individual-Level Interventions

It is important that we ensure breaks from the use of IT (Swanson et al. 1989). Research has shown that the use of IT can become addictive (Amichai-Hamburger and Hayat 2011; Brenner 1997; Chou et al. 2005; Kim 2011; Widyanto and Griffiths 2006; Young 1998; Young and Rodgers 2004). Many people are immersed in IT throughout their entire waking hours. For example, you may use IT extensively at work, have a personal IT device for communicating with family and friends during the day, use IT devices when commuting to and from work, interact with information and entertainment devices after work, and have a home-based IT workstation. In essence, almost every hour of a waking day people can be connected and interacting with IT! There is no break for their brains to "rest" (or recover) from the sensory and mental stimulation from IT. In addition, the constant use of IT can reduce your face-to-face social interaction with family and friends, and this may lead to social isolation and conflicts. It is true that people can have social interaction using IT, but the nature of the interaction differs significantly from face-to-face interaction. Constant, continuous interaction with IT can be stressful, and people need to have breaks away from IT to rest their brains and bodies to reduce their stress (Henning et al. 1989; Swanson et al. 1989).

The blurriness between the work sphere and the personal sphere creates the additional challenge of increased IT use (Messersmith 2007). The cumulative impact of IT use at work with IT use at home and social places may enhance physical stress in the form of musculoskeletal disorders; this is particularly clear among university students (Hupert et al. 2004; Jacobs et al. 2011). We need to go beyond focusing on the impact of IT on quality of working life and begin to examine the impact of IT on quality of life (Hancock and Drury 2011). How can individuals use IT to benefit their overall quality of life?

People may have very limited opportunities to take breaks from IT at work, but they can establish personal rules and behaviors that provide breaks and increase rest from IT while away from work. For example, one rule could be to not use IT while commuting. This has the benefit of increasing transportation safety while also providing rest away from IT. Another break could be established at least one-half hour each night after work for reading a newspaper or a book. Research indicates that reading from hard copy produces different sensory and brain effects than when reading from IT (Dillon et al. 1988). This variation in sensory and mental effects can be positive for recovery from IT use.

One method to break from IT and to also reduce the physical and psychological effects of stress is to take a complete break and to relax using meditation or other related relaxation techniques. Relaxation has been around for centuries, and Edmund Jacobson, an American psychiatrist, wrote an easy-to-read book in 1934 (revised in 1942) that describes the need for regaining momentary mental serenity and how to achieve it for better mental and physical health (Jacobson 1942). For more recent information on relaxation and meditation, Davidson has produced two excellent books describing the need for mental breaks and how meditation produces positive effects (Davidson and Begley 2012; Kabot-Zinn and Davidson 2012).

Another break from IT is face-to-face social interaction with family and friends. This requires turning off and putting away IT devices during the social interaction. Too often IT interrupts face-to-face interaction, which can produce negative responses in the people interacting. This could lead to more stress. So it is best to just turn the IT off and become immersed in the social interaction. Such social interaction has the potential to provide social support, which is a very positive process for stress reduction (House 1981). It has been shown to promote better physical and mental health and longevity (Barth et al. 2010; Cobb 1976; LaRocco et al. 1980; Thoits 2011; Uchino 2009).

7.4 Conclusion

IT can bring both positive and negative outcomes for users. In this chapter, we have highlighted the need to examine the entire system in which IT is implemented and used. This systemic approach as displayed in Fig. 7.1 is necessary to understand the pluses and minuses of IT and devise approaches for balancing IT. Interventions at the society, company, and individual levels were described. The technology is only one element of the work system; other system elements and interactions between the technology and the rest of the system need to be considered for developing effective approaches for balancing IT. Opportunities exist for society, companies, and individuals to benefit from IT and stop the trend of intensification that has been observed in relation to technological change.

References

American Psychological Association. (2012). *Stress in America™: Our health at risk*. Washington, DC: American Psychological Association.

Amichai-Hamburger, Y., & Hayat, Z. (2011). The impact of the Internet on the social lives of users: A representative sample from 13 countries. *Computers in Human Behavior, 27*(1), 585–589.

Bakker, A. B., Demerouti, E., de Boer, E., & Schaufeli, W. B. (2003a). Job demands and job resources as predictors of absence duration and frequency. *Journal of Vocational Behavior, 62* (2), 341–356.

Bakker, A. B., Demerouti, E., Taris, T. W., Schaufeli, W. B., & Schreurs, P. J. G. (2003b). A multigroup analysis of the Job Demands-Resources Model in four home care organizations. *International Journal of Stress Management, 10*(1), 16–38.

Barth, J., Schneider, S., & Von Kanel, R. (2010). Lack of social support in the etiology and the prognosis of coronary heart disease: A systematic review and meta-analysis. *Psychosomatic Medicine, 72*(3), 229–238.

Boivie, I., Blomkvist, S., Persson, J., & Aborg, C. (2003). Addressing users' health issues in software development – An exploratory study. *Behaviour & Information Technology, 22*(6), 411–420.

Brenner, V. (1997). Psychology of computer use: XLVII. Parameters of internet use, abuse and addiction. The first 90 days of internet usage survey. *Psychological Reports, 80*(3), 879–882.

Cannon, W. B. (1915). *Bodily changes in pain, hunger, fear and rage: An account of recent research into the function of emotional excitement*. New York: D. Appleton & Company.

Cannon, W. B. (1927). The James-Lange theory of emotion: A critical examination and an alternative theory. *American Journal of Psychology, 39*, 106–124.

Cannon, W. B. (1931). Again the James-Lange and the thalamic theories of emotion. *Psychological Review, 38*(4), 281–295.

Cannon, W. B. (1932). *The wisdom of the body*. New York: W.W. Norton Company.

Caplan, R. D., Cobb, S., French, J. R. P., Harrison, R. V., & Pinneau, S. R. (1975). *Job demands and worker health*. Washington, DC: US Government Printing Office.

Carayon, P. (1993). Effect of electronic performance monitoring on job design and worker stress: Review of the literature and conceptual model. *Human Factors, 35*(3), 385–395.

Carayon, P. (2007). Healthy and efficient work with computers and information and communication technology – Are there limits? *Scandinavian Journal of Work, Environment and Health, 33*(3), 10–16.

Carayon, P. (2009). The Balance Theory and the work system model... Twenty years later. *International Journal of Human-Computer Interaction, 25*(5), 313–327.

Carayon, P., & Haims, M. C. (2001). Information & communication technology and work organization: Achieving a balanced system. In G. Bradley (Ed.), *Humans on the Net-Information & Communication Technology (ICT), Work Organization and Human Beings* (pp. 119–138). Sweden: Prevent.

Carayon, P., & Smith, M. J. (2000). Work organization and ergonomics. *Applied Ergonomics, 31*, 649–662.

Carayon, P., Smith, M. J., & Haims, M. C. (1999). Work organization, job stress, and work-related musculoskeletal disorders. *Human Factors, 41*(4), 644–663.

Carayon, P., Hundt, A. S., Karsh, B.-T., Gurses, A. P., Alvarado, C. J., Smith, M., et al. (2006a). Work system design for patient safety: The SEIPS model. *Quality & Safety in Health Care, 15* (Supplement 1), i50–i58.

Carayon, P., Schoepke, J., Hoonakker, P. L. T., Haims, M. C., & Brunette, M. (2006b). Evaluating causes and consequences of turnover intention among IT users: The development of a questionnaire survey. *Behaviour and Information Technology, 25*(5), 381–397.

Carayon, P., Hoonakker, P. L. T., & Smith, M. J. (2012). Human factors in organizational design and management. In G. Salvendy (Ed.), *Handbook of human factors and ergonomics* (4th ed., pp. 534–552). Hoboken: Wiley.

Chou, C., Condron, L., & Belland, J. C. (2005). A review of the research on Internet addiction. *Educational Psychology Review, 17*(4), 363–388.

Cobb, S. (1976). Social support as a moderator of life stress. *Psychosomatic Medicine, 38*(5), 300–314.

Davidson, R. J., & Begley, S. (2012). *The emotional life of your brain: How its unique patterns affect the way you think, feel, and live – you can change them.* New York: Hudson Street Press.

Demerouti, E., Bakker, A. B., Nachreiner, F., & Schaufeli, W. B. (2001). The job demands-resources model of Burnout. *Journal of Applied Psychology, 86*(3), 499–512.

Derjani-Bayeh, A., & Smith, M. J. (1999). Effect of physical ergonomics on VDT workers' health: A longitudinal intervention field study in a service organization. *International Journal of Human-Computer Interaction, 11*(2), 109–135.

Dillon, A., McKnight, C., & Richardson, J. (1988). Reading from paper versus reading from screen. *The Computer Journal, 31*(5), 457–464.

Eason, K. (2001). Changing perspectives on the organizational consequences of information technology. *Behaviour and Information Technology, 20*(5), 323–328.

Government Accounting Office. (1997). *Worker protection. Private sector ergonomics programs yield positive results* (Report No. GAO?HEHS-97-163). Washington, DC: Superintendent of Documents.

Grandjean, E. (1968). Fatigue: Its physiological and psychological significance. *Ergonomics in Design, 11*(5), 427–436.

Grandjean, E. (1970). Fatigue. *American Industrial Hygiene Association Journal, 31*, 401–412.

Green, F. (2004). Why has work effort become more intense? *Industrial Relations, 43*(4), 709–741.

Hancock, P. A., & Drury, C. G. (2011). Does human factors/ergonomics contribute to the quality of life? *Theoretical Issues in Ergonomics Science, 12*(5), 416–426.

Harris, K. J., Marett, K., & Harris, R. B. (2011). Technology-related pressure and work–family conflict: Main effects and an examination of moderating variables. *Journal of Applied Social Psychology, 41*(9), 2077–2103.

Harrison, R. V. (1978). Person-environment fit and job stress. In C. L. Cooper & R. Payne (Eds.), *Stress at work* (pp. 175–209). New York: Wiley.

Hendrick, H. W. (1996). Human factors in ODAM: An historical perspective. In O. J. Brown & H. W. Hendrick (Eds.), *Human factors in organizational design and management -V* (pp. 429–434). Amsterdam: Elsevier Science Publishers.

Hendrick, H. W. (2008). Applying ergonomics to systems: Some documented "lessons learned". *Applied Ergonomics, 39*(4), 418–426.

Henning, R. A., Sauter, S. L., Salvendy, G., & Krieg, E. F., Jr. (1989). Microbreak length, performance, and stress in a data entry task. *Ergonomics, 32*(7), 855–864.

House, J. (1981). *Work, stress and social support*. Reading: Addison-Wesley.

Hupert, N., Amick, B. C., Fossel, A. H., Coley, C. M., Robertson, M. M., & Katz, J. N. (2004). Upper extremity musculoskeletal symptoms and functional impairment associated with computer use among college students. *Work: Journal of Prevention, Assessment & Rehabilitation, 23*(2), 85–93.

Jacobs, K., Foley, G., Punnett, L., Hall, V., Gore, R., Brownson, E., et al. (2011). University students' notebook computer use: Lessons learned using e-diaries to report musculoskeletal discomfort. *Ergonomics, 54*(4), 206–219.

Jacobson, E. (1942). *You must relax. A practical method of reducing the strains of modern living*. New York: Whittlesey House (McGraw-Hill).

James, W. (1890). *Principles of psychology* (1983 reprint edition). Boston: Harvard University Press.

James, W. (1913). *Psychology* (Original copyright 1892 ed.). New York: Henry Holt and Company.

Johnson, J. V. (1989). Control, collectivity and the psychosocial work environment. In S. L. Sauter, J. J. Hurrell, & C. L. Cooper (Eds.), *Job control and worker health* (pp. 55–74). New York: Wiley.

Kabot-Zinn, J., & Davidson, R. (Eds.). (2012). *The mind's own physician: A scientific dialogue with the Dalai Lama on the healing power of meditation*. Oakland: New Harbinger Publications, Inc.

Kalimo, R., Lindstrom, K., & Smith, M. J. (1997). Psychosocial approach in occupational health. In G. Salvendy (Ed.), *Handbook of human factors and ergonomics* (pp. 1059–1084). New York: Wiley.

Karasek, R. A. (1979). Job demands, job decision latitude, and mental strain: Implications for job redesign. *Administrative Science Quarterly, 24*, 285–308.

Karasek, R. A., & Theorell, T. (1990). *Healthy work: Stress, productivity and the reconstruction of working life*. New York: Basic Books.

Karsh, B.-T., & Brown, R. (2010). Macroergonomics and patient safety: The impact of levels on theory, measurement, analysis and intervention in patient safety research. *Applied Ergonomics, 41*(5), 674–681.

Karsh, B.-T., Holden, R. J., Alper, S. J., & Or, C. K. L. (2006). A human factors engineering paradigm for patient safety: Designing to support the performance of the healthcare professional. *Quality & Safety in Health Care, 15*(i6), i59–i65.

Kim, S. J. (2011). Conceptualizing personal web usage in work contexts: A preliminary framework. *Computers in Human Behavior, 27*(6), 2271–2283.

Korunka, C., & Vitouch, O. (1999). Effects of the implementation of information technology on employees' strain and job satisfaction: A context-dependent approach. *Work & Stress, 13*(4), 341–363.

Kraut, R., Kiesler, S., Boneva, B., Cummings, J., Helgeson, V., & Crawford, A. (2002). Internet paradox revisited. *Journal of Social Issues, 58*(1), 49–74.

Lange, C. G., & James, W. (1922). *The emotions* (Vol. 1). Baltimore: Williams & Wilkins Company.

LaRocco, J. M., House, J. S., & French, J. R. P. J. (1980). Social support, occupational stress, and health. *Journal of Health and Social Behavior, 21*, 202–218.

Lazarus, R. S. (1974). Psychological stress and coping in adaptation and illness. *International Journal of Psychiatry in Medicine, 5*, 321–333.

Mahmood, M. A., Burn, J. M., Gemoets, L. A., & Jacquez, C. (2000). Variables affecting information technology end-user satisfaction: A meta-analysis of the empirical literature. *International Journal of Human-Computer Studies, 52*(4), 751–771.

Mason, J. W. (1959). Psychological influences on the pituitary-adrenal cortical system. *Recent Progress in Hormone Research, 15*, 345–389.
Mason, J. W. (1971). A reevaluation of the concept of "non-specificity" in stress theory. *Journal of Psychiatric Research, 8*, 323–333.
Mason, J. W. (1975a). A historical view of the stress field. Part 1. *Journal of Human Stress, 1*, 6–12.
Mason, J. W. (1975b). A historical view of the stress field. Part 2. *Journal of Human Stress, 1*, 22–36.
McGrath, J. E. (1976). Stress and behavior in organizations. In M. Dunnette (Ed.), *Handbook of industrial and organizational psychology* (pp. 1353–1395). Chicago: Rand McNally.
Messersmith, J. (2007). Managing work-life conflict among information technology workers. *Human Resource Management, 46*(3), 429–451.
Morganson, V. J., Major, D. A., Oborn, K. L., Verive, J. M., & Heelan, M. P. (2010). Comparing telework locations and traditional work arrangements: Differences in work-life balance support, job satisfaction, and inclusion. *Journal of Managerial Psychology, 25*(6), 578–595.
Murphy, L. R., & Cooper, C. L. (Eds.). (2000). *Healthy and productive work: An international perspective*. London: Taylor & Francis.
Quick, J. C., Wright, T. A., & Adkins, J. A. (2012). *Preventive stress management in organization*. Washington, DC: American Psychological Association.
Sandblat, B., Gulliksen, J., Aborg, C., Boivie, I., Persson, J., Goransson, B., et al. (2003). Work environment and computer systems development. *Behaviour & Information Technology, 22* (6), 375–387.
Sauter, S., Lim, S. Y., & Murphy, L. R. (1996). Organizational health: A new paradigm for occupational stress at NIOSH. *Japanese Journal of Occupational Mental Health, 4*(4), 248–254.
Schachter, S., & Singer, J. (1962). Cognitive, social and physiological determinants of emotional state. *Psychological Review, 69*, 379–399.
Schaufeli, W. B., & Bakker, A. B. (2004). Job demands, job resources, and their relationship with burnout and engagement: A multi-sample study. *Journal of Organizational Behavior, 25*(3), 293–315.
Selye, H. (1956). *The stress of life*. New York: McGraw Hill.
Selye, H. (1974). *Stress without distress*. New York: New American Library.
Siegrist, J. (1996). Adverse health effects of high-effort/low-reward conditions. *Journal of Occupational Health Psychology, 1*(1), 27–41.
Siegrist, J. (2009). Unfair exchange and health: Social bases of stress-related diseases. *Social Theory & Health, 7*(4), 305–317.
Siegrist, J., & Wahrendorf, M. (2009). Quality of work, health, and retirement. *The Lancet, 374* (9705), 1872–1873.
Smith, M. J. (1981). Occupational stress: An overview. In G. Salvendy & M. J. Smith (Eds.), *Machine pacing and occupational stress* (pp. 13–19). London: Taylor & Francis.
Smith, M. J. (1987). Mental and physical strain at VDT workstations. *Behaviour and Information Technology, 6*(3), 243–255.
Smith, M. J., & Beringer, D. B. (1987). Human factors in occupational injury evaluation and control. In G. Salvendy (Ed.), *Handbook of human factors* (pp. 767–789). New York: Wiley.
Smith, M. J., & Carayon, P. (1995). New technology, automation, and work organization: Stress problems and improved technology implementation strategies. *The International Journal of Human Factors in Manufacturing, 5*(1), 99–116.
Smith, M. J., & Carayon, P. (1996). Work organization, stress, and cumulative trauma disorders. In S. D. Moon & S. L. Sauter (Eds.), *Beyond biomechanics – Psychosocial aspects of musculoskeletal disorders in office work* (pp. 23–41). London: Taylor & Francis.
Smith, M. J., & Carayon, P. (2001). Balance theory of job design. In W. Karwowski (Ed.), *International encyclopedia of ergonomics and human factors* (pp. 1181–1184). London: Taylor & Francis.

Smith, M. J., & Carayon, P. (2012). Design of fixed, portable, and mobile information devices. In J. Jacko (Ed.), *The human computer interaction handbook* (3rd ed., pp. 297–311). Boca Raton: CRC Press.

Smith, M. J., & Carayon-Sainfort, P. (1989). A balance theory of job design for stress reduction. *International Journal of Industrial Ergonomics, 4*(1), 67–79.

Smith, M. J., & Derjani-Bayeh, A. (2003). Do ergonomics improvements increase computer workers' productivity? An intervention study in a call center. *Ergonomics, 46*(1), 3–18.

Smith, M. J., & Taveira, A. (2011). Physical ergonomics and the Web. In K.-P. L. Vu & R. W. Proctor (Eds.), *Handbook of human factors in web design* (2nd ed., pp. 65–84). Boca Raton: CRC Press.

Smith, M. J., Cohen, B. G., Stammerjohn, I. W. J., & Happ, A. (1981). An investigation of health complaints and job stress in video display operations. *Human Factors, 23*(4), 387–400.

Smith, M. J., Carayon, P., Sanders, K. J., Lim, S. Y., & LeGrande, D. (1992). Employee stress and health complaints in jobs with and without electronic performance monitoring. *Applied Ergonomics, 23*(1), 17–27.

Swanson, N. G., Sauter, S. L., & Chapman, L. J. (1989). The design of rest breaks for video display terminal work: A review of the relevant literature. In A. Mital (Ed.), *Advances in industrial ergonomics and safety I* (pp. 895–898). London: Taylor & Francis.

Tarafdar, M., Qiang, T. U., Ragu-Nathan, B. S., & Ragu-Nathan, T. S. (2007). The impact of technostress on role stress and productivity. *Journal of Management Information Systems, 24* (1), 301–328.

Thoits, P. A. (2011). Mechanisms linking social ties and support to physical and mental health. *Journal of Health and Social Behavior, 52*(2), 145–161.

Uchino, B. N. (2009). Understanding the links between social support and physical health: A life-span perspective with emphasis on the separability of perceived and received support. *Perspectives in Psychological Science, 4*(3), 236–255.

Widyanto, L., & Griffiths, M. (2006). Internet addiction: A critical review. *International Journal of Mental Health and Addiction, 4*(1), 31–51.

Young, K. S. (1998). Internet addiction: The emergence of a new clinical disorder. *CyberPsychology and Behavior, 1*(3), 237–244.

Young, K. S., & Rodgers, R. C. (2004). The relationship between depression and internet addiction. *American Behavioral Scientist, 48*(4), 402–415.

Zhang, W., & Xu, P. (2011). Do I have to learn something new? Mental models and the acceptance of replacement technologies. *Behaviour and Information Technology, 30*(2), 201–211.

Chapter 8
New Ways of Working: Impact on Working Conditions, Work–Family Balance, and Well-Being

Evangelia Demerouti, Daantje Derks, Lieke L. ten Brummelhuis, and Arnold B. Bakker

8.1 Introduction

It goes without saying that over the past two decades developments in information and communication technology have had a huge impact on working life. Email is arguably the most prevalent form of computer-mediated communication within organizations, but the increasing use of mobile devices in business has given the experience of email a new dimension (Derks and Bakker 2010). Using these technological innovations, more and more organizations have started to redesign their approach to work. Central to this new approach is that employees are asked to organize their work flexibly. Employees are expected to decide for themselves when they work (schedule flexibility), where they work (e.g., telecommuting), and by which communication tool/medium (smartphone, email, videoconference) they work (Baarne et al. 2010; ten Brummelhuis et al. 2012). This implies further that the emphasis has shifted to output, as opposed to face time (just being present). Such a flexible work design, also referred to as "new ways of working" (NWW), has been applauded thus far, as it would lead to more efficient work processes and reduce organizational costs (Rennecker and Godwin 2005). However, whereas the organizational benefits of NWW have been emphasized in previous studies (Sánchez et al. 2007), little is known yet about how NWW influence employees and their

E. Demerouti (✉)
Department of Industrial Engineering and Innovation Sciences, Human Performance Management Group, Eindhoven University of Technology, Eindhoven, The Netherlands
e-mail: E.demerouti@tue.nl

D. Derks • A.B. Bakker
Department of Work and Organizational Psychology, Erasmus University Rotterdam, Rotterdam, The Netherlands
e-mail: Derks@fsw.eur.nl; bakker@fsw.eur.nl

L.L. ten Brummelhuis
Beedie School of Business, Simon Fraser University, Burnaby, Canada
e-mail: lieke@wharton.upenn.edu

C. Korunka and P. Hoonakker (eds.), *The Impact of ICT on Quality of Working Life*, 123
DOI 10.1007/978-94-017-8854-0_8, © Springer Science+Business Media Dordrecht 2014

families. What are the pros and cons of NWW? Do NWW help employees to find a better balance between work and nonwork roles? Using an iPad to check work-related email in the evening at home while watching TV with the spouse may interfere with private life. However, using that same iPad to Skype with the spouse while on a business trip may positively influence work–family balance. Insight into the possible pitfalls and opportunities of NWW may help employees to use NWW in such a way that they enable them to optimally combine their work and nonwork responsibilities.

In this chapter, we examine the impact of NWW on work–family balance. We will first discuss the concept of NWW and their possible advantages and disadvantages. In the next paragraph, we will investigate the impact of NWW on working conditions, work–family balance, and employee well-being. We will then proceed with a discussion of how NWW can be used as an intervention to improve the balance between work and private life.

8.2 New Ways of Working

New ways of working (NWW) have three key characteristics (Baarne et al. 2010). First, the *timing* of work has become more flexible. Employees have more autonomy in deciding when they work. This implies that there are no fixed work schedules as is common in 9 a.m. to 5 p.m. jobs. Second, NWW offer the employee various options for the *place* of work, including the office, home, and during commuting time (e.g., on the train, on the airplane). At the office, employees no longer have fixed workspaces (Kelliher and Anderson 2008). Instead, plain workspaces are provided that are suitable and accessible for every employee who comes to the office. Third, NWW are facilitated by *new media technologies*, such as smartphones and videoconferencing. Thus, NWW offer the employee various options for communication with co-workers, supervisors, and clients, including phone calls, email, online messaging, and (online) virtual meetings (Baarne et al. 2010). Combining these three characteristics, we define NWW as a work design in which employees can control the timing and place of their work while being supported by electronic communication. Strictly speaking, all these characteristics should be present to meet the definition (or criteria) of NWW. Although NWW refer to these three characteristics, this chapter will particularly focus on the last one as the other two characteristics have been more extensively covered by earlier literature on flextime (Baltes et al. 1999) and telecommuting (Golden and Veiga 2005). However, we would emphasize that the distinctive features of NWW are more autonomy over the workday (location, timing, communication) and more flexibility that is facilitated by high-tech communication to guarantee information flow and contact with colleagues and customers.

8.2.1 Pros and Cons

The introduction of NWW has initiated a revolution in the way employees interact with each other on the work floor (Gephart 2002). A significant proportion of communication in organizational life, with clients and colleagues, far away or in close proximity, takes place online (Renaud et al. 2006). Communication by email is supposed to be less time-consuming, more reliable, and more efficient than face-to-face meetings or phone calls (e.g., Berghel 1997). Moreover, people can be reached easily and quickly (Manger et al. 2003) and can collaborate with individuals across geographically distributed locations (Renaud et al. 2006). Furthermore, email enables the receipt of more information from more – and more diverse – sources.

Wireless access to email facilitated by smartphones enables users to engage in email in new ways. The smartphone is one of the newest communication tools in the workplace today (Rennecker and Godwin 2005). For an increasing number of employees, smartphones have become part of everyday work life (e.g., Hassan 2003). A smartphone is a mobile device with the functionality of a pocket PC. It facilitates calendar management, unlimited access to the Internet, making phone calls, and receiving emails anytime, anywhere. The main reason for having a smartphone is to send and receive emails (Middleton 2007). Companies provide their employees with smartphones in the hope of a return on investment. Research has indeed indicated that mobile tools can lead to increased productivity (Locke 2005) and enhanced collaboration (Baron 2005). Other advantages associated with smartphone use are improved responsiveness, the availability of real-time information, faster decision-making, and more flexibility in work schedules. This flexibility can give individual workers the opportunity to better balance their work and home domains, as they can allocate their time over work and family activities in a way that suits their situation best (Parasuraman and Greenhaus 2002).

However, NWW are known to have some drawbacks as well. One such drawback is the possible (information) overload. Hiltz and Turoff (1985) foresaw that when email became widely available for everyone, workers would struggle with managing the inflow of messages. A handful of studies, however, has found that workers' perceived overload stems from aspects of their email use other than, or in addition to, the number and length of messages received (Rennecker and Derks 2012). Other factors contributing to perceived overload have included pressures to respond quickly (Derks and Bakker 2010; Thomas et al. 2006), unanticipated tasks generated by received messages (Thomas et al. 2006), interruptions and task switching associated with responding to emails (Dabbish and Kraut 2006; Russell et al. 2005), numerous and diverse role demands (Derks and Bakker 2010), and lack of control over incoming messages (Allen and Shoard 2005).

Moreover, NWW and particularly the use of electronic communication, i.e., smartphones, may also extend the workday. Fenner and Renn (2004) reported that extending the workday to the home during evenings, weekends, and holidays is of all times. However, the availability of technological tools (e.g., the smartphone) facilitating anytime-anywhere connectedness of employees to their employers is a relatively new tendency. Some studies suggest that employees who use electronic communication outperform employees who refuse to work after hours, because of reduced interruptions from colleagues and increased autonomy (e.g., Venkatesh and Vitalari 1992). However, other studies have shown that employees who engage in such NWW report feelings of isolation, have difficulties in working without structure, experience interruptions by family and friends (Allen et al. 2003), and complain about being overworked (Galinsky et al. 2001).

NWW have advantages and disadvantages not only for the user but also for the organization. The intensive use of smartphones in organizational life creates a norm that is characterized by nomadic working and continual communication (e.g., Hassan 2003). The possibility to stay connected expands into new settings and introduces new options regarding availability, responsiveness, and coordination (Mazmanian et al. 2006). However, this opportunity of accessibility anytime, anywhere, seems to change to availability everywhere, all the time (Katz and Aarhus 2002). There are indications that the blurring of boundaries leads to a deteriorated work–family balance (e.g., Derks and Bakker in press; Jarvenpaa and Lang 2005).

Finally, NWW practices require autonomous and self-managed ways of working, which are thought to benefit both organizational and employee performance. However, previous studies have found contradicting results regarding the impact of flexible working practices on employee outcomes (Golden and Veiga 2005). Some studies have shown favorable effects, e.g., an increased sense of autonomy (De Jonge and Rutte 1999; Gajendran and Harrison 2007), while many other studies found negative outcomes such as an increase in negative emotions, physical health complaints (Mann and Holdsworth 2003), work intensification (Kelliher and Anderson 2010), and reduced privacy and job satisfaction (De Croon et al. 2005). We will now take a closer look at the impact of NWW on working conditions, work–family balance, and employee well-being.

8.3 A Closer Look at the Impact of NWW on Working Life

8.3.1 Impact of NWW on Working Conditions

NWW influence the working conditions in a drastic way. We will use the job demands–resources (JD-R) framework (Bakker and Demerouti 2007; Demerouti and Bakker 2011; Demerouti et al. 2001) to illustrate how NWW impact the work environment. Thus, we use a systematic way not only to describe the changes in the work environment due to NWW but also to explain how these changes may influence work–family balance and well-being. Accordingly, although every work environment is unique, its characteristics can be categorized in two broad dimensions: job demands and job resources. *Job demands* refer to those physical, psychological, social, or organizational aspects of the job that require sustained physical and/or psychological (cognitive and emotional) effort or skills and are therefore associated with certain physiological and/or psychological costs. Examples are a high work pressure, an unfavorable physical environment, and irregular working hours. Although job demands are not necessarily negative, they may turn into job stressors when meeting those demands requires high effort from which the employee fails to recover adequately (Meijman and Mulder 1998). *Job resources* refer to those physical, psychological, social, or organizational aspects of the job that either (1) are functional in achieving work goals; (2) reduce job demands and the associated physiological and psychological costs; or (3) stimulate personal growth, learning, and development. Hence, resources are not only necessary to deal with job demands, but they also are important in their own right. This agrees with Hackman and Oldham's (1980) job characteristics model that emphasizes the motivational potential of job resources at the task level, including autonomy, feedback, and task significance.

NWW may influence both job demands and job resources. With respect to job demands, Derks and Bakker (2010) suggested that NWW increase three kinds of "overload": *information overload*, *work overload*, and *social overload*. Information overload occurs when the amount of information to be consumed and assimilated, particularly with respect to a task or decision, exceeds the individual's information processing capacity. Work overload occurs when the volume of messages received and the time required to respond appropriately exceeds the time available to do so. This may be due to the receipt of a large number of unnecessary messages, a low-trust culture that prompts users to "cc:" many recipients, a worker being engaged in too many simultaneous projects, or a lack of group or organizational norms to promote judicious use of email. Finally, social overload occurs when a worker receives email messages from too many different people evoking too many distinct roles and social contexts, exceeding the recipient's interaction capacity.

Moreover, although the continuous availability can decrease work delays (quick access to information) which leads to increased organization efficiency, at the same time, it may lead to an increase in *work interruptions* and, in turn, to increased disorganization (Rennecker and Godwin 2005). Rubinstein et al. (2001) examined the time cost implications of task familiarity and complexity in task switching. They showed that switching between tasks resulted in a delay before engaging effectively in a new task, even if the worker had been previously engaged in the task. Each fragmentation of a task adds to the total time required to complete it (Rubinstein et al. 2001).

The lack of nonverbal cues in computer-mediated communication implies automatically that not all information is fully transferred (McKenna and Bargh 2000). The messages typically conveyed by these cues are absent in a text-based environment (e.g., Walther 1995), which implies that for the interpretation of messages online we have to rely exclusively on nonverbal information. This may have consequences for the decoding of others' emotions because we cannot make use of nonverbal cues in the interpretation of incoming messages. *Misunderstandings* and *conflicts* between colleagues can be the result of such kind of communication.

At the same time, the lack of nonverbal cues also has consequences for the expression of our own emotions since every emotion has to be verbalized and part of the nonverbal expression happens unconsciously. The strictly task-oriented messages should not suffer that much from these consequences. This makes email a relatively "safe" environment (McKenna et al. 2002).

The lack of nonverbal cues may also have certain advantages in the regulation of emotions. Since many organizations demand that their service employees adhere to strict display rules regarding the emotions they should show to customers, computer-mediated communication may have the potential to make this work easier. Service employees constantly have to regulate their emotional expressions while interacting with customers (Grandey and Brauburger 2002). Hochschild (1983) argued that this form of *emotional labor* is not without costs for the employees because this process requires a lot of effort. It can be argued that the possibility to communicate emotional messages to colleagues and customers mediated by email gives the user more control and autonomy over actions.

One may consider electronic communication as a helpful resource for the sender but as a demand for the recipient. Specifically, a characteristic of email is that it invites the sender to engage in short and shallow messages (Bertacco 2007; Bertacco and Deponte 2005). Wicklund and Vandekerckhove (2000) argued that only speedy communicative media that are also limited in bandwidth, for example, email, would promote shallow communications. Speed-oriented communication gives an individual the sense that the recipient can be reached and dealt with quickly (Manger et al. 2003). Especially in comparison with postal mail, email messages tend to be shallower and more reactive (Bertacco and Deponte 2005). This might bring about important social psychological consequences in that senders abbreviate their interactions and are more egocentric, in that they reduce perspective taking, than individuals who interact face-to-face (Wicklund and Vandekerckhove 2000).

With respect to the impact of NWW on resources, when electronic communication was introduced on the work floor, it was expected not only to replace part of face-to-face communication but also to generate an increase in *communication overall* (Contractor and Eisenberg 1990). Surprisingly, Sarbaugh-Thompson and Feldman (1998) found that the increase in electronic communication was related to a decrease in face-to-face and telephone interactions, producing a net decrease in overall communication in their population of organization members. This decline in volume might suggest that electronic communication is more efficient (see also, Rice and Case 1983). Taking a closer look at the analysis revealed that electronic communication was not more efficient per se but that the reduction in casual communication (e.g., greetings, social talk at the coffee corner) was at the root of the decrease in communication (Sarbaugh-Thompson and Feldman 1998). Thus, although NWW help to increase the efficiency of communication, at the same time they reduce overall communication (which represents an important job resource according to the JD-R model).

According to the JD-R model, social support is an essential job resource that has the potential to buffer the impact of job demands on well-being (e.g., Bakker et al. 2005; Xanthopoulou et al. 2007). In view of the fact that NWW facilitate workers to be separated in time and place, the likelihood that colleagues spend time together in one place is decreasing. The key ingredient of casual conversation, "hanging out together," is missing when employees communicate by email or work from home, which requires intent and planning. These reduced opportunities to give and receive support are also an issue for the increasing number of teleworkers.

Since NWW and in particular electronic communication are very practical in the exchange of documents and information (e.g., Sullivan 1995), it has also become more common to deliver feedback on these documents. Feedback messages can be considered ambiguous because they have an objective, critical component, but also a motivational component in the form of constructive feedback. In organizations, feedback is considered as a first step to improvement and personal development. This makes it an important resource fueling our motivation at work (Bakker and Demerouti 2007). However, if information is likely to be negative, media choice can be crucial when delivering the feedback (Fulk and Mani 1986). In our Western society, it is not done to send negative personal feedback by email. In such a situation, face-to-face interaction is preferred. The mediated environment of electronic communication might decrease the psychological discomfort of the sender during the communication process, and, as a consequence, the feedback might be more straight and honest (Sussman and Sproull 1999). So, people may find it less stressful to deliver negative feedback by email in comparison to face-to-face because they are socially buffered from their communication partners (e.g., Gallupe et al. 1992; Kiesler and Sproull 1992). Sussman and Sproull (1999) experimentally tested the influence of media choice (face-to-face, telephone, synchronous computer-mediated communication) on the perception of feedback (positive or negative). The results showed that individuals using computer-mediated communication to deliver negative feedback distorted it to a lesser extent than individuals communicating face-to-face. Thus, computer-mediated communication facilitates the delivery of more direct and negative feedback, which is sometimes difficult to deliver through face-to-face communication. Because of NWW, individuals do office work away from a central, conventional office during regular office hours (Kraut 1987). NWW replace work done at a central office location. Employees who work from home might experience enhanced autonomy, more flexible working hours, and reduction in costs for transportation (Zedeck and Mosier 1990). Employees who use NWW are also better able to cope with family demands since they can take care of their children while actually working. In this way, they need less day care and can be with their child in case of sickness. However, the biggest concern about telecommuting is the potential for exploitation by the organization (Zedeck and Mosier 1990). According to Zedeck and Mosier, telecommuting contains the danger of restriction of career advancement for the more vulnerable groups of the working population like females with enhanced childcare responsibilities, elderly individuals, and people with disabilities. The reason is that telecommuters are isolated from the organization and their promotion possibilities might therefore be impaired (Demerouti 2006).

In conclusion, NWW seem to have an impact on the quantity and quality of job demands and job resources. Specifically, in terms of job demand overload, interruptions, misunderstandings, and conflict seem to increase, while emotional labor seems to decrease due to the application of NWW. With respect to job resources, while feedback and autonomy seem to increase, social support, overall communication, and career advancement might decline as a result of the introduction of NWW. How does this consequently influence work-life balance and employee well-being? That is what we will discuss next.

8.3.2 Impact of NWW on Work-Life Balance

One of the reasons that more and more organizations introduce NWW is that it would facilitate the integration of employees' work and life roles (Ryan and Kossek 2008). The general idea of why NWW contribute to work-life balance is that, first of all, they give employees control over the scheduling of their workdays. Flexible work schedules allow the employee to use time more efficiently and schedule various activities in a way that suits the employee's situation best (Parasuraman and Greenhaus 2002). Being able to choose a location for work (e.g., working from home) also allows employees to schedule work optimally to minimize work–family interference (Gajendran and Harrison 2007). Furthermore, telecommuting actually saves the employee time because it cuts down on commuting time that cannot be used for work or family activities (Hill et al. 2003). Finally, electronic communication enables employees to stay in touch with work while working from home or on schedules that differ from colleagues or customers (ten Brummelhuis et al. 2012).

Although the potential of NWW for adjusting work and life roles sounds appealing, some critical notes have been made as well. For instance, Perlow (1998) suggested that managers are keen to control the hours that employees work and therefore the temporal boundary between employees' work and life outside of work. The predictions about the effectiveness of telecommuting in reducing problems with balancing work and family as well as the initial research findings were more positive (e.g., Gordon 1976) than in recent studies. Gajendran and Harrison (2007) commented that telecommuting may increase the permeability of boundaries between work and nonwork domains as the physical boundaries between the two environments are eliminated (Shamir and Salomon 1985). Instead of facilitating balance, telecommuting was found to enhance interference between multiple roles (Hill et al. 2003). Also, Duxbury et al. (1996) found that users of telecommuting were more likely to report greater stress and more work–family interference. Similarly, flexible work schedules may cause more stress owing to constantly changing schedules that result in a highly unstructured daily program (Tausig and Fenwick 2001). A blurring of work–family boundaries may particularly occur when flexible work arrangements are combined with increased electronic communication (Katz and Aarhus 2002). Working from home while staying connected through email and smartphone implies that work never stops and intrudes into the family domain. In this way, both the beginning and end times of work are not clearly defined (Hamilton 1987).

Not surprisingly then, empirical studies on the effects of telecommuting, flextime, and electronic communication on work-life balance show a rather mixed picture. In their meta-analysis of studies on telecommuting, Gajendran and Harrison (2007) concluded that telecommuting reduced work–family conflict, although the effect was small. Nevertheless, in some studies it is reported that telecommuters experience more time pressure in the long run while making longer work hours (Peters and Van der Lippe 2007). Glass and Finley (2002) were more explicit about the mixed findings of flexible work schedules. In their review study, they mentioned that previous studies reported both positive and negative effects of flexible schedules on work–family conflict. There is also evidence that mobile devices blur the distinctions between the public and private domains of life (Grant and Kiesler 2001; Green 2002). For instance, Jarvenpaa and Lang (2005) showed that smartphone users reported increased work pressure and the inability to separate and keep distance from work. This might be because boundary management is more difficult for NWW, as blurring role boundaries will occur when working from home is combined with smartphone use (or other forms of continuous connections).

Kattenbach et al. (2010) provided an additional explanation for the mixed findings regarding the effects of flexible working time arrangements and work–family interference. Namely, flexibility in working time contains not only time autonomy (of the employee's) but also his or her temporal restrictions, imposed by others, e.g., the employer. Kattenbach et al. (2010) found that after controlling for various job demands, time autonomy was negatively related, while time restrictions were positively related to work–family conflict.

In sum, in the studies on the key dimensions of NWW (telecommuting, flexible work schedules, and electronic communication), mixed findings were reported on the impact on work–family balance. A possible explanation for these mixed findings is that conditional factors that might influence the success of NWW have rarely been taken into account. Work conditions, family conditions, and personal characteristics (e.g., a boundary management strategy of segmentation or integration of roles; Perlow 1998; Powell and Greenhaus 2010) are all very likely to influence the extent to which NWW actually enhance work-life balance. For instance, organizations propagating a presence culture, while being wary of telecommuters, may rather raise stress than supporting "new workers." ten Brummelhuis and Van der Lippe (2010) showed that employees' family situation also matters, as they reported that telecommuting and flexible work schedules were only effective for singles and not for employees with a partner and/or children. Finally, persons may differ in the extent to which they prefer, but also are able to deal with, enhanced control over their work schedule. Conscientiousness and self-efficacy possibly play an important role here (Raghuram and Wiesenfeld 2004). Future studies are needed to examine the consequences of NWW on work-life balance in different work and family settings and among persons varying in individual characteristics.

8.3.3 Impact of NWW on Recovery

NWW can influence not only interrole management but also the way in which individuals spend their time after work in the form of recovery activities. Recovery occurs during time periods when no demands similar to the preceding job demands are put on the person (Meijman and Mulder 1998), in other words during evenings off (Rook and Zijlstra 2006). The common factor underlying most recovery definitions is that recovery occurs after strain when the stressor is no longer present (Sonnentag and Geurts 2009).

The important role of recovery can be illustrated from the perspective of effort–recovery theory (Meijman and Mulder 1998). Its central assumption is that effort expenditure at work is unavoidably associated with acute load reactions. Under optimal circumstances, these stress-related acute load reactions return to prestressor levels during after-work hours, and recovery is completed before the next working day starts. In this situation, health is not at risk (Meijman and Mulder 1998). However, when stress-related acute load reactions prolong or reoccur during after-work hours, recovery is incomplete. In this situation, the worker will start the subsequent workday in a suboptimal condition and will have to invest compensatory effort in order to perform adequately at work. Following this idea, Sonnentag (2001) showed that employees need leisure time to detach from work in order to properly recover from stress expenditure.

Sonnentag and Fritz (2007) argued that people might differ in the activities (e.g., low-effort, social, or physical activities) they experience as recovering. They suggest that recovery experience consists of four different dimensions. Psychological detachment (1) includes activities aimed to disengage oneself mentally from work. Relaxation (2) is characterized by low activation and increased positive affect. Deep physical and mental relaxation can be achieved by deliberately practicing relaxation techniques, for example, meditation (Grossman et al. 2004). Mastery experiences (3) refer to challenging experiences in other domains that provide opportunities for learning and success (Sonnentag et al. 2008). Finally, control or autonomy (4) refers to an individual's ability to choose an action from multiple options. Or, the degree to which an individual can decide which activity to pursue during leisure time, as well as how and when to engage in this activity (Sonnentag and Fritz 2007).

It is questionable to what extent intensive smartphone users really experience evenings off. Derks et al. (2014) examined whether intensive smartphone users have more difficulties to actively engage in recovery activities. It was hypothesized that it might be very difficult for intensive smartphone users to engage in recovery activities (e.g., low-effort or social activities) in response to high work–home interference. In other words, especially when employees need recovery the most, the probability that they will succeed in undertaking activities aimed at recovery decreases. This hypothesis was examined in a study among 80 employees (40 smartphone users, 40 controls). Participants completed a 6-day diary questionnaire over a time period of 2 weeks. Results showed that for the control group, T1 work–home interference was positively related to recovery (i.e., psychological detachment, relaxation, mastery, and control over time), whereas smartphone users facing high work–home interference did not succeed in engaging in these recovery activities. This implies that being connected to work in the evening hours through smartphones has consequences for the extent to which employees succeed in adopting recovery strategies. This finding is explained by the fact that in most cases the request to work initiated by the smartphone is external and uncontrollable and continues the confrontation with work-related matters (Duxbury et al. 1994).

Research on job-stress recovery suggests that recovery experiences during leisure time provide opportunities to unwind from work (Geurts and Sonnentag 2006; Westman and Eden 1997). Empirical research has shown that employees who successfully detach from work during after-work hours experience higher levels of life satisfaction and well-being (Sonnentag and Fritz 2007) and show better performance (e.g., Binnewies et al. 2009; Demerouti et al. 2009; Meijman and Mulder 1998). Continuous preoccupation with work during after-work hours and the inability to switch off from work are part of an unhealthy pattern characterized by high levels of fatigue, sleep complaints, and other indicators of poor well-being (Grebner et al. 2005; Van Hooff et al. 2006). Derks and Bakker (in press) argued that work–home interference and the inability to switch off are stronger related to poor well-being for intensive smartphone users in comparison to less intensive users. Assuming that intensive smartphone users use their smartphones during evening hours, they drain the same energy resources during the evening as during the workday, which accelerates the fatigue process. Since employees who decide to stay connected have no prior information about the frequency and quantity of requests that will be made on them, they might experience low levels of control (Middleton and Cukier 2006). In addition, the smartphone facilitates working overtime. As a result, it is plausible that extensive smartphone use during evening hours contributes to the prolonged exposure to work demands and its associated negative consequences. With a daily diary study, Derks and Bakker (in press) found that for intensive smartphone users daily work–home interference was more positively related to daily exhaustion than for employees who abstained from smartphone use during evening hours. In other words, the costs of high work–home interference are disproportionally loaded on the intensive smartphone user. The explanation for this effect is that because smartphone users will be more inclined to check their work-related emails during nonwork time, they ruminate more about their work, are more involved in work while being at home, and consequently recover less.

Taken together, it seems that the empirical evidence regarding the impact of NWW on recovery is not sufficient to provide a clear picture of the way in which the different dimensions of NWW influence recovery after work. It seems that NWW have both positive and negative effects on work–family interaction. The positive effects are due to the flexibility (in location and hours of working) that NWW enable, while the negative effects are due to the increased risk that individuals are constantly busy with their work during nonwork times.

8.3.4 Impact of NWW on Employee Well-Being and Performance

In a recent diary study, ten Brummelhuis et al. (2012) examined the effects of NWW on work engagement and exhaustion and investigated whether communication quality mediated these relationships. The results of a 5-day diary study ($n = 550$) showed that daily use of NWW was positively related to daily engagement and negatively to daily exhaustion due to increased effective and efficient communication. In addition, NWW enhanced connectivity among co-workers, resulting in enhanced daily engagement and reduced exhaustion. However, ten Brummelhuis et al. (2012) also found a positive relationship between NWW and exhaustion, because NWW increased interruptions during the work process. This means that although NWW have the potential to foster work engagement during the workday, some caution is needed. Namely, NWW make employees engaged but at the same time cost a lot of energy, which consequently may exhaust them at the end of the workday.

Similarly, Kattenbach et al. (2010) found that after controlling for various job demands, time autonomy was negatively related, while time restrictions (e.g., incidental overtime) were positively related to exhaustion. Moreover, the authors showed that time autonomy and time restrictions were unrelated to self-reported as well as peer-rated in-role and extra-role performance. The only trend that was found (on $p < .06$) was that the more time autonomy employees reported, the more negative their extra-role performance was rated by their colleagues. The authors explained this finding by the fact that highly flexible working times can interfere with communication and cooperation among colleagues because employees are not at work during the same time period (Nollen 1981). Such problems can arise particularly when tasks are highly interdependent (Ronen and Primps 1981).

8.4 NWW as a Work–Family Balance Intervention

"New workers" are allowed to determine their working times, their location of work, as well as the communication media they use to keep in contact with the office. This enhanced control over the workday provides employees with the opportunity to tune work hours to family responsibilities. For instance, employees may decide to work from home and use the time they save on traveling for doing groceries. Or they schedule their work hours around their children's schooltimes, enabling them to bring and pick up the children. Meanwhile, email, phone, and instant messaging can be used to stay in touch with co-workers or clients. NWW thus allow employees to efficiently distribute their time over various responsibilities. Moreover, the feeling of being in control lowers stress (Lazarus and Folkman 1984), thereby indirectly contributing to work-life balance.

Paradoxically, the pitfalls of NWW lie also in their flexibility. For most people, a certain separation between work and leisure time helps them to recover from work (Geurts and Sonnentag 2006). Working from home removes such a clear separation between work and home and may impede the recovery process. Moreover, highly irregular day schedules may also cause stress, as they raise uncertainty and a feeling of restlessness (ten Brummelhuis et al. 2010). Finally, the advanced communication technologies that support NWW blur the home–work boundary even further because one is constantly in contact with work and messages from work intrude the home domain (Grant and Kiesler 2001). Not only does this constant connection with work impede employee recovery, family members may also be annoyed by the employee's preoccupation with work (Middleton 2008). When we review the opportunities and pitfalls of NWW, it seems that NWW have the potential to contribute to work-life balance, provided they are used in a considerate and moderate way. In other words, NWW can be beneficial for employees and their families if boundaries to separate work and family life are created. The following steps may help employees to adopt such a strategy:

1. Map the means. Like all behavioral changes, the first step to change is awareness of current behavior (Bandura 1977). Therefore, employees first are asked to estimate their current NWW behavior by reconstructing an average workday. This means making a scheme of one's work time slots (beginning and end times of each work block), the location of work, and the communication techniques used (e.g., hours spent on email, phone calls).
2. Map the goals. The next step is to make an overview of one's responsibilities; thus all tasks that need to be done as well as other activities one wants to be involved in (work hours, household chores, care tasks, volunteering, sports, etc.). This overview can be further completed by an estimation of the actual hours spent on each activity and the preferred hours spent. For an estimation of preferred hours to spend on each activity, it can be helpful to rank activities on a scale from high priority to lower priority. For instance, one may prefer to limit the amount of time spent on smartphone use during the evening while increasing undisturbed time spent with family members.
3. Compile the optimal daily schedule. As described above, NWW can be used to design an efficient daily schedule, in which responsibilities are scheduled efficiently. The extent to which employees can plan their work times and location can be seen as a means to reach their goals (i.e., spending enough time to prioritized activities). For example, if one attaches great value to picking up the children from school and having dinner with the whole family, but also working 8 h a day, one may decide to schedule work in a "scattered" workday (e.g., working between 10 a.m. and 3 p.m. at the office and from 8 p.m. to 11 p.m. at home).
4. Report the actual schedule. Because intentions often do not match reality, in the next step a record is kept of one's actual weekly schedule. This can be done by using an online daily reconstruction tool (Oerlemans et al. 2011) in which employees report during five consecutive workdays the timing and duration of

activities they engaged in each day. At the end of the week, an overview of one's actual behavior is obtained. It is then possible to compare the actual schedule to the optimal schedule (e.g., whether one picked up the children on time or managed to work 8 h on a day or exercised two times a week).

5. Evaluate, adjust, and fine-tune. The final step comprises of adjusting any gaps between the actual (point 4) and optimal work schedules (point 3). If goals are not met, one can reflect on whether this is due to a lack of means or may result from having set unrealistic goals. When the latter is the case, lower priority goals may be adjusted (e.g., skipping a training, outsourcing household chores, or working less hours a week). Also, the use of NWW may be fine-tuned. For example, when the weekly records reveal that one uses the smartphone at home more than preferred, one can more consciously try to limit its use. Finally, it should be noted that there is a limit to flexibility (Hill et al. 2003). This means that, although NWW may foster efficient time use, they do not create an additional hour to the 24 h that a day counts.

8.5 Conclusion

Because organizations embrace NWW although the exact pros and cons are still unclear, more research is needed on the impact of NWW on working life. First of all, it would be interesting to examine the role of control over communication. The findings of ten Brummelhuis et al. (2012) suggest that harmful effects of NWW may be attenuated when employees can control when and where they are connected to work, while uncontrolled communication, such as interruptions, are energy consuming. Studies are needed to test this hypothesis. Furthermore, it is important to design longitudinal research to investigate the long-term effects of NWW. In such a design, the frequency of or time spent on NWW can be related to work–family balance, recovery after work, well-being, and job performance over time, for example, over the course of 6 months. This would allow an examination of the causal direction of the relationship.

Another suggestion for future research is to examine the role of personality or other individual characteristics (like boundary management strategies). For example, it is conceivable that individuals who are more open to new experiences will profit more from NWW, experiencing more work engagement while costing them less energy to adopt this new work design. Conscientiousness may also play a role, as highly disciplined persons are probably better able to work efficiently at home and schedule their workday. In contrast, NWW may be stressful for individuals scoring high on extraversion, since they would miss the face-to-face contact with their colleagues. Finally, future studies could use a study design in which employees using NWW are compared with employees who do not use NWW (yet). Such a design will enable to address more explicitly how job demands and resources and work outcomes differ between NWW users and nonusers. Thus, a more conclusive understanding of how NWW influence employee well-being and recovery after work and family life can be gained. Such an understanding is vital to design NWW effectively and in a way that they stimulate positive outcomes for both organizations and employees.

References

Allen, D. K., & Shoard, M. (2005). Spreading the load: Mobile information and communication technologies and their effect on information overload. *Information Research 10*, paper 227. http://InformationR.net/ir/10-2/paper227.html. Accessed 15 Jan 2011.

Allen, D., Renn, R., & Griffeth, R. (2003). The impact of telecommuting design on social systems, self-regulation, and role boundaries. In J. Martocchio & G. Ferris (Eds.), *Research in personnel and human resources management* (Vol. 22, pp. 125–163). Oxford: Elsevier.

Baarne, R., Houtkamp, P., & Knotter, M. (2010). *Het nieuwe werken ontrafeld* [Unraveling new ways of working]. Assen: Koninklijke Van Gorcum/Stichting Management Studies.

Bakker, A. B., & Demerouti, E. (2007). The Job Demands-Resources model: State of the art. *Journal of Managerial Psychology, 22*, 309–328.

Bakker, A. B., Demerouti, E., & Euwema, M. (2005). Job resources buffer the impact of job demands on burnout. *Journal of Occupational Health Psychology, 10*, 170–180.

Baltes, B., Briggs, T. E., Huff, J. W., Wright, J. A., & Neuman, G. A. (1999). Flexible and compressed workweek schedules: A meta-analysis of their effects on work-related criteria. *Journal of Applied Psychology, 84*, 496–513.

Bandura, A. (1977). Self-efficacy: Toward a unifying theory of behavioral change. *Psychological Review, 84*, 191–215.

Baron, A. (2005). Build technology into strategy. *Strategic Communication Management, 9*, 13.

Berghel, H. (1997). E-mail – The good, the bad and the ugly. *Communications of the ACM, 40*, 11–15.

Bertacco, M. (2007). Social norms and behavioral regulation in asynchronous communication: The shift of attention during speed communication. *Human Computer Interaction, 22*, 299–324.

Bertacco, M., & Deponte, A. (2005). E-mail as a speed-facilitating device: A contribution to the reduced-cues perspective on communication. *Journal of Computer-Mediated Communication, 10*. http://jcmc.indiana.edu/vol10/issue3/bertacco.html. Accessed 17 Mar 2009.

Binnewies, C., Sonnentag, S., & Mojza, E. J. (2009). Daily performance at work: Feeling recovered in the morning as a predictor of day-level job performance. *Journal of Organizational Behavior, 30*, 67–93.

Contractor, N. S., & Eisenberg, E. M. (1990). Communication networks and new media in organizations. In J. Fulk & C. Steinfeld (Eds.), *Organizations and communication technology* (pp. 143–172). Newbury Park: Sage.

Dabbish, L. A., & Kraut, R. E. (2006, November). Email overload at work: An analysis of factors associated with email strain. In *Proceedings of the 2006 20th anniversary conference on computer supported cooperative work* (pp. 431–440). New York: ACM.

De Croon, E. M., Sluiter, J. K., Kuijer, P. P., & Frings-Dresen, M. H. (2005). The effect of office concepts on worker health and performance: A systematic review of the literature. *Ergonomics, 48*, 119–134.

De Jonge, J., & Rutte, C. (1999). Een quasi-experimenteel veldonderzoek naar de psychologische effecten van een flexibel kantoorconcept [A quasi-experiment investigating the psychological effect of desk-sharing]. *Gedrag en Organisatie, 12*, 427–444.

Demerouti, E. (2006). Human resource policies for work-personal life integration. In R. Burke & C. Cooper (Eds.), *The human resources revolution: Why putting people first matters* (pp. 147–169). Oxford: Elsevier.

Demerouti, E., & Bakker, A. B. (2011). The Job Demands-Resources model: Challenges for future research. *South African Journal of Industrial Psychology, 37*, 1–9.

Demerouti, E., Bakker, A. B., Nachreiner, F., & Schaufeli, W. B. (2001). The Job Demands-Resources model of burnout. *Journal of Applied Psychology, 86*, 499–512.

Demerouti, E., Bakker, A. B., Geurts, S. A. E., & Taris, T. W. (2009). Daily recovery from work-related effort during non-work time. In S. Sonnentag, P. L. Perrewé, & D. C. Ganster (Eds.), *Current perspectives on job-stress recovery: Research in occupational stress and well being* (Vol. 7, pp. 85–123). Bingley: JAI Press.

Derks, D., & Bakker, A. B. (2010). The impact of e-mail communication on organizational life. Cyberpsychology. *Journal of Psychosocial Research on Cyberspace, 4*(1). http://cyberpsychology.eu/view.php?cisloclanku=2010052401&article=1

Derks, D., & Bakker, A. B. (in press). Smartphone use, work–home interference, and burnout: A diary study on the role of recovery. *Applied Psychology: An International Review*.

Derks, D., Ten Brummelhuis, L. L., Zecic, D., & Bakker, A. B. (2014). Switching on and off...: Does smartphone use obstruct the possibility to engage in recovery activities? *European Journal of Work and Organizational Psychology, 23*, 80–90.

Duxbury, L. E., Higgins, C. A., & Lee, C. (1994). Work-family conflict: A comparison by gender, family type, and perceived control. *Journal of Family Issues, 15*, 449–466.

Duxbury, L. E., Higgins, C. A., & Thomas, D. R. (1996). Work and family environments and the adoption of computer-supported supplemental work-at-home. *Journal of Vocational Behavior, 49*, 1–23.

Fenner, G. H., & Renn, R. W. (2004). Technology-assisted supplemental work: Construct definition and a research framework. *Human Resource Management, 43*, 179–200.

Fulk, J., & Mani, S. (1986). Distortion of communication in hierarchical relationships. In M. McLaughlin (Ed.), *Communication yearbook 9* (pp. 483–510). Newbury Park: Sage.

Gajendran, R. S., & Harrison, D. A. (2007). The good, the bad, and the unknown about telecommuting: Meta-analysis of psychological mediators and individual consequences. *Journal of Applied Psychology, 92*, 1524–1541.

Galinsky, E., Kim, S., & Bond, J. (2001). *Feeling overworked: When work becomes too much*. Paper presented at the Conference Board/Families and Work Institute's Work-Life 2001 Conference, New York, NY.

Gallupe, R. B., Dennis, A. R., Cooper, W. H., Valacich, J. S., Nunamaker, J. F., & Bastianutti, L. (1992). Electronic brainstorming and group size. *Academy of Management Journal, 35*, 350–369.

Gephart, R. P. (2002). Introduction to the brave new workplace: Organizational behavior in the electronic age. *Journal of Organizational Behavior, 23*, 327–344.

Geurts, S. A. E., & Sonnentag, S. (2006). Recovery as an explanatory mechanism in the relation between acute stress reactions and chronic health impairment. *Scandinavian Journal of Work, Environment & Health, 32*, 482–492.

Glass, J. L., & Finley, A. (2002). Coverage and effectiveness of family-responsive workplace policies. *Human Resource Management Review, 12*, 313–337.

Golden, T. D., & Veiga, J. F. (2005). The impact of extent of telecommuting on job satisfaction: Resolving inconsistent findings. *Journal of Management, 31*, 301–318.

Gordon, F. (1976). Telecommunications: Implications for women. *Telecommunications Policy, 1*, 68–74.

Grandey, A. A., & Brauburger, A. L. (2002). The emotion regulation behind the customer smile. In A. S. DeNisi, R. L. Dipoye, K. J. Klein, R. J. Klimoski, C. Ostroff, & R. D. Pritchard (Eds.), *Emotions in the workplace* (pp. 260–294). San Francisco: Jossey-Bass.

Grant, D., & Kiesler, S. (2001). Blurring the boundaries: Cell phones, mobility and the line between work and personal life. In B. Brown, R. Harper, & N. Green (Eds.), *Wireless world: Social and interactional aspects of the mobile age* (pp. 121–131). New York: Springer.

Grebner, S., Semmer, N. K., & Elfering, A. (2005). Working conditions and three types of well-being: A longitudinal study with self-report and rating data. *Journal of Occupational Health Psychology, 10*, 31–43.

Green, N. (2002). On the move: Technology, mobility, and the mediation of social time and space. *The Information Society, 18*, 281–292.

Grossman, P., Niemann, L., Schmidt, S., & Walach, H. (2004). Mindfulness-based stress reduction and health benefits: A meta-analysis. *Journal of Psychosomatic Research, 57*, 35–43.

Hackman, J. R., & Oldham, G. R. (1980). *Work redesign*. Boston: Addison-Wesley.

Hamilton, C. (1987). Telecommuting. *Personnel Journal, 66*, 90–101.

Hassan, R. (2003). Network time and new knowledge epoch. *Time and Society, 12*, 225–241.

Hill, E. J., Ferris, M., & Martinson, V. (2003). Does it matter where you work? A comparison of how three work venues influence aspects of work and personal/family life. *Journal of Vocational Behavior, 62*, 220–241.

Hiltz, S. R., & Turoff, M. (1985). Structuring computer-mediated communication systems to avoid information overload. *Communications of the ACM, 28*, 680–689.

Hochschild, A. R. (1983). *The managed heart: Commercialization of human feeling*. Berkeley: University of California Press.

Jarvenpaa, S., & Lang, K. (2005). Managing the paradoxes of mobile technology. *Information Systems Management Journal, 22*, 7–23.

Kattenbach, R., Demerouti, E., & Nachreiner, F. (2010). Flexible working times: Effects on employees' exhaustion, work-nonwork conflict and performance. *Career Development International, 15*, 279–295.

Katz, J. E., & Aarhus, M. A. (2002). Making meaning of mobiles: A theory of apparatgeist. In J. E. Katz & M. Aarhus (Eds.), *Perpetual contact: Mobile communication, private talk, public performance* (pp. 301–318). Cambridge: Cambridge University Press.

Kelliher, C., & Anderson, D. (2008). For better or for worse? Analysis of how flexible working practices influence employees perceptions of job quality. *The International Journal of Human Resource Management, 19*, 419–431.

Kelliher, C., & Anderson, D. (2010). Doing more with less? Flexible working practices and the intensification of work. *Human Relations, 63*, 83–106.

Kiesler, S., & Sproull, L. (1992). Group decision making and communication technology. *Organizational Behavior and Human Decision Processes, 52*, 96–123.

Kraut, R. (1987). Telework as a work style innovation. In R. E. Kraut (Ed.), *Technology and the transformation of white collar work* (pp. 49–64). Hillsdale: Lawrence Erlbaum.

Lazarus, R. S., & Folkman, S. (1984). *Stress, appraisal, and coping*. New York: Springer.

Locke, P. (2005). *A tool for assessing corporate intranets to increase the productivity of mobile knowledge workers: An evaluation of a handheld wireless device*. Unpublished dissertation, Capella University.

Manger, T., Wicklund, R. A., & Eikeland, O. (2003). Speed, communication and solving social problems. *Communications, 28*, 323–337.

Mann, S., & Holdsworth, L. (2003). The psychological impact of teleworking: Stress, emotions and health. *New Technology, Work and Employment, 18*, 196–211.

Mazmanian, M., Orlikowski, W. J., & Yates, J. (2006). *Crackberrys: Exploring the social implications of ubiquitous wireless e-mail devices*. Paper presented on the EGOS Conference, Bergen.

McKenna, K. Y. A., & Bargh, J. A. (2000). Plan 9 from cyberspace: The implications of the internet for personality and social psychology. *Personality and Social Psychology Review, 4*, 57–75.

McKenna, K. Y. A., Green, A. S., & Gleason, M. E. J. (2002). Relationship formation on the internet: What's the big attraction? *Journal of Social Issues, 58*, 9–31.

Meijman, T. F., & Mulder, G. (1998). Psychological aspects of workload. In P. J. D. Drenth & H. Thierry (Eds.), *Handbook of work and organizational psychology* (Work psychology, Vol. 2, pp. 5–33). Hove: Psychology Press.

Middleton, C. (2007). Illusions of balance and control in an always-on environment: A case study of BlackBerry users. Continuum. *Journal of Media & Cultural Studies*. http://www.tandf.co.uk/journal/titels/. Accessed 17 Mar 2009.
Middleton, C. A. (2008). Illusions of balance and control in an always-on environment: A case study of BlackBerry users. *Journal of Media & Cultural Studies, 21*, 165–178.
Middleton, C. A., & Cukier, W. (2006). Is mobile email functional or dysfunctional? Two perspectives on mobile email usage. *European Journal of Information Systems, 15*, 252–260.
Nollen, S. D. (1981). The compressed workweek: Is it worth the effort? *Industrial Engineer, 13*, 58–64.
Oerlemans, W. G. M., Bakker, A. B., & Veenhoven, R. (2011). Finding the key to happy aging: A day reconstruction study of happiness. *Journal of Gerontology: Psychological Sciences, 66B*, 1–10.
Parasuraman, S., & Greenhaus, J. H. (2002). Toward reducing some critical gaps in work–family research. *Human Resource Management Review, 12*, 299–312.
Perlow, L. A. (1998). Boundary control: The social ordering of work and family time in a high-tech corporation. *Administrative Science Quarterly, 43*, 328–357.
Peters, P., & Van der Lippe, T. (2007). The time-pressure reducing potential of telehomeworking: The Dutch case. *International Journal of Human Resource Management, 18*, 430–447.
Powell, G. N., & Greenhaus, J. H. (2010). Sex, gender, and the work-to-family interface: Exploring negative and positive interdependencies. *Academy of Management Journal, 53*, 513–534.
Raghuram, S., & Wiesenfeld, B. (2004). Work-nonwork conflict and job stress among virtual workers. *Human Resource Management, 43*, 259–277.
Renaud, K., Ramsay, J., & Hair, M. (2006). You've got mail. . .Shall I deal with it now? Electronic mail from a recipient's perspective. *Journal of Human-Computer Interaction, 21*, 313–332.
Rennecker, J., & Derks, D. (2012). Email overload: Fine tuning the research lens. In D. Derks & A. B. Bakker (Eds.), *The psychology of digital media @ work*. London: Psychology Press.
Rennecker, J., & Godwin, L. (2005). Delays and interruptions: A self-perpetuating paradox of communication technology use. *Information and Organization, 15*, 247–266.
Rice, R. E., & Case, D. (1983). Electronic message systems in the university: A description of use and utility. *A Journal of Communication, 33*, 131–152.
Ronen, S., & Primps, S. B. (1981). The compressed workweek as organizational change behaviours and attitudinal outcomes. *Academy of Management Review, 6*, 61–74.
Rook, J. W., & Zijlstra, F. R. H. (2006). The contribution of various types of activities to recovery. *European Journal of Work and Organizational Psychology, 15*, 218–240.
Rubinstein, J. S., Meyer, D. E., & Evans, J. E. (2001). Executive control of cognitive processes in task switching. *Journal of Experimental Psychology. Human Perception and Performance, 27*, 763–797.
Russell, W., Purvis, L. M., & Banks, A. (2005). Describing the strategies used for dealing with email interruptions according to different situational parameters. *Computers in Human Behavior, 23*, 1820–1837.
Ryan, A. M., & Kossek, E. E. (2008). Work-life policy implementation: Breaking down or creating barriers to inclusiveness? *Human Resource Management, 47*, 295–310.
Sánchez, A. M., Pérez, M., De Luis Carnicer, P., & Vela Jiménez, M. J. (2007). Teleworking and workplace flexibility: A study of impact on firm performance. *Personnel Review, 36*, 42–64.
Sarbaugh-Thompson, M., & Feldman, M. S. (1998). Electronic mail and organizational communication: Does saying "hi" really matter? *Organizational Science, 9*, 685–698.
Shamir, B., & Salomon, I. (1985). Work-at-home and the quality of working life. *Academy of Management Review, 10*, 455–464.
Sonnentag, S. (2001). Work, recovery activities, and individual well-being: A diary study. *Journal of Occupational Health Psychology, 6*, 196–210.

Sonnentag, S., & Fritz, C. (2007). The recovery experience questionnaire: Development and validation of a measure for assessing recuperation and unwinding from work. *Journal of Occupational Health Psychology, 12*, 204–221.

Sonnentag, S., & Geurts, S. A. (2009). Methodological issues in recovery research. In S. Sonnentag, P. L. Perrewe, & D. C. Ganster (Eds.), *Current perspectives on job-stress recovery* (pp. 1–37). Bingley: JAI Press.

Sonnentag, S., Binnewies, C., & Mojza, E. J. (2008). "Did you have a nice evening?" A day-level study on recovery experiences, sleep, and affect. *Journal of Applied Psychology, 3*, 674–684.

Sullivan, C. (1995). Preferences for electronic mail in organizational communication tasks. *Journal of Business Communication, 32*, 49–64.

Sussman, S. W., & Sproull, L. (1999). Straight talk: Delivering bad news through electronic communication. *Information Systems Research, 10*, 150–164.

Tausig, M., & Fenwick, R. (2001). Unbinding time: Alternate work schedules and work-life balance. *Journal of Family and Economic Issues, 22*, 101–119.

ten Brummelhuis, L. L., & Van der Lippe, T. (2010). Effective work-life balance support for various household structures. *Human Resource Management, 49*, 175–195.

ten Brummelhuis, L. L., Haar, J. M., & van der Lippe, T. (2010). Collegiality under pressure: The effects of family demands and flexible work arrangements in the Netherlands. *International Journal of Human Resource Management, 21*, 2831–2847.

ten Brummelhuis, L. L., Bakker, A. B., Hetland, J., & Keulemans, L. (2012). Do new ways of working foster work engagement? *Psicothema, 24*, 113–120.

Thomas, G. F., King, C. L., Baroni, B., Cook, L., Keitelman, M., Miller, S., & Wardle, A. (2006). Reconceptualizing e-mail overload. *Journal of Business and Technical Communication, 20*, 252–287.

Van Hooff, M. L. M., Geurts, S. A. E., Kompier, M. A. J., & Taris, T. W. (2006). Work-home interference: How does it manifest itself from day to day? *Work & Stress, 20*, 145–162.

Venkatesh, A., & Vitalari, N. (1992). An emerging distributed work arrangement: An investigation of computer-based supplemental work at home. *Management Science, 38*, 1687–1706.

Walther, J. B. (1995). Relational aspects of computer-mediated communication: Experimental observations over time. *Organizational Science, 6*, 186–203.

Westman, M., & Eden, D. (1997). Effects of a respite from work on burnout: Vacation relief and fade out. *Journal of Applied Psychology, 82*, 516–527.

Wicklund, R. A., & Vandekerckhove, M. M. P. (2000). Delay of gratification in Interaction rituals. In T. Postmes, R. Spears, M. Lea, & S. Reicher (Eds.), *SIDE issues centre stage: Recent developments in studies of de-individuation in groups* (pp. 191–202). Amsterdam: Koninklijke Nederlandse Akademie van Wetenschappen Verhandelingen, Afd. Letterkunde, Nieuwe Reeks, deel 183.

Xanthopoulou, D., Bakker, A. B., Demerouti, E., & Schaufeli, W. B. (2007). The role of personal resources in the Job Demands-Resources model. *International Journal of Stress Management, 14*, 121–141.

Zedeck, S., & Mosier, K. L. (1990). Work in the family and employing organization. *American Psychologist, 45*, 240–251.

Chapter 9
Trust in Complex Work Systems: A Focus on Information and Communication Technologies

Enid Montague and Erin K. Chiou

9.1 Introduction

Trust is an integral component of all relationships and successful organizations. However, existing research and scholarship have not adequately addressed the complexity of context, perspective, and interconnectedness in understanding trust. The complexity of understanding trust is magnified in work organizations with multiple human and technological components. These organizations are complex sociotechnical systems composed of people, groups, technology, and suborganizations. Trust in one work system may form differently than in other work systems, particularly different types of work systems. In a complex work system, diverse user groups may have differing views of the system based on their work-related roles and histories of engagement and interaction. In these work systems, multiple types of users are integral to system success, including, but not limited to, workers, managers, technicians, and customers (Vicente 1999).

Existing scholarship shows that attitudes about technology and relationships with technology are constructed through the work system in which the user is a member (Davis 1989). Additionally, the presence of technology has been found to affect interpersonal relationships within the system. For example, in the health system, information and communication technology use among patients has been found to impact the relationship with their care providers (McMullan 2006; Murray et al. 2003). Trust can impact communication, affect working relations, or result in anxiety or increased stress in the workplace. The sociotechnical systems framework adopted in this paper will illustrate the potential effects of information and communication technologies on interpersonal organizational relationships. The

E. Montague (✉)
Feinberg School of Medicine, Northwestern University, Chicago, IL, USA
e-mail: enid.montague@northwestern.edu

E.K. Chiou
Industrial and Systems Engineering, University of Wisconsin-Madison, Madison, WI, USA
e-mail: chiou2@wisc.edu

C. Korunka and P. Hoonakker (eds.), *The Impact of ICT on Quality of Working Life*, DOI 10.1007/978-94-017-8854-0_9,

interconnectedness of these concepts is important for measuring trust in work systems, creating trust that enhances technological interventions, and understanding the effects of work system interventions on trust outcomes such as quality of working life.

To address the role trust plays in mediating new and existing information and communication technology and its impact on quality of working life, types of trust in complex work systems will be identified. These types of trust include trust between individuals (Anderson and Dedrick 1990), in organizations (Mayer et al. 1995), and technology (Montague et al. 2009; Timmons et al. 2008). A model of trust that accounts for multiple types of users, in work systems that include or implement information and communication technologies, will be presented. This integrated model serves as a framework for understanding how trust affects information and communication technology use and quality of working life.

9.2 Defining Trust in Complex Work Systems

Trust has myriad definitions depending on the discipline or construct. For example, trust has been defined as a psychological state, a more general attitude or expectancy, or a multidimensional construct that includes affective and motivational components (Kramer 1999). In complex work systems, a suitable definition of trust can be the "expectation by one person, group, or firm of ethical behavior – that is, morally correct decisions and actions based upon ethical principles of analysis – on the part of the other person, group, or firm in a joint endeavor or economic exchange" (Hosmer 1995, p. 399). This definition of trust is independent of disciplines or context and emphasizes both interpersonal and organizational relationships, as well as the idea of shared enterprise (Kasper-Fuehrera and Ashkanasy 2001). Furthermore, it addresses the idea of a shared understanding of ethical behavior or social norms. The absence of social norms may cause changes in behavior and decision-making in communication mediated by technology (Kiesler et al. 1984).

9.2.1 Interpersonal Trust

Interpersonal trust is largely defined as the expectation that an individual or group can be relied on (Rotter 1967). Other scholars have defined interpersonal trust as including a sense of vulnerability to another person; there may be a penalty if that vulnerability is abused or a gain if the other person does not abuse the trustor's vulnerability (Zand 1972). In complex work systems, interpersonal trust is integral to work system outcomes such as quality of work, safety, productivity, and satisfaction. In some contexts, it is important for workers to develop trust relationships with their clients or customers, where they can trust their customers and their customers can trust them. An example of this type of work environment would be health-care systems, where physicians develop trust relationships with their patients and vice versa (Hall et al. 2001, 2002).

9.2.2 Organizational Trust

In Mayer et al.'s (1995) integrative model of organizational trust, trust is defined as the willingness of a trustor to be vulnerable to the actions of a trustee based on the expectation that the trustee will perform a particular action. Mayer et al.'s (1995) model is built upon the constructs ability, benevolence, integrity, propensity to trust, and perceived risk. Other scholars have looked at trust in organizations based on the target of trustworthiness or trustee. For example, to assess organizational trust, Athos and Gabarro (1978) look at a worker's trust in an employer and define organizational trust as an employee's belief that the employer has integrity and is truthful, fair, and honest.

Cook and Wall (1980) define trust in terms of a worker's belief that their peers or managers are reliable and capable. Scott (1980) developed measures of trust that look at an individual worker's trust in multiple levels of the organization, from trust in the immediate supervisor, work unity, top management, and consultants. This measure may be particularly important when attitudes of distrust originate from one level of the organization to another, for example, workers' distrust in top-level management or consultants. This level of focus on groups of workers allows trust-related interventions to be more easily targeted to the appropriate organizational entity. Other researchers have evaluated factors related to trust in organizations such as availability, competence, consistency, fairness, honesty, maintenance of commitments, integrity, reliability, and concern (Butler and Cantrell 1984; Cummings and Bromiley 1996; Shaw 1997).

9.3 Defining Information and Communication Technologies

Information and communication technologies (ICT) are tools that aid in the integration or transfer of knowledge from one person to another. When the tool is multicomponent, it is often called a system. The term ICT may be used interchangeably with information technology (IT) and information systems (IS) and encompass inter-organizational systems, such as electronic data interchange (EDI) and group decision support systems (GDSS) (Avgerou et al. 2004). Knowledge management systems (Maier 2004; Alavi 1999) or computer-mediated communication systems (Grudin 1994) are also associated terms. While knowledge, information, and data overlap in many aspects, they have distinct characteristics in the information systems literature: knowledge is information thought to be true, information is data interpreted into a meaningful framework, and data is raw numbers and facts (Alavi 1999). Some definitions of ICT refer specifically to electronic forms of text-based communication that allows information to be copied with minimal effort and reused for various purposes (Shortis 2001). Broadly speaking, information and communication systems support knowledge-based work, particularly in knowledge-based organizations that depend on individual workers' expertise and the networks between these individuals to create value for customers (Maier 2004).

An organization's ability to sustain competitive advantage in a hypercompetitive market depends on its ability to integrate and apply specialized knowledge (Grant 1996). It is thus unsurprising that isolated knowledge has limited organizational value. ICT promises efficient means of knowledge sharing by closing geographic distance or time differences between knowledge workers. However, understanding when and how meaningful knowledge is shared requires a closer look at how ICT affects motivation for knowledge sharing (Hendriks 1999). Selwyn (2003) describes the importance of social context in understanding technology use or nonuse. Other factors, such as technology usability, usefulness, reliability, and organizational context, may impact workers' acceptance and subsequent use of the ICT (Carayon 2007).

9.4 Trust and ICTs

There are different types of trust that are relevant to ICT (see Table 9.1). These include interpersonal trust or trust between people (Anderson and Dedrick 1990), organizational trust or trust in organizations (Mayer et al. 1995), and trust in technologies (Montague et al. 2009; Timmons et al. 2008).

9.4.1 Interpersonal Trust and ICTs

ICTs can affect interpersonal trust by allowing workers to communicate more efficiently and effectively, but they might also negatively impact trust, by inhibiting communication cues, quality, and duration. Several scholars have described trade-offs between decisions making using technologies to share information and communication. In communicative encounters between two or more people, ICTs can be used at (1) the same time and same place, such as face-to-face interactions; (2) same time and different place, such as video- or audio-based concurrent communication; (3) different time and same place, such as whiteboards or digital message boards; or (4) different time and different place, such as email or other message-based communication systems (Johansen 1988). Organizations can better

Table 9.1 Types of trust and examples

Type of trust	Definition	Example
Interpersonal trust	A person's belief that another person will not fail them	An individual's belief that they can trust another person in the work system. These individuals can be workers or customers in the system
Organizational trust	A person's belief that the organization and the people in that organization will not fail them	A worker's belief that their supervisor will not fail them A worker's trust in the organization they work
Technological trust	A person's belief that a tool or technology will not fail	A worker's trust in a technology

understand the potential effects of ICT on interpersonal trust by exploring the use of technologies during same time or same place interactions.

When considering work system designs that facilitate interpersonal trust, one ICT may be better suited to a specific organization than another. For example, in a system where individuals must develop rapport in a short amount of time, technologies that allow for the full range of communicative behaviors may be preferable. These technologies would allow individuals to communicate at the same time and same place using verbal and nonverbal communication methods, reducing the risk of emotional and literal miscommunication. In a fast-paced environment such as an emergency department, a tool such as a digital whiteboard that allows for efficient communication using information artifacts, and can be clearly seen by all members of a team, may facilitate interpersonal trust more effectively. However, it should be noted that these technologies are only effective if they complement workflow, are properly implemented into the system with appropriate training, and are useable by workers.

9.4.2 *Organizational Trust and ICTs*

In an information systems environment, like the kind where virtual organizations exist, trust can be a central construct in understanding these complex systems and how they function (Kasper-Fuehrera and Ashkanasy 2001). Trust encourages cooperation and facilitates transactions, while distrust can inhibit these activities. For example, in virtual team environments, trust can diminish the negative impact of geographic distance between team members. The same is true in virtual interaction between workers and customers. This ultimately leads to better outcomes for the work organization and the people the organization serves, in terms of overcoming geographic barriers. However, distrust among workers, or workers' distrust of technology, may lead to inappropriate or nonuse of the technology, impeding cooperation and heightening the disadvantages of geographic barriers in business operations.

Trust building – or trustworthiness – in complex organizations can be facilitated or impeded by communication technologies. For example, information sharing – or knowledge sharing – is often mediated by varying forms of communication technology, such as telephone, conference call, or email. When improper representations of knowledge are shared, however, information sharing can be detrimental to knowledge (Hendriks 1999). This may lead to distrust among people or of organizational components. Understanding the quality of knowledge shared requires consideration of technology's effects on knowledge transfer as well as the motivation of knowledge sharing.

ICTs can influence trust at the organizational level in two ways. ICTs that make workplaces more efficient, safe, and easier to work in can positively impact an individual or groups of workers' trust in the organization (Breaugh and Farabee 2012). For example, work systems that allow workers to work remotely and during nontraditional work hours using ICTs improve quality of work life for workers who would like to continue working while managing family or other types of demands. In these systems, employees may appreciate the organization's commitments to increasing the quality of the work environment for the employees and therefore trust that the organization has their best interest in mind. Conversely, newly introduced technologies that reduce efficiency, decrease safety, and are difficult to use can negatively impact employee trust in the organization. These technologies can also negatively impact trust between workers, as workers may become more cautious of the potential impact of errors on their performance measures and be reluctant to share information about mistakes or errors that might improve the overall organization. In systems with ICTs that negatively impact productivity, workers may be reluctant to help each other accomplish work-related goals, as their extra effort is expended on accomplishing goals that have grown increasingly difficult with the introduction of a difficult-to-use technology.

9.5 Factors of Trust in ICTs

Various researchers have looked at trust in technologies generally and proposed factors that contribute to trust. Jian et al. (1998) discovered that trust between humans is similar to how humans evaluate the trustworthiness of machines. However, the literature makes distinctions between measures that evaluate trust in a specific entity or a person's inclination to trust a technology (Jian et al. 1998). Several factors have been defined in trust in technology literature as antecedents of the construct trust in technology such as the technology's predictability, reliability, dependability, and trustworthiness (Jian et al. 1998; Larzelere and Huston 1980; Lee and See 2004; Muir 1994; Muir and Moray 1996). Others have identified features of the technology or environment that contribute to an individual's level of trust in the technology. These features include an individual's ability to use the technology effectively, familiarity with the technology, how easy the technology is to understand, the degree the intent of the technology is clear, and the usefulness of the technology to the individual (Sheridan 1988).

9.6 Trust in Technologies and Potential Consequences

One of the more important features of trust in technologies in work systems is the notion of appropriate trust. In work systems, over-trust or overreliance can be equally detrimental to work system outcomes as under-trust. Parasuraman and Riley (1997) describe this notion in terms of automation use, misuse, disuse, and abuse, where trusting attitudes can lead to either using technologies appropriately, using them in ways they were not designed for, or overusing them; distrusting attitudes can lead to disuse. Consequently, when workers are required to use technologies they do not trust, they may use work-arounds, which can lead to errors. When workers over-trust technologies, they may become complacent, and errors can also occur (Parasuraman et al. 1993). These system inefficiencies can contribute to organizational distrust and result in poor worker satisfaction or turnover. Mismatches in perceptions about technologies between workers that must work together can also diminish interpersonal trust.

9.7 Integrated Models of Trust

An integrated model of trust in complex work systems with ICT would include the following premises:

- Interpersonal relationships are important in complex organizations, and ICTs have the ability to positively or negatively impact the formation and maintenance of interpersonal trust.
- Appropriate technology can positively impact interpersonal trust relationships in the work system by facilitating or inhibiting interactions between individuals to achieve efficiency, safety, and productivity.
- Introduction of new ICTs can impact organizational trust, where ICTs that are difficult to use, challenging to learn, unsafe, or inefficient may lead to work distrust in other workers and management.
- Appropriate trust in ICTs is important and should be the goal for organizations seeking to implement new technologies. Over-trust and under-trust can both negatively impact the formation and maintenance of trust in organizations.

9.8 Importance of Trust in ICTs for Quality of Working Life

Existing scholarship shows that attitudes about technology and relationships with technology are constructed through the work system in which the user is a member (Davis 1989). The presence of technology has been found to affect interpersonal relationships within the system (McMullan 2006; Murray et al. 2003). Organizations should carefully consider the impact of ICTs on potential organizational outcomes. When considering the introduction of new ICTs, organizations should consider the effects on interpersonal trust and consider designs that will optimize interpersonal trust. Organizations should also consider the effects of ICTs on worker trust in the organization and ability to work in teams. These factors should be considered with a dedication to implementing ICTs that are both useful and useable, which will positively impact trust. Finally, organizations should be weary of designing for complete trust in technologies as over-trust can contribute to complacency and distrust can contribute to technology disuse and trust in the organization and lead to poor quality of working lives, low satisfaction, low commitment to the organization, stress, and turnover.

References

Alavi, M. (1999). Knowledge management systems: Issues, challenges, and benefits. *Communications of the Association for Information Systems, 1*(7), 1–37.

Anderson, L. A., & Dedrick, R. F. (1990). Development of the trust in physician scale: A measure to assess interpersonal trust in patient-physician relationships. *Psychological Reports, 67*(3.2), 1091–1100.

Athos, A. G., & Gabarro, J. J. (1978). *Interpersonal behavior: Communication and understanding in relationships*. Englewood Cliffs: Prentice Hall.

Avgerou, C., Ciborra, C., & Land, F. (Eds.). (2004). *The social study of information and communication technology: Innovation, actors, and contexts*. New York: Oxford University Press.

Breaugh, J., & Farabee, A. (2012). Telecommuting and flexible work hours: Alternative work arrangements that can improve the quality of work life. In M. J. Sirgy, N. P. Reilly, & C. A. Gorman (Eds.), *Work and quality of life: Ethical practices in organizations* (pp. 251–274). New York: Springer Science + Business.

Butler, J. K., & Cantrell, R. S. (1984). A behavioral decision theory approach to modeling dyadic trust in superiors and subordinates. *Psychological Reports, 55*(1), 19–28.

Carayon, P. (2007). Healthy and efficient work with computers and information and communications technology – Are there limits? *Scandinavian Journal of Work, Environment & Health, 33* (3), 10–16.

Cook, J., & Wall, T. (1980). New work attitude measures of trust, organizational commitment and personal need non-fulfillment. *Journal of Occupational Psychology, 53*(1), 39–52.

Cummings, L. L., & Bromiley, P. (1996). The organizational trust inventory (OTI): Development and validation. In *Trust in organizations: Frontiers of theory and research* (pp. 302–330). Thousand Oaks: Sage.

Davis, F. D. (1989). Perceived usefulness, perceived ease of use, and user acceptance of information technology. *MIS Quarterly, 13*(3), 319–340.

Grant, R. M. (1996). Prospering as in integration environments: Organizational capability knowledge. *Organization Science, 7*(4), 375–387.

Grudin, J. (1994). Computer-supported collaborative work: History and focus. *IEEE Computer, 27* (5), 19–26.

Hall, M. A., Dugan, E., Zheng, B., & Mishra, A. K. (2001). Trust in physicians and medical institutions: What is it, can it be measured, and does it matter? *Milbank Quarterly, 79*(4), 613–639. doi: 10.1111/1468-0009.00223.

Hall, M. A., Zheng, B., Dugan, E., Camacho, F., Kidd, K. E., Mishra, A., & Balkrishnan, R. (2002). Measuring patients' trust in their primary care providers. *Medical Care Research and Review, 59*(3), 293–318. doi:10.1177/1077558702059003004.

Hendriks, P. (1999). Why share knowledge? The influence of ICT on the motivation for knowledge sharing. *Knowledge and Process Management, 6*(2), 91–100.

Hosmer, L. T. (1995). Trust: The connecting link between organizational theory and philosophical ethics. *Academy of Management Review, 20*(2), 379–403.

Jian, J. Y., Bisantz, A. M., & Drury, C. G. (1998). *Towards an empirically determined scale of trust in computerized systems: Distinguishing concepts and types of trust*. Paper presented at the Human Factors and Ergonomics Society annual meeting proceedings, Amherst.

Johansen, R. (1988). *Groupware: Computer support for business teams*. New York: The Free Press.

Kasper-Fuehrera, E. C., & Ashkanasy, N. M. (2001). Communicating trustworthiness and building trust in interorganizational virtual organizations. *Journal of Management, 27*(3), 235–254.

Kiesler, S., Siegel, J., & McGuire, T. W. (1984). Social psychological aspects of computer-mediated communication. *American Psychologist, 39*(10), 1123–1134.

Kramer, R. M. (1999). Trust and distrust in organizations: Emerging perspectives, enduring questions. *Annual Review of Psychology, 50*, 569–598.

Larzelere, R. E., & Huston, T. L. (1980). The dyadic trust scale: Toward understanding interpersonal trust in close relationships. *Journal of Marriage and the Family, 42*(3), 595–604.

Lee, J. D., & See, K. A. (2004). Trust in automation: Designing for appropriate reliance. *Human Factors, 46*(1), 30–80.

Maier, R. (2004). *Knowledge management systems: Information and communication technologies for knowledge management*. Berlin: Springer.

Mayer, R. C., Davis, J. H., & Schoorman, F. D. (1995). An integrative model of organizational trust. *Academy of Management Review, 20*(3), 709–734.

McMullan, M. (2006). Patients using the internet to obtain health information: How this affects the patient – Health professional relationship. *Patient Education and Counseling, 63*(1–2), 24–28.

Montague, E., Kleiner, B. M., & Winchester, W. W. (2009). Empirical evaluation of the construct trust in medical technology. *International Journal of Industrial Ergonomics, 39*(4), 628–634.

Muir, B. (1994). Trust in automation: Part 1. Theoretical issues in the study and human intervention in automated systems. *Ergonomics, 37*, 1905–1923.

Muir, B., & Moray, N. (1996). Trust in automation. Part II. Experimental studies of trust and human intervention in a process control simulation. *Ergonomics, 39*(3), 429–460.

Murray, E., Lo, B., Pollack, L., Donelan, K., Catania, J., White, M., et al. (2003). The impact of health information on the internet on the physician-patient relationship: Patient perceptions. *Archives of Internal Medicine, 163*(14), 1727–1734.

Parasuraman, R., & Riley, V. (1997). Humans and automation: Use, misuse, disuse, abuse. *Human Factors: The Journal of the Human Factors and Ergonomics Society, 39*, 230–253.

Parasuraman, R., Molloy, R., & Singh, I. L. (1993). Performance consequences of automation-induced complacency. *The International Journal of Aviation Psychology, 3*(1), 1–23.

Rotter, J. B. (1967). A new scale for measurement of interpersonal trust. *Journal of Personality, 35* (4), 651–665.

Scott, C. L. (1980). Interpersonal trust: A comparison of attitudinal and situational factors. *Human Relations, 33*(11), 805–812.
Selwyn, N. (2003). Apart from technology: Understanding people's non-use of information and communication technologies in everyday life. *Technology in Society, 25*(1), 99–116.
Shaw, R. B. (1997). *Trust in the balance: Building successful organizations on results, integrity, and concern.* San Francisco: Jossey-Bass.
Sheridan, T. B. (1988). *Trustworthiness of command and control systems.* Paper presented at the IFAC/IFIP/IEA/IFORS conference on Analysis; Design and Evaluation of Man-machine Systems, Oulu, Finland.
Shortis, T. (2001). *The language of ICT: Information and communication technology*. London: Routledge.
Timmons, S., Harrison-Paul, R., & Crosbie, B. (2008). How do lay people come to trust the automatic external defibrillator? *Health, Risk & Society, 10*(3), 207–220.
Vicente, K. J. (1999). *Cognitive work analysis.* Mahwah: Lawrence Erlbaum Associates.
Zand, D. E. (1972). Trust and managerial problem solving. *Administrative Science Quarterly, 17* (2), 229–239.

Chapter 10
Aging, Changes, and Quality of Working Life

Nathalie Greenan, Mathieu Narcy, and Serge Volkoff

10.1 Introduction

The issue we would like to deal with stems from a contradiction which could arise from three phenomena. These phenomena, if confirmed, are hardly compatible and might become less and less so in the future: (1) changes in technologies and work organization modes tend to accelerate; (2) the working population in industrialized countries is shifting to older ages; (3) but these frequent changes are known as "age selective." They supposedly reinforce aging workers' deficiencies and alter the benefits of their experience and therefore the quality of their working life.

We shall not dwell here on the first observation: the search for flexibility in corporate structures and the growing frequency of technical or organizational changes. This issue is widely developed in other chapters all along this book.

The second one is well grounded also. The overall aging of the workforce in industrialized countries is general and ongoing, even though its magnitude and timing may vary from one country to another (OECD 1998). It is mainly due to the evolution of birthrate in the second half of the twentieth century: the high birthrates following the Second World War (also known as the Baby Boom generation)

N. Greenan (✉)
Centre d'Etudes de l'Emploi (CEE), Noisy le Grand, France

TEPP-CNRS, Noisy le Grand, France
e-mail: nathalie.greenan@cee-recherche.fr

M. Narcy
Centre d'Etudes de l'Emploi (CEE), Noisy le Grand, France

TEPP-CNRS, Noisy le Grand, France

ERUDITE, University of Paris-Est Créteil, Créteil, Paris, France
e-mail: mathieu.narcy@cee-recherche.fr

S. Volkoff
Centre d'Etudes de l'Emploi (CEE), Noisy le Grand, France
e-mail: Serge.volkoff@cee-recherche.fr

C. Korunka and P. Hoonakker (eds.), *The Impact of ICT on Quality of Working Life*,
DOI 10.1007/978-94-017-8854-0_10, © Springer Science+Business Media Dordrecht 2014

dropped after the 1960s. The 40s, 50s, and 60s age groups are the largest in number. This factor accounts in itself for an aging of the demographic structure in the labor force. Furthermore, the oldest in these groups have reached or are about to reach retirement age. Given their number, and the increase in life expectancy, this raises a pension funding problem. In many countries, due to this need for funding, public policy aims at promoting active aging by lengthening professional life and raising the employment rate of "senior workers."

For both these reasons, the third statement (changes in technologies and organization are "age selective") is worth a more in-depth study. Therefore, the aim of this chapter is to examine whether the changes implemented by firms affect differentially the quality of working life according to employees' age. By quality of working life, we mean work-related aspects of quality of life or characteristics of work experience that are likely to be crucial for well-being (Green 2006). We capture the quality of working life through three dimensions: the feeling of fair work recognition, the opportunity to learn new things at work, and the feeling of work overload.

10.2 Aging and Changes: Main Concerns

To begin with, we may recall that the problems encountered by aging workers in these situations constitute one of their negative characteristics in the eyes of many employers (Yeatts et al. 1999). Employers' assessments of older workers vary according to economic conditions and the tensions on the employment market. However, we are going to see that surveys in different countries and at different times have identified recurring views that are widely accepted though nonetheless difficult to justify: the fears of employers concern the supposedly negative attitude of older workers to change and the difficulty they experience in learning new skills. Reduced physical capacity is also mentioned, but less often. In the context of changing technologies and organizations, these negative opinions are a major handicap for older people.

This has been documented in various periods and countries. A pioneer study in that field has been conducted in the USA by Rosen and Jerdee (1977). They proposed to 6,000 subscribers of the Harvard Business Review a series of virtual human resource-managing exercises, with two versions of the questionnaire, the only change being the age of the employee concerned. It appeared that when the employee was supposedly old, fewer managers considered she was able to change her behavior or found it reasonable to send her to a training course. In the UK during the 1990s, according to Walker and Taylor (1992), 43 % of employers thought that the elderly had "difficulties to learn," and 40 % thought that they could not "adapt themselves to new technologies." More or less the same percentages have been found more recently in a survey carried out by the French Ministry of Employment (Defresne et al. 2010): 42 % of employers answered that employees aged 50 or more were disadvantaged as for their "capacity to adapt to new technologies," comparatively to younger ones. The criticisms are however counterbalanced by skills they are recognized to possess: experience, know-how, and professional dedication.

These problems are echoed – which perhaps exacerbates them – in the reluctance of elderly employees themselves or at least part of them to adapt to a changing workplace. Difficulties linked to the characteristics of the new technology or organization, and some specific anxiety in apprenticeship situations, at least in the beginning, intermingle and reinforce each other, leading to a deterioration in the quality of their working lives, as it has been shown, for example, in a field research conducted among employees of an important town in Finland (Hukki and Seppala 1992).

Knowledge about evolution of functional mental capacities with aging cannot on its own explain the problems faced by older workers when the nature of their job actually changes or in learning situations. Work psychology provides some explanation for their reluctance, suggesting fears for their jobs, worries about damaging equipment, apprehension when faced with learning situations, and competing with younger employees (Marquié et al. 1994). Furthermore, the literature in ergonomics shows the advantages older employees could derive from familiarizing themselves with the task, and with the consistency between its various components, in order to avoid excessive stress on basic mental processes (Delgoulet and Marquié 2002).

All these studies emphasize therefore the characteristics of the new technology itself, the conditions of the changes or training, and the way in which these changes and learning situations are prepared and conducted (Cau-Bareille et al. 2012). When "apprenticeship conditions" are sound, change even appears as a resource for the elderly. It helps them in avoiding some wear and tear in physically demanding jobs, produces cognitive stimulation (Marquié et al. 2010), reinforces their feeling of self-efficacy (Reed et al. 2005), and favors the desire to work longer.

Keeping in mind these aspects of age/change relationship, we intend here to analyze the differences (or similarities) between young and elderly employees in their exposure to technological and organizational changes and in the links between this exposure and the quality of their working life. These analyses will be achieved by using the French linked employer/employee survey about organizational changes and computerization (COI survey). We shall build our hypotheses and interpret the results by referring to research in ergonomics and work psychology, as mentioned above.

10.3 Data and Measurement Frame

The COI survey is a linked employer/employee survey about organizational changes and computerization.[1] The employer section of the survey seeks to identify changes in organizations and examine how they mobilize a wide range of

[1] See Greenan et al. (2012) and http://www.enquetecoi.net/ for more details about the COI survey.

Table 10.1 Diffusion between 2003 and 2006 of ICT and management tools used in the composite measures of change

13 managerial tools			15 ICT tools		
% of firms	2003	2006	% of firms	2003	2006
Contractual commitment to provide a product or a service within a fixed deadline	66.1	68.5	Website	61.2	73.3
Long-term relationships with suppliers	51.7	54.7	Local area network (LAN)	61.3	66.7
Contractual obligation for certain suppliers to provide the product or service in fixed deadlines	51.5	53.5	Use of software or in-house application for HRM	63.4	65.3
Quality certification (ISO 9001)	36.3	41.4	Intranet	47.9	57.8
Satisfaction surveys of customers	32.9	38.7	Use of software or in-house application for conception and development	47.4	49.8
Autonomous teams or work groups	30.7	33.8	Tools for data analysis	39.5	47.1
Tools for tracing the product or service	28.3	32.9	Electronic data interchange system (EDI)	36.2	45.8
Tools for labeling goods and services	28.3	30.8	Database(s) on HRM	34.5	38.5
Call or contact centers	25.5	28.0	Extranet	25.0	30.2
Just-in-time production	22.9	24.3	ERP	26.6	29.6
Methods of problem solving (FMEA)	17.3	20.9	Databases for conception and development	26.1	28.8
Customer relationship management	9.7	14.3	Database and application interface tools	21.1	28.6
Environmental (ISO 14001) or ethical certification	9.7	12.9	Filing/automated data search tools	21.4	27.4
			Groupware tools	15.1	21.0
			Process modeling and automation tools	8.8	12.7

Source: Survey on organizational change and computerization (COI 2006), INSEE, DARES, CEE
Coverage: Private sector French firms with 20 employees or more, $N = 6{,}342$ firms, weighted statistics

management tools, such as just-in-time or quality certification, or information and communication technologies (ICTs) such as enterprise resource planning (ERP) or e-commerce. Indeed, when a manager implements a new tool based on a management concept, he or she has the intention to modify the way the company operates and the implementation itself is a marker of organizational change. The COI survey captures changes that occurred between 2003 and 2006 in a representative sample of private sector French companies with 20 or more employees. From this part of the survey, we compute two composite indexes of change, measuring respectively the cumulative implementation of management tools (out of a list of 13 tools) and of computer tools (out of a list of 15 tools). Descriptive statistics on employer use of ICT and managerial tools in 2003 and 2006 are given in Table 10.1 (see also Bigi et al. 2012). We dichotomize the two composite indexes to distinguish firms with no or only marginal change in each dimension from firms with ICT or managerial changes, respectively. Finally, we build a typology of company changes in four categories: ICT changes only, managerial changes only, ICT and managerial changes, and no or only marginal changes in both dimensions that we label "inertia." We also build an indicator of global change by grouping these three categories of change.

The employee section of the COI survey has a threefold objective: capture employee's perspective on organizational change, collect data on both the job and the employee, and measure employees' experiences and outcomes within the firm. The employer and employee samples are the result of a two-stage sampling frame. A list of employers has first been randomly selected and postal questionnaires were sent in 2006. Responding firms have then been identified in a linked employer/employee register from which small random samples of employees (between 2 and 15 depending on company's size) have been selected. Then telephone or face to face interviews with employees took place. In this research, we are going to analyze the work experience of employees who were still affiliated with the same firm at the time of their interview, which took place around 1 year after they were selected (and the firm was interviewed). They are thus representative of rather stable employees, with at least 1 year of seniority in our sample of firms.

The two sections of the COI survey received high response rates (82 % for employers, 70 % for employees), leading to working samples of 6,342 firms and 14,101 employees. In our analysis, we use weighted statistics and take into account the complex sampling frame in order to ensure the representativity of our results.

10.4 Age-Related Selection Linked to Changes?

A couple of decades ago, surveys on technology and work organization in France showed that ICT use decreased significantly with age, including when controlling for variables such as gender, nationality, occupation, or educational attainment (Moatty 1993). This observation, also valid for the use of industrial robots (Marquié and Baracat 1998), raised two questions, related to one another: Did it reflect a generation effect, because the employees with average age at that time had not been academically trained in these technologies? Were these disparities specific to technological innovations, or were they also observed for other types of company transformations: changes in product range, in strategy, and in organization?

Since then, many other results have confirmed this general trend. Results from the second and third European Working Conditions surveys[2] show that between 1995 and 2000, the proportion of European workers – in the EU15, at that time – who declared that they "never" used computers at work had certainly declined between the two dates but continued to display definite differences by age group (Molinié 2003). These differences showed up again in the fourth survey in 2005 (Parent-Thirion et al. 2007; Villosio et al. 2008), and other disparities between age groups were highlighted, for different types of "new" work practices, with a downward trend from the age of 40–45 years: Internet use, for example, but also job rotation, access to training, or learning opportunities at work.

The first step of our analysis must therefore be to examine how our own data confirm this differentiated distribution of the workforce by age, with regard to forms of "change." Considering the usual age thresholds in the literature on aging and the labor market, we distinguish two age groups of sufficient size to go deeper into the analysis: up to 45 and older than 45 years of age. The second group of employees is the less numerous in our sample, with 4,363 observations whereas the first group adds up to 9,738 observations. Table 10.2 gives the distribution of firms and employees according to the type of change implemented by the employer between 2003 and 2006, as well as the share of older employees for each category of firm in this distribution.

Inert firms are the more numerous in our sample. They represent 73 % of firms and their workforce gathers together 61 % of employees. Compared with the mid-1990s covered in the previous edition of the COI survey, the turn of the century seems to be characterized in the French competitive sector by a distinct deceleration of the dynamics of change, leading to a higher incidence of inertia (Greenan and Walkowiak 2010). We observe that the most frequent type of employer change involves new ICTs only: 15 % of firms are in this category and their workforce represents 20 % of employees. Firms that implemented managerial changes only and both managerial and ICT changes are, respectively, 7 % and 5 %. When we compare the share of employees over 45 years old in the four types of firm, we note slight differences. This share is smaller in firms with ICT changes only (30 %, $n = 1{,}202$) than in any other categories. But the only significant differences between shares (respectively, with a significance t-stat threshold of $p < 0.1$ and $p < 0.05$) are with inert firms (34 %, $n = 4{,}071$) and firms with managerial changes only (36 %, $n = 493$), suggesting that older workers are under more adaptation pressure when they face technological changes than when they face managerial changes. However, if we leave aside firms with ICT changes only, differences are too small on the whole to reflect a significant age selection process related to the employer changes that we measure.

As a matter of fact, the time period we cover with this survey has been seldom explored with quantitative data. Most of the results available in the literature,

[2] This survey is produced every five years by the European Foundation for the improvement of living and working conditions.

Table 10.2 Distribution of types of changes at the employer level over the samples of firms and employees

Type of change at the employer level	% firms (among the whole sample)	% employees (among the whole sample)	% employees over 45 (among employees in this type of firm)	Number of firms	Number of employees
Inertia	73	61	34	4,071	8,669
ICT and/or managerial changes	27	39	32	2,271	5,432
ICT changes only	15	20	30	1,202	2,798
Managerial changes only	7	11	36	493	1,390
ICT and managerial changes	5	8	33	576	1,244

Source: see Table 10.1

Coverage: private sector French firms with 20 employees or more and their employees with at least 1 year of seniority, 6,342 firms and 14,101 employees, weighted statistics

including some of the ones we quoted above, are based on survey data that was collected in the mid-1990s. The beginning of the millennium is a different time period in many respects: first, the computer literacy issue is less acute as most of the older generation in employment has been accustomed to working in a computerized work environment; second, ICT changes that occurred at the turn of the century have more to do with software than with hardware; and third, managerial changes are more related to transversal issues in organizations, like optimizing overall processes or improving relations with customers and suppliers, than focused on a given area like production. These results could mitigate the age selection process observed in the period of rapid changes of the mid-1990s and in particular the rapid ICT changes linked to the diffusion of the Internet.

10.5 Changes and Quality of Working Life according to Age

Episodes of change in a workplace may be experienced differently by older and younger workers (Marquié and Baracat 1998). These differences derive both from earlier career paths and from future prospects. On the one hand, indeed, initial training is more recent for younger workers. It could enable them to acquire knowledge about emerging technology. Knowledge of older workers, in contrast, is more likely to be considered obsolete, or even to be really difficult to mobilize, when work methods are heavily modified. This disadvantage is particularly marked when their professional trajectory was relatively poor in opportunities to grow and learn.

On the other hand, older and younger workers are not at the same point in their career and therefore do not have the same outlook. For young people a change can be a turning point for a route to come. The elderly have a greater probability of reaching an end position or at least limited opportunities for advancement. Worse, they have more reason to fear that a change is a prelude to restructuring, with potential implications for their jobs and skills. It may happen, probably more often for older workers, that a new situation "calls into question the psychological, cognitive and relational balances, previously acquired, sometimes dearly" (Paumès et al. 1998). The transformation of work may, for these workers, generate a subjective impact in terms of degradation of self-image, with the fear of having to "start from scratch," at a moment in their working life when they are not ready for that. Based on these elements, we can expect that membership in a changing workplace can contribute rather positively to the quality of working life for young workers and rather negatively for older workers.

We are going to consider three different employee outcomes in our analysis of the quality of working life, which cover complementary dimensions of work experience: the feeling of fair work recognition, the opportunity to learn new things at work, and the feeling of work overload. The precise formulations for the questions and item responses from which these three binary variables derive are given in Appendix A.1. These questions are asked toward the end of the questionnaire after the employee has described her job and the main characteristics of work organization. The first question to appear is the one about opportunities to learn new things at work, in a section of questions about skill development. The question on work overload comes in the last section of the questionnaire where the employee is asked to give a general review of her work experience. The question on fair work recognition is the last question which aims at synthesizing the balance between effort and reward with a reference to fairness of treatment: does the employee feel that his contribution is justly valued by the employer?

Seventy-one percent of the employees covered by the survey indicate that their job gives them "opportunities to learn new things," 27 % have to cope with work overload "every day" or "at least once a week," and 44 % have a feeling of fair work recognition (Table 10.3). When we break down these statistics between the two age groups we considered, we note that the older employees report less learning opportunities at work, less frequent feeling of work overload, and more recognition for their contribution than younger ones.

The objective of our research is to explore the sensitivity of these results concerning quality of working life to the context of change within companies, using our typology. Table 10.4 computes the average quality of working life indicators for the two age groups in changing firms of each type compared to inertia which is our benchmark case. The lines entitled "change gap" give the difference in quality of working life for these two organizational contexts.

First, we observe no significant differences in "opportunities to learn new things at work" between changing and inert firms, whatever the type of change, and for

Table 10.3 Quality of working life and age

%	Feeling of fair work recognition	Opportunities to learn new things at work	Feeling of work overload	Number of employees	Number of firms
All samples	43.6 %	71.0 %	27.3 %	14,101	6,342
46–59 years old	45.3 %	70.7 %	25.2 %	4,363	3,051
20–45 years old	43.1 %	72.8 %	28.6 %	9,738	5,392
Age gap	2.2*pp	−2.1*pp	−3.4**pp	–	–

Source: See Table 10.1
Coverage: employees with at least 1 year of seniority in private French firms with 20 employees and more
Note: The age gap is the difference in each of the three components of well-being between employees aged 46–59 and employees aged 20–45. It is expressed in percentage points (pp). Significance thresholds for this difference (*t*-stat): $^{**}p < 0.05$, $^{*}p < 0.10$

Table 10.4 Quality of working life and employer level changes according to age: means and mean differences

	Feeling of fair work recognition		Opportunities to learn new things at work		Feeling of work overload	
	46–59 years old	20–45 years old	46–59 years old	20–45 years old	46–59 years old	20–45 years old
Inertia	47.4 %	44.1 %	71.3 %	72.3 %	24.2 %	29.4 %
ICT and/or managerial change	41.8 %	41.6 %	69.8 %	73.5 %	26.9 %	27.3 %
Change gap	−5.6*pp	−2.4pp	−1.5pp	1.2pp	2.7pp	−2.2pp
ICT change only	37.1 %	37.5 %	67.8 %	72.5 %	25.9 %	29.4 %
Change gap	−10.3*pp	−6.5#pp	−3.5pp	0.1pp	1.7pp	0.0pp
Managerial change only	50.1 %	49.1 %	74.1 %	73.9 %	28.2 %	24.8 %
Change gap	2.7pp	5.0*pp	2.8pp	1.5pp	4.0pp	−4.6*pp
ICT and managerial change	40.5 %	42.6 %	68.0 %	75.8 %	27.3 %	25.0 %
Change gap	−6.9*pp	−1.5pp	−3.3pp	3.4pp	3.1pp	−4.4**pp
Number of employees	4,363	9,738	4,363	9,738	4,363	9,738

Source: see Table 10.1; for coverage, see Table 10.3
Note: The change gap is the difference in each of the three components of well-being for an age group between firms that implemented some changes and firms that remained inert or nearly so between 2003 and 2006. It is expressed in percentage points (pp). Significance thresholds for these differences (*t*-stat): $^{**}p < 0.05$, $^{*}p < 0.10$, $^{\#}p < 0.15$

younger workers as well as older ones. But differences related to the organizational context do appear in the two other dimensions of the quality of working life. For older workers, it is the feeling of fair work recognition that is sensitive to employer changes, whereas for younger workers, it is the feeling of work overload. However, the outcomes of change take opposite directions for the two groups of workers, in

Table 10.5 Quality of working life and employer level changes according to age: marginal effects from logit regression models

	Feeling of fair work recognition		Opportunities to learn new things at work		Feeling of work overload	
	46–59 years old	20–45 years old	46–59 years old	20–45 years old	46–59 years old	20–45 years old
Model 1						
Inertia	Ref.	Ref.	Ref.	Ref.	Ref.	Ref.
ICT and/or managerial changes	−4.9*	−3.3	−1.8	−1.2	2.7	−2.9#
Model 2						
Inertia	Ref.	Ref.	Ref.	Ref.	Ref.	Ref.
ICT changes only	−8.0*	−6.2	−1.2	−0.9	2.7	−1.2
Managerial changes only	0.4	2.3	−1.4	−3.2	3.6	−4.4#
ICT and managerial changes	−5.5	−3.2	−3.9	0.3	1.6	−5.0**
Number of employees	4,363	9,738	4,363	9,738	4,363	9,738

Source: see Table 10.1; for coverage, see Table 10.3

Note: Two sets of regressions are given in the table: a first one with a dummy indicating the existence of any type of change at the employer level and a second one where we distinguish between our three types of change. The two regressions include the set of controls given in Appendix A.1, but we do not show the associated coefficients in the table: company size, employee personal characteristics, employment characteristics, and work organization characteristics. Marginal effects are multiplied by 100. They can be read in terms of % of growth in the incidence of the dependent variable when a given change is implemented by the firm. Significance thresholds for the marginal effects (z-scores): $^{**}p < 0.05$, $^{*}p < 0.10$, $^{\#}p < 0.15$

terms of quality of working life: older workers feel lower fair work recognition whereas younger ones feel less work overload. Interestingly, older workers are sensitive to ICT changes only, whereas younger ones react to changes that incorporate managerial ingredients. In other words, ICT changes tend to deteriorate the balance between effort and reward for older workers whereas managerial changes help younger workers to better cope with their duties. The strongest correlation is observed for older workers in organizational contexts where only ICT have changed: there is a significant difference of 10 percentage points in feeling of fair work recognition for older workers between this type of change and inertia. We also note that younger workers have a more frequent feeling of fair working recognition when their employer implements managerial changes only.

These descriptive results match the findings of the more qualitative research that we mentioned earlier on. Are they robust to structural controls? We estimated two sets of logit regressions where the dependent variables are the quality of working life indicators and where the regressors described in Appendix A.1: are the employer level of changes and a set of structural controls at the employer and employee levels company size at the employer level, personal characteristics, employment characteristics, and work organization characteristics at the employee level. Apart from the fact that the correlation between organizational change and quality of working life may stem from a different distribution of these characteristics among firms that have changed and firms that have remained inert, some of these variables may also mediate the relation between organizational change and quality of working life. In the first set of regressions (Model 1), we use an indicator of overall change and in a second set (Model 2), our typology of changes ("ICT changes only," "managerial changes only," and "ICT and managerial changes"). Inertia is the reference category for the discrete change variable in the two models. We see from Table 10.5 that the main results concerning feeling of fair work recognition for older workers and feeling of work overload for younger ones remain valid once controls have been taken into account.

Since our purpose here is to focus on older workers, we are now going to look closer into our main result for this age group, by identifying what factors contribute to explaining the fair work recognition gap among them, between inert and changing firms.

10.6 Explaining Differences in Feeling of Fair Work Recognition for Older Workers Facing Changes in Their Work

In the relationship between age and changes in work, as in all age/work relationships, the effects are in general "conditional": they depend on several characteristics of the work environment which may increase or decrease the age-related impairments. They can help or hinder the construction of experience-based resources as well as their mobilization by older workers.

We shall now see how these characteristics or attributes can intervene by inquiring the reasons for which the feeling of fair work recognition is lower for older workers when their firms implement changes, and more particularly ICT changes. The feeling of fair work recognition derives from a perceived balance between efforts spent by the workers and rewards received from the work environment. According to Siegrist (1996), a perceived imbalance between effort and reward is a source of increased health hazards. The feeling of fair work recognition depends upon a set of observable characteristics: individual characteristics, which shape how the employees value their involvement (sex, age, years of education); employment characteristics, which define the type of membership to the organization that employers offer to employees (contractual conditions, employer size); and work organization characteristics, which structure the conditions of work performance (work pace, social support, training, etc.).[3] We will use this set of characteristics or attributes in our analysis of fair work recognition gap among older workers, between inert and changing firms.

[3] Appendix A.1 displays the questions and item responses for the variables that capture these characteristics. They have been used as controls in the regressions presented in Table 10.5.

Table 10.6 The aggregate decomposition of the observed fair work recognition gap for older workers facing changes

	ICT and/or managerial changes vs. inertia		ICT changes vs. inertia		ICT and managerial changes vs. inertia	
	Change gap	%	Change gap	%	Change gap	%
Total	−5.6*pp	100.0	−10.3*pp	100.0	−6.9*pp	100.0
Aggregate characteristics effect	−0.9pp	16.1	−2.1pp	20.4	−2.4pp	34.8
Aggregate coefficients effect	−4.7*pp	83.9	−8.2*pp	79.6	−4.5pp	65.2
Number of employees	4,363		3,544		3,074	

Source: see Table 10.1

Note: The measured change gap and its decomposition are expressed in terms of percentage points (pp). Significance thresholds for the change gap and its decomposition (t-stat): $*p < 0.10$

Coverage: Employees with at least 1 year of seniority of 46–59 years old in private French firms with 20 employees and more that implemented different types of changes

This analysis will be based on the decomposition method suggested by Yun (2004, 2005), which extends the Oaxaca-Blinder technique, well known in wage discrimination research, to the case of a binary outcome (see Appendix A.2). This decomposition can be done at aggregate and detailed levels.

At the aggregate level, the change gap is assigned, on the one hand, to differences in the distribution of observable characteristics among older workers between organizations that have undergone changes (changing firms) and organizations that have not materially changed (inert firms) and, on the other hand, to differences in the impact of characteristics or attributes between the two samples of firms. The first source is labeled the "characteristics effect" and the second one, the "coefficients effect." Table 10.6 presents the results of this aggregate decomposition for changes, ICT changes only and ICT and managerial changes. The fair work recognition gap for managerial changes only is not decomposed here, because it is not statistically significant (see Tables 10.4 and 10.5).

The more salient finding of this decomposition is that the observed fair work recognition gap is largely explained by the "coefficients effect." In fact, if we consider the first column of Table 10.6, feeling of fair work recognition among older workers in firms that have implemented changes is 5.6 % points lower than among older workers in inert firms and 83.9 % of this gap is due to the coefficients effect. On the contrary, the contribution of the differences in older worker characteristics is very small (16.1 %) and not statistically significant. We find similar percentages when we consider the observed fair work recognition gap for older workers between firms that have only implemented ICT changes and inert ones (column 2). Finally, the aggregate coefficients effect is smaller (but still important) and not significant when we decompose the loss of fair work recognition for older workers facing both ICT and managerial changes (column 3). Hence, the lower feelings of recognition that we observe among older workers in changing firms compared to older workers in inert firms are not explained by differences in observable individual and employment characteristics between these two populations. It is rather due to a differing contribution of employment relations and work organization characteristics in shaping the balance between effort and reward in both contexts. Indeed, older workers seem to have different behavioral responses in terms of recognition depending on whether or not they are confronted with change.

The decomposition method we use allows us to go one step further in the analysis by investigating, through a detailed decomposition, which are the attributes or characteristics giving rise to the most pronounced differences in behavioral responses of older workers, and therefore contributing the most to the explanation of the observed difference of fair work recognition.

The results of the detailed decompositions are presented in Fig. 10.1a–c. Figure 10.1a focuses on total changes, and Fig. 10.1b, c concern, respectively, ICT changes only and ICT and managerial changes. The left side of each figure represents the characteristics or attributes leading to behavioral differences that contribute to widen the recognition gap for older workers between changing and inert firms (aggravating behavioral responses). In contrast, characteristics or attributes that contribute to narrow the recognition gap are represented on the right side of each figure (improving behavioral responses).

In each figure, the intercept appears as the main factor explaining the recognition gap for older workers. It can be taken as an assessment of the propensity of older workers to declare being poorly recognized in their work when they face changes in their company, regardless of their characteristics. If so, this result indicates that employer changes, and notably when they incorporate ICT changes, generate for older workers a strong increase of the tendency to feel poorly recognized at work.

Higher pay, and the fact of having a permanent job, more strongly influence – and in a positive sense – older workers' feeling of fair work recognition within changing than within inert firms, so these two elements contribute to reducing the observed recognition gap (Fig. 10.1a). Traditional components of the employment relation thus play an important role in comforting the feeling of fair work recognition of older workers when they face changes. However, there are differences according to the type of changes. Higher pay helps to reduce the loss of recognition only among firms that have experienced both ICT and managerial changes, (Fig. 10.1c) while the fact of having a permanent job can help reduce this loss among firms that experienced ICT changes only (Fig. 10.1b).

Having to follow strict work targets reduces the feeling of fair work recognition of older workers and especially when they belong to changing firms (Fig. 10.1a) and to firms with ICT changes only (Fig. 10.1b). The following explanation could prevail: The issue for older workers facing a change is to reuse personal work strategies that they have forged along their professional path, adapting them to new circumstances (Gaudart 2000). This objective is undermined if the change takes place in a context of increasing prescription to streamline, to standardize, and to draw more strictly labor practices.

We also note that, when firms implement changes and especially changes in ICT tools only, it is better for the feeling of fair work recognition of older workers that

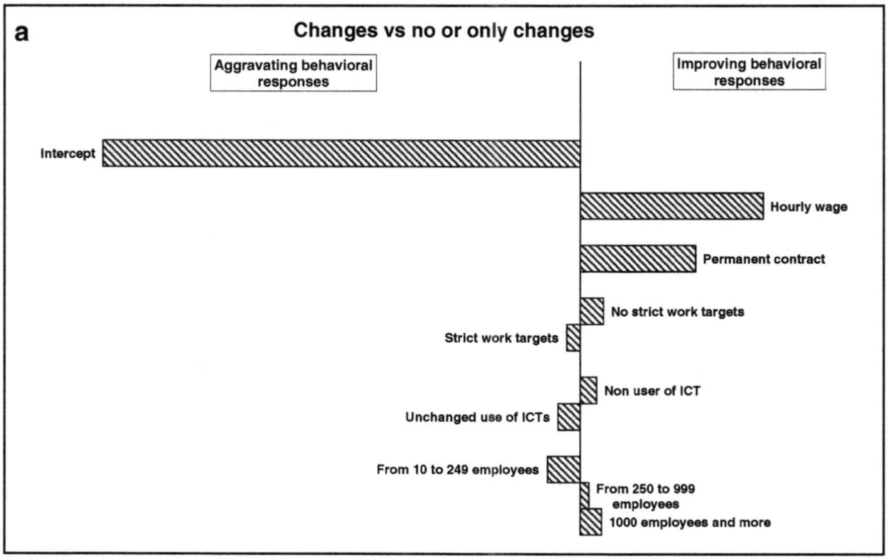

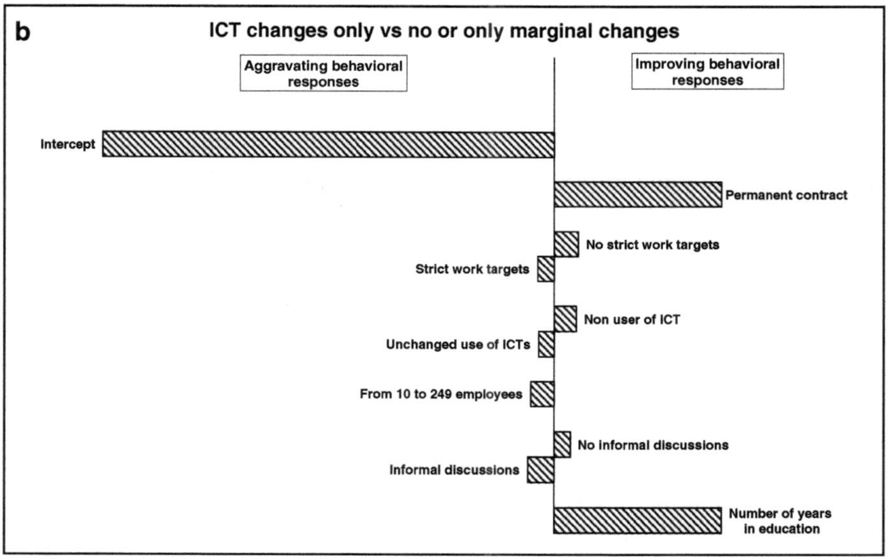

Fig. 10.1 (continued)

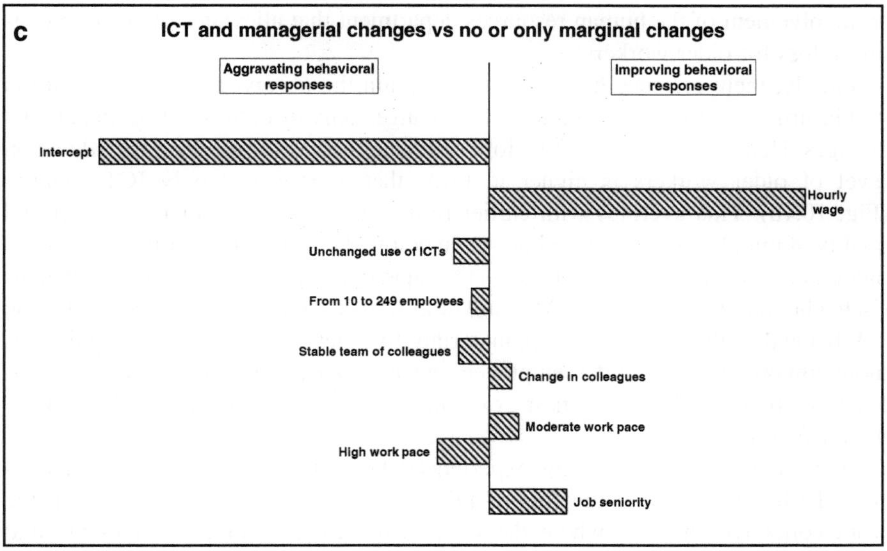

Fig. 10.1 (**a–c**) The characteristics that contribute the most to the differences in behavioral responses to recognition gap for older workers facing changes
Source: See Table 10.1; for coverage, see Table 10.6
Note: The figure displays the characteristics leading to behavioral differences that contribute the most to the explanation of the observed difference of fair work recognition for older workers between changing and inert firms. The length of the bar is proportionate to the strength of the contribution of each characteristic.

they (themselves, personally) do not use any computers, and using computer equipment that has not changed over the past year in this case is particularly detrimental. This could reflect both the difficulties associated with age in the appropriation of new ICT tools and the symbolic value of new equipment in the process of work recognition.

Firm size has a positive influence on the feeling of fair work recognition of older workers within changing firms and a negative one within inert ones. Therefore, when firms are changing, it is better for the feeling of recognition of older employees that they evolve within firms whose size is greater than 250 employees rather than in small structures. A negative relationship between firm size and the feeling of fair work recognition for older workers has been described by empirical research using the European SHARE survey (Lengagne 2011). The author advocates the fact that smaller organizations have a greater ability to favor a balance between efforts and rewards because of more direct communication between employees and thus a better common knowledge of the share of the work burden. However, improved working and employment conditions in bigger structures could counterbalance this common knowledge effect. It could be the case that when changing firms have a bigger size, change management is better organized, with an involvement of the human resources department that alleviates the work recognition loss for older workers.

Finally, there are specific factors that explain the observed loss of recognition within firms that experienced either ICT changes only or both ICT and managerial changes. Hence it appears that the loss of recognition is lower when the education level of older workers is higher in firms that experienced only ICT changes (Fig. 10.1b). This overlaps with earlier results, according to which the level and quality of initial and further training – even before the considered company change – moderate the negative effects of age on the capacity to appropriate technical changes (Behaghel and Greenan 2010; Marquié et al. 2010; Paumès et al. 1998; Salthouse 1990). On the other hand, and in a counterintuitive manner, this loss of recognition is more important where older employees have opportunities to discuss with colleagues, perhaps because these exchanges encourage them to share their dissatisfaction.

If we consider firms having experienced both ICT and managerial changes (Fig. 10.1c), we see that the loss of fair work recognition is reduced when the work collective changes, where the work is not carried out under pressure and among older workers with high seniority in the post. Conversely, the loss of recognition is aggravated by the fact of working with the same colleagues and under high pressure. These findings are consistent with more general knowledge: when the time pressure at work is high, older workers always experience more difficulties (Volkoff et al. 2010) because they have fewer opportunities to mobilize the resources gained through their experience, even though these resources are valuable to anticipate emergencies. This applies to learning situations, because the training times are then smaller and more difficult to plan, prepare, and preserve, because of the lack of sufficient staff, for example. But research in occupational psychology have long shown that older people sometimes need a learning time a little longer than the younger people (Czaja et al. 1989). However, compared with older workers in firms that change ICT equipment only, older workers in firms that change both ICT equipment and managerial tools are still able to valorize as an asset the experience accumulated on the job. This confirms some previous research results on training needs for older workers facing different types of company changes (Behaghel and Greenan 2010). The positive contribution of the renewal of the work collective could indicate that new colleagues are a resource to cope with change for older workers. This implies potential knowledge transfers between older workers and new recruits that contribute to increase their feeling of fair work recognition.

10.7 Conclusion

Our results suggest that changes in ICTs and/or managerial techniques have less negative impact than what could be expected on employees' quality of working life, especially among older employees. Indeed, between the three dimensions of quality of working life considered, only the feeling of fair work recognition is negatively correlated with company changes – especially ICT changes – for older workers. Furthermore, the feeling of work overload of younger workers is lower when companies change, especially when they change their managerial tools.

In this chapter, we have also explored the reasons for which the feeling of fair work recognition is lower for older workers when their firms implement changes, and more particularly ICT changes. We show that this change gap in the feeling of fair work recognition is not explained by differences in observable characteristics of older workers employed in the two types of firm. It is rather due to a differing contribution of employment relations and work organization characteristics in shaping the balance between effort and reward in both contexts. As a result, some characteristics of work and employment counterbalance the deficit of fair work recognition experienced by older workers in changing firms and thus narrow the change gap: higher pay, the fact of having a permanent job and of belonging to firms which size is greater than 250 employees, as well as moderate time pressure in work activity. More specifically, when firms implement changes in ICT tools only, it is better for the feeling of fair work recognition of older workers not to be a computer user whereas using computer equipment that has not changed over the past year is particularly detrimental.

As a whole, our results suggest that changes in technologies and organizations at work might be less "age discriminating" than what preconceived ideas would let one suppose. Older workers are just as frequently present in firms which have managed such changes as in those that have not. And as far as quality of working life is concerned, we find no differences for older workers between changing and inert firms in terms of learning opportunities at work or feeling of work overload and a moderate change gap in the feeling of fair work recognition, in particular in firms having implemented only new ICTs compared with inert firms.

For sure, experience-related work strategies are often based on a certain familiarity with the task: it is most valuable to have accomplished the task itself or similar tasks repeatedly and to know beforehand the effects of specific actions on one's own well-being and one's own efficiency. Therefore, when an older worker encounters a new work environment because of work being reorganized, or a technical change, she has to consider a means of transferring part of her previous strategies and/or developing new ones. That is why senior workers, more than the younger ones, share the concern to develop a "controlled" approach to the new context, ways of doing things that will allow them to feel comfortable and not let the job become too tiring. These two concerns (to learn the job and to learn to feel comfortable with it) partly explain why older workers require longer learning periods than the younger ones and may feel ill at ease (or "ill recognized") during this period. This learning time allows the fine-tuning of a revisited balance between effort and reward. But it does not mean that they cannot adapt to "new" work environments.

Many studies in the field of work or learning have shown the effectiveness of operating modes based on experience and the substantial role they play in preserving well-being. However the possibility for workers – especially the older ones – to implement them and, consequently, their chances of success will depend on the organization of work that is chosen. Hence the overall changes in working conditions must be taken into account. In particular, work intensification (Green and McIntosh 2001) puts the importance of experience-related strategies at the forefront, but at the same time, it hinders their implementation.

Therefore, while it is important to take into consideration the potential deterioration of well-being resulting from the various aspects of professional life, another component of the age/work/well-being relationship is just as essential (Vendramin et al. 2012): career paths can favor or hinder capacities to face changes (Shani et al. 2002). One of the key questions in the coming years will be whether the organization of work in companies will preserve and value professional experience, by encouraging its development and its implementation, namely, when changes are planned.

Acknowledgements We acknowledge the financial support of the French National Research Agency (ANR) for this research that is part of the COI-COSA project.

Appendix A.1: Variables Included in the Analysis

A.1.1 Dependent Variables: Employee Level

Feeling of fair work recognition: When the employee makes a balance of what she brings to the company and the benefits she gets back, she thinks that she is fairly recognized.

Opportunities to learn new things at work: The employee's job allows her to learn new things at work.

Feeling of work overload: There are moments at work every day or at least once a week when the employee feels unable to cope or overloaded.

A.1.2 Independent Variables: Employer Level

Employer-level changes: Categorical variable deriving from two composite indicators measuring, respectively, the cumulative implementation of management tools and of computer tools – ICT changes only, managerial changes only, ICT and managerial changes, and inertia.

Company size: from 10 to 249, from 250 to 999, and more than 1,000 employees.

A.1.3 Independent Variables: Employee Level

A.1.3.1 Personal Characteristics

Sex: male, female.

Number of years in education: number of years in education starting from primary schools.

A.1.3.2 Employment Characteristics

Fixed-term contract: The employee is on a fixed-term contract.
Permanent contract: The employee is on a permanent contract.
Part-time work: The employee works part time.
Log of hourly wage: Log of the net daily wage divided by the usual number of daily hours.
Job seniority and seniority squared: Computed from the declared year when the employee started to hold her current job.

A.1.3.3 Work Organization Characteristics

Training: The employee has taken training courses in the company in 2003, 2004, or 2005.
High work pace: The work pace of the employee is set by demands needing immediate response.
Strict work targets: The employee has to achieve set work targets and has no latitude to change them.
Strict quality procedures: The employee has to follow strict quality procedures.
Technical support on the job: Since 2003, the employee's colleagues or her boss showed her or gave her explanations about the operation of a slightly complex piece of machinery or the course of a slightly complex procedure or about how to deal with customers.
Operational support: When facing a temporary excess workload or when having trouble doing a complicated task, the employee receives support either internal or external to the company.
Continuous improvement: The employee or his colleagues have made, in the last 12 months, suggestions to improve operations, procedures, or machines, and they have been taken into account.
Informal discussion: The employee is able to discuss informally what happens in the company with his colleagues.
Change in colleagues: Over the past 12 months, some or most of the employee's colleagues have changed.
Change in used ICTs: Over the past 12 months, the employee's computer equipment or software has changed.
Unchanged use of ICTs: The employee uses ICTs, but equipment and software have not changed over the past 12 months.
Nonuser of ICT: The employee does not use ICTs at work.

Appendix A.2: The Decomposition Method of Yun (2005)

In this chapter, we perform the nonlinear decomposition method proposed by Yun (2005) in order to decompose the observed fair work recognition gap between older workers in changing firms and their counterparts in inert firms into "explained" and "unexplained" components. This decomposition can be done at aggregate and detailed levels.

A.2.1 Aggregate Decomposition

The aggregate decomposition presents the same form as that of the traditional Oaxaca (1973) and Blinder (1973) decomposition in wage discrimination research. In fact, the difference in average probability of feeling fair work recognition $\overline{I}_j$ between older workers in changing firms ($j = C$) and their counterparts in inert firms ($j = NC$) can be expressed as

$$\overline{I}_c - \overline{I}_{NC} = \left[\overline{\Phi(X_C\hat{\beta}_{NC})} - \overline{\Phi(X_{NC}\hat{\beta}_{NC})}\right] + \left[\overline{\Phi(X_C\hat{\beta}_C)} - \overline{\Phi(X_C\hat{\beta}_{NC})}\right] \quad \text{(A.2.1)}$$

where X_j is a raw vector of individual, job, and employer characteristics for an older worker belonging to a firm of type j ($j = C, NC$). $\hat{\beta}_j$ is the corresponding vector of coefficient estimates. Φ is the standard normal cumulative distribution function and "over bar" represents the value of sample's average. The first term in square brackets corresponds to the part of the fair work recognition gap due to differences in the observed characteristics of older workers between the two types of firms (the aggregate characteristics effect or the "explained" component). It can be seen as the gap in the feeling of fair work recognition that would be observed if the impact of the observed characteristics was homogeneous depending on whether or not firms have experienced changes. The second term in square brackets represents the part due to differences in coefficients, i.e., differences in the behavioral responses of older workers to the observed characteristics depending on whether or not their firms have implemented changes (the aggregate coefficients effect or the "unexplained" component). This can be seen as the gap in the feeling of fair work recognition that would be observed if older workers had not differed in their observed characteristics according to the type of firms. The decomposition described in (A.2.1) is done at the aggregate level. We note that the explained part is computed with logit estimates obtained using the sample of older workers in inert firms. In this study, we are also concerned with decomposing the fair work recognition gap at a detailed level.

A.2.2 Detailed Decomposition

To evaluate the individual contribution of each characteristic included in the vector X to the overall gap, we use the following detailed decomposition equation suggested by Yun:

$$\begin{aligned}\overline{I}_c - \overline{I}_{NC} = &\sum_{i=1}^{K} W^i_{\Delta X}\left[\overline{\Phi(X_C\hat{\beta}_{NC})} - \overline{\Phi(X_{NC}\hat{\beta}_{NC})}\right] \\ &+\sum_{i=1}^{K} W^i_{\Delta\hat{\beta}}\left[\overline{\Phi(X_C\hat{\beta}_C)} - \overline{\Phi(X_C\hat{\beta}_{NC})}\right]\end{aligned} \tag{A.2.2}$$

with $W^i_{\Delta X} = \frac{\left(\overline{X}^i_C - \overline{X}^i_{NC}\right)\hat{\beta}^i_{NC}}{\left(\overline{X}_C - \overline{X}_{NC}\right)\hat{\beta}_{NC}}$, $W^i_{\Delta\hat{\beta}} = \frac{\overline{X}^i_C\left(\hat{\beta}^i_C - \hat{\beta}^i_{NC}\right)}{\overline{X}_C\left(\hat{\beta}_C - \hat{\beta}_{NC}\right)}$, and $\sum_{i=1}^{K} W^i_{\Delta X} = \sum_{i=1}^{K} W^i_{\Delta\hat{\beta}} = 1$.

The weights $W^i_{\Delta X}$ and $W^i_{\Delta\hat{\beta}}$ are, respectively, the individual relative contributions of characteristic i ($i = 1,\ldots, K$) to the aggregate characteristics and coefficient effects.

Yun uses normalized regressions in computing weights in order to tackle the identification problem that occurs when the detailed decomposition of the aggregate coefficient effect is undertaken. In fact, normalized regressions have the advantage of being invariant to the "left-out" reference category in computing the contribution of dummy variables to the detailed coefficient effect. Moreover, the method of Yun overcomes the "path dependence" problem implying that in nonlinear decomposition, the independent contribution of one variable to the overall difference depends on the order in which the other variables are entered into the decomposition.

References

Behaghel, L., & Greenan, N. (2010). Training and age-biased technical change. *Annals of Economics and Statistics, 99/100*, 317–342.

Bigi, M., Greenan, N., Lanfranchi, J., & Hamon-Cholet, S. (2012). *Changements organisationnels et évolution du vécu au travail: une comparaison entre secteur privé et fonction publique d'Etat* [Organisational changes and the evolution of working life quality: A comparison between the private sector and the state civil service]. Rapport de Recherche, CEE, n°75.

Blinder, A. S. (1973). Wage discrimination: Reduced form and structural variables. *Journal of Human Resources, 8*, 436–455.

Cau-Bareille, D., Gaudart, C., & Delgoulet, C. (2012). Training, age and technological change: Difficulties associated with age, the design of tools, and the organization of work. *Work, 41*, 127–141.

Czaja, S. J., Hammond, K., Blascovitch, J. J., & Swede, H. (1989). Age related differences in learning to use a text-editing system. *Behavior and Information Technology, 8*(4), 309–319.

Defresne, M., Marioni, P., & Thévenot, C. (2010). *L'opinion des employeur sur les seniors* [The views of employers on senior workers]. Dares, Analyses, n° 55.

Delgoulet, C., & Marquié, J.-C. (2002). Age differences in learning maintenance skills: A field study. *Experimental Aging Research, 28*, 25–37.
Gaudart, C. (2000). Conditions for maintaining ageing operators at work – A case study conducted at an automobile manufacturing plant. *Applied Ergonomics, 31*(5), 453–462.
Green, F. (2006). *Demanding work: The paradox of job quality in the affluent economy*. Princeton: Princeton University Press.
Green, F., & Mcintosh, S. (2001). The intensification of work in Europe. *Labour Economics, 8*(2), 291–308.
Greenan, N., & Walkowiak, E. (2010). La dynamique des changements à long terme [The long term dynamics of changes]. *Réseaux, 62*(4), 231–273.
Greenan, N., Narcy, M., & Robin, S. (2012). Changements au sein des entreprises et accès des seniors à la formation continue dans les années 1990 et 2000 [Changes within companies and access of older workers to further training in the 1990's and 2000's]. *Revue Française d'Economie, 27*(1), 129–162.
Hukki, K., & Seppala, P. (1992, May 28–30). Utilization of user's experience in the introduction of information technology: A study in a large municipal organization. In J. Ilmarinen (Ed.), *International scientific – Symposium on aging and work*, Haïkko, Finland.
Lengagne, P. (2011, June). *Récompense au travail ressentie et santé des seniors* [Feeling of reward at work and health of senior workers]. Questions d'économie de la sante, n°166.
Marquié, J. C., & Baracat, B. (1998). Being over forty-five in an ever-changing technological context. In J. C. Marquié, D. Paumès, & S. Volkoff (Eds.), *Working with age* (pp. 273–284). London: Taylor & Francis.
Marquié, J. C., Thon, B., & Baracat, B. (1994). Age influence on attitudes of office workers faced with new computerized technologies. *Applied Ergonomics, 25*(3), 130–142.
Marquié, J. C., Rico Duarte, L., Bessières, P., Dalm, C., Gentila, C., & Ruidavets, J. B. (2010). Higher mental stimulation at work is associated with improved cognitive functioning in both young and older workers. *Ergonomics, 53*(11), 1287–1301.
Moatty, F. (1993). *Qui utilise l'informatique au travail?* [Who uses computer equipment at work?]. Cahiers du Centre d'Etudes de l'Emploi, n°51.
Molinié, A. F. (2003). *Age and working conditions in the European Union*. Dublin: European Foundation for the Improvement of Living and Working Conditions.
Oaxaca, R. (1973). Male-female wage differentials in urban labor markets. *International Economic Review, 14*(3), 693–709.
OECD. (1998). Work-force ageing in OECD countries. In *Employment Outlook* (pp. 123–151). Paris: OECD.
Parent-Thirion, A., Fernandez Macias, H., Hurley, J., & Vermeylen, G. (2007). *Fourth European working conditions survey. Conditions*. Luxembourg: European Foundation for the Improvement of Living and Working Conditions.
Paumès, D., Cau-Bareille, D., & Marquié, J. C. (1998). Ageing workers, learning and job training. In J. C. Marquié, D. Paumès, & S. Volkoff (Eds.), *Working with age* (pp. 297–311). London: Taylor & Francis.
Reed, K., Doty, D. H., & May, D. R. (2005). The impact of aging on self-efficacy and computer skill acquisition. *Journal of Managerial Issues, 16*(2), 212–228.
Rosen, B., & Jerdee, T. H. (1977). Too old or not too old. *Harvard Business Review, 55*(6), 97–106.
Salthouse, T. A. (1990). Influence of experience on age differences in cognitive functioning. *Human Factors, 32*(5), 551–569.
Shani, A. B., Docherty, P., & Forslin, J. (2002). *Creating sustainable work systems – Emerging perspectives and practices*. London: Routledge.
Siegrist, J. (1996). Adverse health effects of high-effort/low-reward conditions. *Journal of Occupational Health Psychology, 1*(1), 27–41.

Vendramin, P., Valenduc, G., Molinié, A. F., Volkoff, S., Ajzen, M., & Léonard, E. (2012). *Sustainable work and the ageing workforce*. Luxembourg: Publications Office of the European Union.

Villosio, C., Di Pierro, D., Giordanengo, A., Pasqua, P., & Richiardi, M. (2008). *Working conditions of an ageing workforce*. Dublin: European Foundation for the Improvement of Living and Working Conditions.

Volkoff, S., Buisset, C., & Mardon, C. (2010). Does intense time pressure at work make older employees more vulnerable? A statistical analysis based on a French survey "SVP50". *Applied Ergonomics, 41*, 754–762.

Walker, A., & Taylor, P. (1992). *The employment of older people: Employers' attitudes and practices'*. ESRC conference on Past, Current and Future Initiatives on Ageing, London.

Yeatts, D. E., Folts, W. E., & Knapp, J. (1999). Older worker's adaptation to a changing workplace: Employment issues for the 21st century. *Educational Gerontology, 24*, 331–347.

Yun, M.-S. (2004). Decomposing differences in the first moment. *Economics Letters, 82*, 275–280.

Yun, M.-S. (2005). A simple solution to the identification problem in detailed wage decompositions. *Economic Inquiry, 43*, 766–772.

Chapter 11
Boon and Bane of ICT Acceleration for Vulnerable Populations

Harald Weber and Klaus J. Zink

11.1 The Bane: New Risks of Exclusion Through Acceleration of ICT

11.1.1 Acceleration

Today's economies are characterised by a steady growth of the importance of informational activities and information intensive industries. The more information becomes a central part of economies, the more it impacts on societies as a whole as well. Strategic policy papers often use terminology like 'information society' or 'knowledge society' to attribute a positive connotation to, and to assume a socially acceptable and desirable course, the process of transformation. Some often highlighted expectations with regard to the target state of this transformation are to overcome barriers certain populations are currently facing, like spatial distribution, language or knowledge barriers, handicaps resulting from disabilities or environmental conditions, social status or economic power.

Yet, the picture of a future society based heavily upon data, information and knowledge is at best – and unsurprisingly – vague. From today's point of view, it seems that the only potent forces that shape and drive the transformation are the ICT industries. Each new ICT device, technology or application stimulates new or activates current markets, which in consequence stimulate even further developments of devices, technologies and applications. This industry has shown a higher than average growth rate for many years (e.g. 4.3 % in 2011), and it is estimated that the worldwide market of ICT reached 1,000 billion Euro in 2011 (BITKOM 2012). To keep this 'chain reaction' alive, speed of innovation and time to market are crucial for ICT developers. It seems that *being the first on the market* is still the

H. Weber (✉) • K.J. Zink
Institute of Technology and Work (ITA), University of Kaiserslautern, Kaiserslautern, Germany
e-mail: harald.weber@ita-kl.de; klaus.j.zink@ita-kl.de

C. Korunka and P. Hoonakker (eds.), *The Impact of ICT on Quality of Working Life*, DOI 10.1007/978-94-017-8854-0_11,

dominating – and economically more successful – strategy compared to *being the best on the market* in this dynamic environment of information and communication technology. To define what is meant by 'being the best' however requires a shared agreement on what the measure should be, i.e. a common and societal desirable vision of the future society and the role of ICT in this context.

Obviously, current industry strategies with regard to new ICT products contradict with proactive approaches in ICT design and development. Proactive approaches recognise the requirements of all potential users (i.e. citizens) with regard to an ICT product throughout the whole design and development process, leading to products that meet users' needs to a wide extent. Although proactive approaches are known to contribute to making a product available to all target user groups at the same time and providing high levels of utility and usability and fewer changes due to design errors that are necessary after market entry, the time to market takes longer compared to other approaches. In consequence, current design approaches often seem to address mainly on few but influential customers, namely early adopters, 'techies' or 'nerds', as these are often effective multipliers and promoters for the ICT industry.

11.1.2 The Digital Divide

These industry strategies produce, and widely disseminate, technology that is inaccessible for certain groups of users. Unintentionally, the ICT industry is 'creating' or 'designing' a new disadvantaged group that is excluded from full participation in the knowledge economy and society. Even if it is difficult to characterise this new type of vulnerable population, it becomes visible, for example, by looking at different societal groups and their access to the Internet. The so-called digital divide that describes the gap between those able to benefit from ICT and those who cannot splits regions, countries and society as a whole. The ability to partake in the benefits of ICT depends on many factors among which economic reach, available infrastructure and appropriate training and qualification are prominent. Figure 11.1 shows the digital divide on the example of students in different countries. For this analysis, students are split into two groups, one with socio-economically disadvantaged students and one with socio-economically advantaged students. The figure shows the percentage of students from both groups who reported having access to the Internet at home. For many countries, the percentages of both groups widely differ and imply that students with a socio-economically disadvantaged background might have fewer opportunities in a knowledge-based economy/society than others. Although the gap between 'onliners' and 'nonliners' seems to get smaller each year, the continuing message is that a certain part of the society is left behind, deprived for whatever reasons from using ICT for improving their quality of work and life.

A particularly vulnerable group is the group of people with disabilities. While already disadvantaged through barriers or poorly designed products, services or

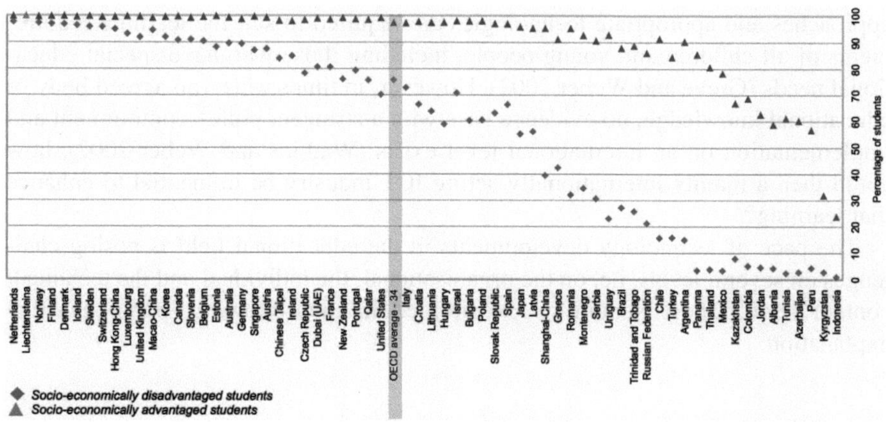

Fig. 11.1 Digital divide and socio-economic background (percentage of students who reported having access to the Internet at home, by socio-economic background (OECD 2011))
[a]Difference between socio-economically advantaged and disadvantaged students (*top* and *bottom* quarters of the PISA index of economic, social and cultural status) is statistically not significant

environments, ICT can pose additional challenges to them. These challenges are in the areas of physical handling and operation of ICT devices (e.g. typing, clicking, touching), of sensory perception (e.g. seeing, hearing) or of cognitive comprehension (e.g. complexity of interaction). ICT that can be used by people with disabilities in simple terms is labelled 'accessible'. Although the group of people with disabilities moved into the focus of ICT policy since at least 20 years, there is still a long way ahead to provide accessible ICT in all areas of a society, not to speak about the unused potentials inherent in this technology for less visible groups of people within the disability community.

11.1.3 Implications of ICT Acceleration on the Example of Education

Education is a good example of highlighting the continuing challenges of accessibility for people with disabilities. We assume that the aim to use ICT in educational settings is to enhance learning by addressing and reaching a wider learner community and making learning (and teaching) more effective, efficient and/or satisfying. These technologies are, e.g. beginning to open doors to new ways of learning. Yet the opportunities which new technologies can offer in terms of richer educational experiences, wider curricula or individually tailored learning are not generally available, nor are they always usable or accessible to all learners yet. Certain groups of learners are at risk of not being fully involved in new ways of learning, either because of their social disadvantages or their disability – or both. In order to build a socially inclusive society based on participation for all, new pedagogical approaches and appropriate technologies are required to suit the learning requirements of all children and young people, including those who have special educational needs (Greve and Weber 2002). However, in times where no agreed body of educational knowledge, no evidence base with a stringent policy commitment and implementation on an international level exists (Watkins and Weber 2002), how could then a mainly internationally acting ICT industry be influential to enhance that learning?

The pace of technology developments in the educational field is posing challenges on several levels, i.e. on the organisational, the individual and the technical/content level. These should be exemplified in the following, non-exhaustive explanation.

11.1.3.1 Challenges on an Organisational Level

For Germany, data from 2010 shows that 82 % of all companies have access to the Internet, 62 % have an own website, 44 % perform purchases via the Internet and 23 % sell products online (Statistisches Bundesamt 2011). A comparison of European countries with regard to the availability of 20 basic ICT-mediated government services (e-government) shows that although huge steps forward have been taken in the past, there is still a long way to achieve broad coverage in this field. Just about half of the German companies with Internet access used e-government offers (for comparison: Finland 95 %, Ireland 91 %), dominated by the download of form sheets or collecting administrative information (Statistisches Bundesamt 2009). In comparison, in education 99 % of German schools of different educational levels are equipped with ICT to be used in teaching/learning, with nine learners on average sharing a single computer (Empirica 2006). However, the PISA results of 2009 shed a different light on these data. While about 95 % of German learners (OECD average: 94 %) at that time used ICT and Internet at home, only 65 % (OECD average: 71 %) used ICT and the Internet in the school context as well (OECD 2011). The comparison of computer use at home between learners from advantaged (Germany 98.8 %, OECD 97.4 %) and disadvantaged (Germany 89.5 %, OECD 75.8 %) socio-economic backgrounds highlights that the digital divide is still a topic of concern, especially in educational settings (OECD 2011) (Fig. 11.2).

Technologies used in educational settings often do not represent the latest ICT available on the markets, but showcase those hardware and software that have a record of successful use, that already have been assessed in the educational field, that have been trained to the administrative and teaching staff and that promise some continuity for the future as well. Education with regard to the use of ICT is rarely a field for experimentation, but for an established technology; therefore, the ICT level of hardware, software and its implementation in teaching processes is lagging behind the state of the art in ICT. While this would not be any problem in the application of ICT in school administration, a gap between the ICT used by learners at home and the technologies used in schools is creating tensions both on

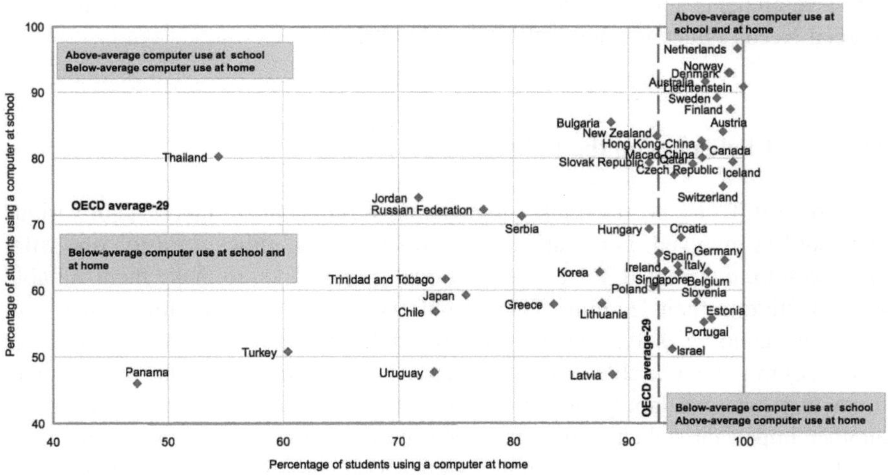

Fig. 11.2 Percentage of students who reported using a computer at home and at school (OECD 2011)

the organisational and the individual teachers' levels. The challenge for an organisation is to keep the right balance between continuity and change, to foresee the costs and benefits of the use of latest ICT, to maintain and support the teachers' encouragement and ability for learning new ICT skills and to keep the focus on learning instead of the use of ICT.

While all of this has been discussed for learners in general, the situation with regard to students with special educational needs (SEN) is even more complicated. The two relevant communities – i.e. the ICT and SEN communities – with their differing constituencies and frames of reference have hitherto lacked easy, open and direct access to the knowledge and networks of the other. Although a debate between both communities on the fundamental questions concerning pedagogy and technology-enabled learning would be necessary, close links and intensive dialogues are still uncommon (Greve and Weber 2002; Greve et al. 2003). However, as there is hardly any exact data on numbers of students with special educational needs (SEN) available due to different legal definitions of SEN in countries (European Agency for Development in Special Needs Education 2010), statistics on the use of ICT at home or at school for this group are not available.

Current reviews still emphasise that the end users of technology – people with disabilities and their families and caregivers – must be involved in the design and development of ICT in the educational field. This is true for major technological research projects, as well as simple adaptations and adjustments to existing technology. A need to support networks involving all stakeholders in the use of ICT in education for people with disabilities is highlighted. Facilitating contact and sharing of experiences between different stakeholder groups – particularly designers of ICT, people with disabilities and the educational staff that support them – is critical for developments and new innovation (European Agency for Development in Special Needs Education and UNESCO IITE 2011).

11.1.3.2 Challenges on the Individual Level

The use of ICT in education makes high demands on the individual level of various stakeholders involved. For example, students with disabilities need to cope with, and adapt to, different ICT-based educational frameworks, to make them suitable and effective to their learning. They might encounter incompatibility issues with assistive technologies (e.g. screen reader that reads aloud the content of a computer screen) or might not be able to afford the costs of ICT to make learning accessible to them (e.g. adapted laptop or communication devices like 'talkers'). Parents as another important stakeholder group need to cope with the pace of technologies available to support learning, need to understand the possibilities and limitations of ICT for the learning of their children and need to accompany their children to become media competent, to name a few of the challenges for them. Teachers belong to another relevant stakeholder group on which the following will focus a bit more.

Teachers find themselves in a difficult role. ICT has the potential to improve individualised teaching and learning in class contexts with an increasing diversity. Teacher competences need to cover general skills in education and pedagogy, as well as inclusive education approaches, with appropriate consideration of the use of ICT in education generally, as well as the use of ICT for learners with disabilities specifically. However, learners often acquire ICT skills faster and earlier than teachers and make innovative and unexpected use of it. Educational organisations are generally slow in adapting to these changes, and the educational field does not provide appropriate and timely training, support, resources and practical experiences in using ICT (European Agency for Development in Special Needs Education and UNESCO IITE 2011).

With regard to training of educational staff, teacher education would need to provide information that makes clear the theory and rationale for using ICT to support learning of people with disabilities, as well as practical experiences in implementing ICT tools and approaches. All teachers should be prepared to use ICT to support learners with SEN in their initial training and have access to further, in-service training later in their careers in order to develop the knowledge and skills to enhance their practice in this area (European Agency for Development in Special Needs Education and UNESCO IITE 2011). As knowledge in this field has a short half-life, teachers need support to keep that knowledge and the respective skills up to date, so that investments in teacher qualification are lasting. However, work intensification is also a topic in education, so answers are required how all of this can fit in today's teaching patterns. Questions about psychological stress that comes with an increased pressure to keep up with all the technological and educational progress and its impact are also unanswered currently.

11.1.3.3 Challenges on the Technical and Content Level

Many disabilities affect the access to ICT applications, appliances and content, e.g. cognitive or sensory impairments, while other types of disabilities do not impair this access (e.g. motor impairments of the lower limbs, difficult heart conditions). The barriers that many people with disabilities still face include difficulties to handle input or output devices, to operate software (e.g. web browser) and to access content (Weber 2006). For many years, however, accessibility recommendations and guidelines have focussed on providing access to ICT for motor or sensor impaired users. It was argued that guidelines and checkpoints of the Web Accessibility Guidelines (World Wide Web Consortium 1999) in version 1 – a de facto standard worldwide for many years – pertaining to cognitive disabilities are lacking in practical techniques and tending to the general, treating all cognitive disabilities as cases of low literacy and/or low intelligence (Seeman 2002). Guidelines for designing accessible ICT are still vague, when the target group of people with learning disabilities is addressed (Weber and Edler 2010).

In this context, not just technology potentially poses a barrier, but content as well. Content and its preparation and management have developed into one of the central concerns regarding efficient use, e.g. of the Internet (Weber and Stephanidis 2001; Proctor et al. 2002). This is particularly a concern in the educational field. The challenge is to find ways to prepare and manage content in such a way that the full range of learners will be able to access the information that they need, effectively, efficiently and with satisfaction. Content preparation is critical to the success of ICT endeavours in the educational field, yet it requires, among others, skilled and keen to learn personnel, state-of-the-art technology and sufficient financial resources. It is a matter of fact that this preparation process requires effort, and human intervention is still needed for high-quality content preparation. The speed of change of technological progress might undermine the willingness of stakeholders to invest these additional efforts in content preparation, if the life expectancy of enhanced contents is estimated short, compared to traditional media (like books or other physical educational materials).

This example in the field of education highlights a few of the challenges that come with an accelerating pace of technological progress. It has not even touched the area of special or segregated educational settings. These are still common in many countries, and technology use is often way behind in respective organisations in comparison to common settings, with teachers and staff often less ICT skilled and experienced compared to mainstream settings.

11.1.4 The Evolution of New Types of Disabilities

Studies commissioned by highest national levels in some European countries sum up that the best way to overcome the before-mentioned digital divide is to persuade people of the benefits of ICT and to train them. Indeed, trends seem to indicate that the gap between those able to benefit from digital technologies and those who cannot is getting smaller every year. However, whether this is caused by providing better information and training or other variables is unclear. But a few simple thoughts show that expecting the digital divide to disappear by solely training and information campaigns is insufficient to solve the issue.

Being able to benefit from digital technologies involves several preconditions. For example, physical access to ICT, physical and sensory abilities to operate ICT, having the financial resources to own ICT, being trained to use ICT or feeling competent to master ICT are key determinants to take into consideration. If, for instance, technology is provided in a geographically remote area, or if technology is poorly designed, if it does not provide a physical and sensory interaction that the user is capable of performing or sensing, or if the complexity of the technology and applications is overtaxing the users' cognitive abilities, then 'persuasion and training' strategies are obviously insufficient.

Some authors are claiming that societies need to be patient, as it might need a generation to overcome the problem of a digital divide, at least when it comes to the ICT usage rates of elderly citizens compared to the remaining part of society. As many jobs meanwhile involve the use of computers, it is expected that once people have learnt to master ICT during their work, they will carry this knowledge and experience into their retirement phase. Although this argument seems to be conclusive, it ignores two facts: the acceleration of ICT developments and progress devaluates previous knowledge at a rapid pace and the digital divide touches upon many more aspects than just age.

Indeed, the digital divide makes it quite difficult to find an appropriate typology to distinguish certain user groups in view of adequately addressing the access issue. While some dimensions like age, gender or geographical location might be obvious, they are nevertheless meaningless when it comes to develop strategies to overcome the digital divide. For example, when labour offices moved towards publishing job vacancies online, those who would have benefitted most from this direct access to up-to-date and highly relevant information not necessarily had the same level of access than others seeking employment. Reasons for not having access or for having delayed or only partial access to the information were manifold. Socio-economic background, long-time unemployment, immigrant status or age of job seekers seemed to be some of the determinants with regard to access. Yet, not *all* people belonging to these – easy to identify – groups were facing access barriers. Rather, other characteristics within those groups were of relevance, like experiences with using ICT, language skills or attitudes towards using ICT, to name a few. However, these characteristics are not equally easy to identify in larger, sometimes even anonymous, user/customer groups.

This has several implications for the design task. First, as we do not know exactly whom we are talking about, we can hardly involve representatives of these groups to work on effective access strategies. Second, the inability to define and characterise the groups makes it impossible to treat them as groups and to ensure their representation, their visibility and lobbying if necessary. The consequence of both is that the relevance to deal with these groups is not acknowledged, resulting in leaving certain parts of the society behind. This, to some extent, repeats the history of people with disabilities, being ignored, concealed and denied full participation in society for too long. Indeed, poor design of ICT unintentionally creates new types of disabilities, yet in this case without a medical cause, but context induced.

11.2 The Boon: ICT as a Platform to Put Design for All into Practice

11.2.1 Design for All

Design for all is an endeavour to the proactive design of environments, products and services with the aim that everybody, independent, e.g. of age, sex, capacities or cultural background, can fully participate in society. Design for all approaches can be found in technical and non-technical areas. For example, news broadcasts or instruction leaflets for medical drugs often make use of reduced thesauri or simplified language to make it understandable for as many users as possible. With regard to technologies, design for all is a prime design objective for instance in creating ticket machines, public kiosk systems or public telephones.

Design for all has a compelling attractiveness as it addresses the requirements, preferences, needs and skills of all potential users of a product, service or environment from the very beginning of the design stage and, therefore, makes it available for all users at virtually no additional costs or delay (Weber 2006). While design for all comes to its limits when designing physical goods, the combination of a multifunctional and high-performance device with powerful software and a wider palette of interaction schemes make ICT an ideal platform that can interface with the user in any imaginable way. The ICT market currently seems to be a highly volatile, dynamic and innovative arena for testing new types of devices, new interaction paradigms and new areas into which ICT could further permeate.

It is in this context that some of these technologies empower vulnerable groups and provide them with equal or at least comparable opportunities. These opportunities might touch upon participation in working life, might relate to access to information and education or might provide those with a voice who had no platform so far to speak out or to be heard. To some extent, ICT is increasingly forming an environment, an ICT-based extension of the real-world society. This environment allows the participation in work, leisure or educational activities, even if participation via traditional means is difficult or even impossible. Developments in ICT already delivered solutions serving certain groups of users and empowered them for an improved participation in the society. However, as there seems to be no 'big plan' or common strategy behind these developments that particularly focuses on these groups at risk, there is at least hope that exactly this speed of innovation and the vast amount of new products and services thrown to the markets might bring up – by coincidence – solutions for them as well, as a kind of desirable side effect.

11.2.2 Empowered by Design

A statement of Caplan (1992) defined disability as the inability to accommodate to the world as it is currently designed. Vanderheiden (1997) paraphrased this – under the impression of new perspectives, ICT adds to the concept of design for all/universal design – by defining disability as the inability to accommodate poor design. While for centuries it was taken for granted that a medical cause is the reason for a disadvantage a person with disability is facing, Vanderheiden questions this. While the agreement still holds that a mismatch between individuals and the environment is the origin of a disadvantage, now the appropriate (re-)design of the environment moves into the centre of attention.

A simple example shows the change of mind set and its implications. With the availability of personal computers in offices, new job opportunities for blind people suddenly arose. Before that time, blind people were restricted to work in few vocations only (e.g. in switchboards). But with text-based computers and operating systems, and with alternative output devices, their inability to read visual displayed information from a screen became irrelevant. For example, text written on a computer screen could be read aloud by a synthetic speech output or sent to a Braille output made up of up to six embossed dots per character to be sensed by the user's fingers. Suddenly, the handicapping factor in that particular context was removed, although employees were still blind and still had to face disadvantages outside the work environment. Proper design of the work environment and the tools to be used completely eliminated the impact of a medical cause. (It is an irony of computer history that the further invention and quick spread of graphic-based operating systems later on created again an insurmountable barrier for blind people, and it took many years for software companies and quite some political pressure to ensure a similar level of accessibility to these new operating systems again.)

Examples can be found in any other area as well. Mobility restrictions that prevented a user to go where information is available (e.g. to a library) can be compensated by the mobility of information and communication (e.g. by having access to an electronic library). Sensory restrictions (e.g. blindness, deafness) can be bypassed by the provision of redundant information on alternative sensory channels. For example, deaf users can access audio information in a visual format as well, if sign language videos are provided or videos have captions. Specific aids like hearing aids or glasses are taken for granted, but computers and mobile devices are even more powerful and will eventually become an equally self-evident assistant for all populations.

While for sure this basic idea of design-induced empowerment does not work for all types of disabilities, it puts the focus on a long-neglected aspect of what constitutes good design. The strategies to deal with a mismatch between people and products/services/environments in the past have been often to try changing the individual (e.g. by training) or to bridge the gap with suitable assistive technologies (e.g. hearing aids or communicators). But with ICT, for the first time, technologies are within reach to customise and suit shared environments to the individual needs, abilities and limitations of all its potential users, to finally implement the vision of design for all (Weber 2003).

11.2.3 Design for Really All?

The outlook provided in this chapter on the role of ICT and the acceleration in the development of it was a positive one so far, but was it too optimistic? A design for all, implemented via ICT, is still a vision. Yet, the percentage of citizens being able to use ICT has grown continuously. In this section a specific case will be discussed, as a template and example for other groups of citizens not yet fully enjoying access to ICT and its services. It highlights the potential but also the accompanying measures that are required to fully exploit the benefits of ICT access for groups at risk of exclusion.

The case is about people with learning disabilities who are currently rarely benefitting from ICT. As there is no internationally agreed disability terminology available, and national definitions are often broad and not well defined, no statistically comparable data can be used to determine the size of this target group. The group comprises of people with learning/cognitive disabilities (IQ lower than 70) including people with autism or deaf and blind people with cognitive problems, yet without people who are mentally ill. Members of this group are usually able to communicate by spoken language, but their cognitive ability such as attention, cognition, perception, conclusion, memory, abstraction or logic is limited by the disability. Using the World Health Organization's ICD-10 terminology, the target group consists of people with moderate and mild mental retardation.

A multiplicity of research projects and initiatives has focused on accessibility of ICT for people with disabilities in the previous 15–20 years. In Europe, the Telematics Applications Programme as part of the 4th Framework Programme (1994–1998) included the 'Technology/Telematics for the Integration of Disabled and Elderly people' initiative. Later, accessibility and the inclusion of the requirements of people with disabilities in ICT research and development projects were highlighted as obligatory for all projects to be funded. Yet, the number of research projects and resulting design guidelines for people with learning disabilities is minimal, compared to the prevalence of learning disabilities in society.

While some of these few projects still wonder if – and how – people with learning disabilities will be able to operate ICT, reality already answered this question. Young people with learning disabilities aged between 11 and 23 years were asked about their experiences with ICT (Weber and Edler 2010). More than 60 % reported to have a computer at home, and more than 56 % have Internet access as well. Accordingly, the interviewees scored their own IT experience above average (3.5 on a scale from 1 'not at all' to 5 'very good'). Being asked of how often per week they go online, the participants responded with 3.2 times per week in average. Preferred activities online were: watching videos (65 %), listening to music (53 %), gaming (47 %), chatting (29 %), writing/reading e-mails (29 %), reading (18 %) and searching for photos (15 %). Additionally, parents report that they consider the mobile phone the biggest step forward in ICT to assist their children with learning disabilities. These phones provide a 'hotline' to the parents whenever and wherever the child needs support, or whenever the parents need to get in touch with their children. The improved usability of the phones, their wide functional spectrum (e.g. video calls, picture taking, picture-based call initiation) and the social status that comes together with using mobile/smartphones have improved people's independence and self-confidence without surrender of back-up in need of help and support.

In a survey to explore the potentials of ICT use in vocational education and training (VET) of young people with disabilities, VET staff from 28 sheltered workshops for people with disabilities in Germany provided feedback. Numerous application examples have been developed and proposed by the respondents, and it is a surprise that hardly any project deals with these exciting ideas. Areas that are considered relevant for ICT use are, for instance, to recall and work with training contents, to repeat lessons anytime and anywhere, to enquire databases, to contact colleagues, to connect to other ICT systems, to plan and structure work processes and many other ideas.

While this again sounds very positive, a further examination shows issues not properly dealt with yet. Most of the young people have not been taught to use computers or the Internet; they rather learnt it by themselves or by peers. This highlights the potential of this target group, but it indicates shortcomings of teaching young people (with and without disabilities) at home, at school or at institutions the skills required in manoeuvring safely in a knowledge-based society. The survey among institutions also provided another statement on an aggregated level. How is it possible that some institutions have a very positive yet critical outlook on the potential use of properly designed ICT, while others at the same time are strong opponents of this and emphasise all potential risks while ignoring potential opportunities? To what extent do ICT skills, experiences, preferences or worries of individual staff in these institutions determine if complete groups of young people with disabilities are granted access to ICT or not? Taking into consideration that the institutions involved in that survey are responsible for providing vocational education and training to +10,000 people with disabilities, the magnitude of this impact is considerable.

Teachers or carers who are not willing to update their skills and knowledge in ICT, parents who are underestimating the abilities of their children and who are acting overprotective and a research and industry environment in which this target group is considered irrelevant and is invisible at all are elements of a setting in which still quite some progress is needed. However, if the acceleration of ICT developments brings up opportunities for this and other vulnerable groups to uncover their unknown potentials, then this should be considered a strong side of acceleration as well.

11.3 Summary

Acceleration in ICT development creates chances and problems, specifically for vulnerable populations. Especially mobile devices triggered the opportunity – and illustrated the necessity – to finally break the chains of the desktop metaphor that was constricting innovation for too long. Since then, a kind of gold rush fever is fuelling a permanent flow of innovative products and approaches. With these smartphones, smart glasses, wearables or 'invisible' devices seamlessly integrated into the environment, ICT developers test out innovative interaction techniques and hardware and software designs in new contexts of use. This can be seen as an experimental setting in which those products that succeed 'in the field' will be further developed. But succeeding does not necessarily go together with certain quality criteria like accessibility or usability. Both criteria, however, are preconditions for certain vulnerable populations to benefit from the services provided via ICT. But at times of high throughput on the ICT market and not-yet established standards for interfaces and interaction, this trial-and-error approach (coincidentally?) produces also exciting applications that specifically support or empower these vulnerable groups.

The challenges are twofold. On the one hand, it is necessary to identify those applications and appliances that have an added value for vulnerable groups and to understand and make available its innovation and approach for future software and hardware designs. And on the other hand, the prevailing practice of ex post, i.e. reactive approaches in software and hardware design, needs to be shifted to a more systematic, proactive approach as promoted by the concept of design for all in order to address the needs of all users in early stages of the design of new products and services.

References

BITKOM. (2012). *ITK-Markt international, 2012*. http://www.bitkom.org/de/markt_statistik/64013.aspx. Accessed 8 Aug 2012.

Caplan, R. (1992). Disabled by design. *Interior Design, 63*, 88–91.

Empirica. (2006). *Benchmarking access and use of ICT in European schools 2006*. Final report from head teacher and classroom teacher surveys in 27 European countries. http://europa.eu.int/information_society/eeurope/i2010/docs/studies/final_report_3.pdf. Accessed 8 Aug 2012.

European Agency for Development in Special Needs Education. (2010). *Special needs education country data 2010*. Odense: European Agency for Development in Special Needs Education.

European Agency for Development in Special Needs Education and UNESCO IITE. (2011). *ICTs in education for people with disabilities – Review of innovative practice. Practice review – Executive summary*. Odense: European Agency for Development in Special Needs Education.

Greve, J., & Weber, H. (2002). Bridging the information gap between IST and SEN – A practical approach on European level. In K. Miesenberger, J. Klaus, & W. Zagler (Eds.), *Computers helping people with special needs*. Eighth international conference, ICCHP 2002 (pp. 115–116). Heidelberg: Springer.

Greve, J., Soriano, V., & Weber, H. (2003). Providing ICT/IST professionals with access to resources in Special Educational Needs (SEN) and vice versa – A European network approach. In C. Stephanidis (Ed.), *Universal access in HCI – Inclusive design in the information society* (pp. 1103–1107). London: Chapman and Hall.

OECD. (2011). *PISA 2009 results. Students on line: Digital technologies and performance* (Vol. VI). Paris: OECD Publishing.

Proctor, R. W., Vu, K.-P. L., Salvendy, G., Degen, H., Fang, X., Flach, J. M., Gott, S. P., Herrmann, D., Krömker, H., Lightner, N. J., Reeves, L., Rudorfer, A., Stanney, K., Stephanidis, C., Strybel, T. Z., Vaughan, M., Wang, H., Weber, H., Yang, Y., & Zhu, W. (2002). Content preparation and management for web design: Eliciting, structuring, searching and displaying information. *International Journal of Human-Computer Interaction, 14*(1), 25–92.

Seeman, L. (2002). *Inclusion of cognitive disabilities in the web accessibility movement*. WWW2002 Alternate Paper Tracks Proceedings. http://www2002.org/CDROM/alternate/689/index.html. Accessed 8 Aug 2012.

Statistisches Bundesamt. (2009). *Informationsgesellschaft in Deutschland*. Wiesbaden: Statistisches Bundesamt.

Statistisches Bundesamt. (2011). *Informationsgesellschaft*. https://www.destatis.de/DE/ZahlenFakten/GesellschaftStaat/EinkommenKonsumLebensbedingungen/_Grafik/IKTNutzung.html. Accessed 8 Aug 2012.

Vanderheiden, G. C. (1997). Design for people with functional limitations resulting from disability, aging or circumstance. In G. Salvendy (Ed.), *Handbook of human factors and ergonomics* (pp. 2010–2052). New York: Wiley.

Watkins, A., & Weber, H. (2002). National information and communication technology policies – Their impact upon the use of ICT in Special Needs Education (SNE). In K. Miesenberger, J. Klaus, & W. Zagler (Eds.), *Computers helping people with special needs* (pp. 68–75). Heidelberg: Springer.

Weber, H. (2003). A draft roadmap to improve the current definition of accessibility. In H. Luczak & K. J. Zink (Eds.), *Human factors in organizational design and management – VII* (pp. 425–428). Santa Monica: IEA Press.

Weber, H. (2006). Providing access to the internet for people with disabilities. Short and medium term research demands. *Theoretical Issues in Ergonomics Science, 5*, 491–498.

Weber, H., & Edler, C. (2010). Supporting the web experience of young people with learning disabilities. In K. Miesenberger, J. Klaus, W. L. Zagler, & A. I. Karshmer (Eds.), *ICCHP 2010*. Proceedings Part I, LNCS 6179 (pp. 649–656). Berlin: Springer.

Weber, H., & Stephanidis, C. (2001). Enabling universal access – Minimum requirements for content preparation. In M. J. Smith, G. Salvendy, D. Harris, & R. J. Koubek (Eds.), *Usability evaluation and interface design. Cognitive engineering, intelligent agents and virtual reality* (pp. 1390–1393). Mahwah: Lawrence Erlbaum Associates.

World Wide Web Consortium. (1999). *Web content accessibility guidelines 1.0. W3C recommendation*. Web Accessibility Initiative (WAI). http://www.w3.org/TR/WCAG10/. Accessed 8 Aug 2012.

Chapter 12
Beyond the Optimal Flow: Pause, Detachment, Serendipity, and Action

Sebastiano Bagnara, Simone Pozzi, and Patrizia Marti

12.1 Introduction

In one of the scenes of the movie *The Social Network* (about the story of Facebook's founder), we see a young software coder, completely immersed in his programming task. He is absorbed by the computer screen, with an almost physical connection through the headset cable. Two other characters are on stage, with one of the two telling the second not to bother the programmer because "he's wired in."

This scene is a nice and clear representation of one the most popular notions in the human-computer interaction (HCI) field that is the notion of the *optimal flow*. The term has been initially introduced by Csikszentmihalyi (1990) and then made widely popular by the works of Don Norman (1993), to describe the state of full engagement that we sometimes experience while interacting with technologies. Our actions stay on the flow, neither too slow nor too quick, and so is the task demand, which remains challenging without becoming too hard and frustrating. According to Norman, when we experience the optimal flow, our attention stays focused and we remain completely immerged in our tasks. The external world and its other stimuli disappear and we live only for what we are doing at the present moment

S. Bagnara
Faculty of Architecture, University of Sassari-Alghero, Alghero, Italy

Institute of Cognitive Sciences and Technologies, National Research Council, Rome, Italy
e-mail: sebastiano.bagnara@gmail.com

S. Pozzi (✉)
Faculty of Architecture, University of Sassari-Alghero, Alghero, Italy

Deep Blue Research and Consultancy, Rome, Italy
e-mail: Simone.pozzi@gmail.com

P. Marti
Department of Communication Science, University of Siena, Siena, Italy

Eindhoven Technical University, Eindhoven, The Netherlands
e-mail: patrizia.marti@unisi.it

C. Korunka and P. Hoonakker (eds.), *The Impact of ICT on Quality of Working Life*,
DOI 10.1007/978-94-017-8854-0_12,

(i.e., our task). The optimal flow is an intense, pleasing, and productive state, one that suits both the workplace and also the free time.

Designing for the optimal flow has almost become a goal in itself, one of the primary goals to pursue in HCI. An immersive experience is often considered an attribute of successful design products, with the user so connected to the product that she/he desires to interact with it as long as possible, with no interruptions. Yet, the popularity of the notion seems to be diminishing. If we search "optimal flow" in the books published in the last 20 years (by means of Google Books Ngram), there is a peak of citations around the mid-1990s and then a slow, but continuous, descent till today.

Many researchers and practitioners start proposing design goals and frameworks that do not fit well with the optimal flow and sometimes are even in open contradiction with it. For instance, Danzico (2010a) speaks of the importance of pauses and transition moments, while Fullerton (2010) advocates the need of designing for solitude. These are just two instances, but they are, in our opinion, clear indications that some HCI researchers and practitioners have moved their focus from immersive interactions to the design of moments of reflection, to what we may name the *design for reflection.*

In the rest of this contribution, we will discuss a strand of human-computer interaction approaches concerned with the idea that design should foster reflective thinking.

12.2 Some (Tacit) Assumptions About the User

The way the user is conceived in the design for the optimal flow has some peculiarities that deserve a full analysis. First of all, her/his well-being passes through a complete coupling with a technological tool. It is as if we were tacitly assuming that a rewarding experience happens whenever the whole person is reduced to one or few aspects, those aspects that can be "wired in" a technological tool and those aspects that can be fulfilled by performing a task at our maximum potential.

This is more the description of a workaholic (or of a hacker), someone who is fully motivated by her/his work, who does not experience fatigue or boredom, and stays absorbed in her/his task.

We are probably rendering an oversimplified description of what the optimal flow proponents consider as being their users. Still, few in this area have ever questioned the possibility that a radical interpretation of the optimal flow might lead to a simplistic model of users. Among them, Don Norman has complemented the idea of optimal flow with the one of emotional design, to address also other aspects of human life (Norman 2004). Most of the practitioners seem instead to assume that good designs remove all the interaction obstacles, smooth the human-computer interaction to the point where users can engage in the optimal flow. Traditional usability approaches aim for maximum efficiency and efficacy; user experience approaches include aesthetic aspects and amusement, but all of them do not really question the key design objective: to optimize the human-machine fit or to maximize the user performance by minimizing her/his cognitive load.

12.3 The Risks of Optimal Flow

The aim of this contribution is not to question the relevance of the optimal flow notion for successful design. Many technological tools are today designed with the goal of supporting the optimal flow, and they indeed succeed in doing that for our pleasure and benefit. Our aim is to discuss whether there is more than optimal flow to design for and to show some of the drawbacks of such a conception.

Just like any other design approach, the optimal flow implies design choices and the primacy of some design directions over others. This section will review some of the tensions that these design choices cannot resolve or have exacerbated. We will briefly outline only some of the most relevant tensions, without any pretense of completeness or depth of analysis.

12.3.1 Everything that Matters Is Happening Today

The mission of Google (one of the companies that best represents the last 10 years of technological developments) is to organize the world information and make it easily, universally and instantaneously available and accessible. This mission is particularly relevant in the age of information deluge, where we are constantly running the risk of information overload and we need to keep scanning the available information to make sure we are not missing the important pieces.

However, there is a drawback to this overabundance. Most of the information we gather and process will become old in a very brief period of time, no matter what its value is, it will decay very quickly in a short time. For instance, we keep learning new software and Internet applications, only to discover that a new version has been released. We learn new skills and interaction modes, but we cannot rely on them. What we have learned yesterday is already old, and will not serve to any purpose tomorrow. Our skills do not add up, we have no time (nor incentive) to master and deeply appropriate them. Instead, they require constant upgrade and revision.

The pace of innovation is so high that our memory runs the risk of becoming a burden. We need to forget in order to effectively learn, in order not to be constrained by the old habits. We are facing the paradoxical situation where we need to voluntarily "erase" skills and competences on which we invested time and efforts (Bagnara et al. 2009). We need to forget in order to achieve the optimal flow with the new technologies, in order to be able to quickly learn new skills.

Our memory lives in a fast moving present, where technologies do not give us any indication to consciously choose what to remember and what to forget (Bannon 2006).

12.3.2 Is Multitasking Making Us Stupid?

The overabundance of information stimulates skills such as multitasking or the capability to cope with continuous interruptions. We need to be able to quickly move from one information flow to the next one, so quickly that we are almost paying attention to two or three flows at the same time. It is the skill of *parallel thinking* that becomes fundamental to engage in multiple tasks, to carry out several different projects with different audiences and teams. Not a new skill but one on which we are more and more relying to cope with the current technological scenario.

The drawback in this case is the loss of reflective thinking, of the capability to engage in complex speculations, to stay focused on only one specific topic. In one famous essay, Carr (2008) describes a scenario in which we all engage only in superficial reading, far from the concentration required to read an old-fashioned book, much more similar to "a form of skimming activity, hopping from one source to another."

Carr mentions some selected studies to support his argument but admits that there is no scientific long-term proof of such changes. Still, for the sake of this contribution, it should not appear too much controversial to state that if we design technologies to support "skimming behaviors," we are likely to penalize more linear ways of reading and to offer cues (to skim and hop) that are likely to disrupt the old-fashioned reading rhythm.

12.3.3 Too Many Weak Ties

The Internet has made the creation of virtual community an easy endeavor. New communities keep being born and new social networks aggregate large numbers of users.

But most of these communities are short lived and tend to dissolve in few years. These communities are based on the idea that being connected is what constitutes a community, without any other form of stronger bonds. There is little (or no) emotional elaboration in such communities, most of the communication acts actually communicate little else than the contact itself. The *like/dislike* function on Facebook is a good example of the primacy of the contact function on the communication contents. Likewise, we may mention the short format (on average) of Facebook posts. Few persons are going to invest time and resources in long posts, when they know their post will disappear from their friends' main page after few hours.

For these reasons, community members find it easy to leave a community. They have not made any real investment in it, so the *opt-out* costs are low. And they can afford to move to another community.

The consequences on the psychological life in those communities are too complex to be discussed here, but it is worth mentioning how such dynamics also impact on the self-perception of our bodies. According to Sherry Turkle (2011), being immerged in a continuous flow of interaction with new technologies causes our bodies to almost disappear. The optimal flow is so engaging that we forget our bodily matter, we are wholly absorbed by the computer interface to the point that we forget that our self also resides in our body and not only in our computer-mediated interactions.

12.4 The Digital Wisdom and Slow Technologies

The tensions we have briefly discussed in the preceding section are becoming more and more a matter of concern in the HCI community. It is probably for this reason that the last years have seen the growth of research directions that critically questioned the relationship between humans and machines. These researchers are advocating a less frantic interaction with technologies, more concerned with the quality of our life than with productivity.

Since the end of the 1990s, human-computer interaction has been extending its traditional focus from the design of efficient, effective, and satisfactory tools (ISO 9241-11 1998; Nielsen 1993) to encompassing a wider range of attributes, most of these less oriented towards a specific goal but more oriented to designing tools that "simply" stir positive emotions and feelings in the user. This approach is named user experience and may include a clear emphasis on fun, creativity, motivation, aesthetic pleasure, engagement, and so on (Blythe et al. 2003; McCarthy and Wright 2004; Norman 2004).

The hallmark of these approaches is that the quality of human-computer interaction cannot be evaluated by simply considering whether a goal is achieved but should also consider less objective criteria, the so-called "nonfunctional" or "soft" ones. Such a shift has an impact on the design goals, rather than aiming for "a fast paced, at-the-moment, connected life" (Cheng et al. 2011), the designer should now consider designing "slow technologies."

Slow technologies are defined as technologies that favor reflection, aesthetic, and ludic aspects, over functionality and absence of obstacles in the interaction:

> Slow technology is technology that is slow in various degrees [...] What is important to note here is that the distinction between fast and slow technology is not a distinction in terms of time perception; it is a metaphorical distinction that has to do with time presence. When we use a thing as an efficient tool, time disappears, i.e. we get things done. Accepting

> an invitation for reflection inherent in the design means on the other hand that time will appear, i.e. we open up for time presence. (Hallnäs and Redström 2001)

Slow technologies do not aim to improve the productivity by making the user more efficient or by focusing on one specific goal. Rather, their aim is to improve the user experience by strengthening all the aspects that are usually left out by the optimal flow approach.

12.4.1 The Digital Wisdom

A complementary discussion has also developed outside the HCI academic community. For instance, in a recent article, Premsky (2009) notes how technology does not only make us smarter, but it can also make us wiser. The digital sapiens accepts the symbiosis with technology as an integral fact of human existence. She/he also uses technology wisely, to better her/his decisions or to enhance innate abilities. Digital wisdom transcends the generational boundary between digital natives and digital immigrants; it is more about the attitude with which we interact with technologies.

Digital wisdom may be seen as a natural reaction to the information overload of the Web era. In order to cope with the massive amount of fragmented information, the user has to develop an effective means of filtering. This is exactly what Premsky defines as one of the aspects of wisdom, i.e., "the capability of knowing what is important," or sound judgment.

One example is the use of news aggregators, to filter and select among the continuous flow of updates. For instance, applications like News360 or Pulse take the contents from selected Web sites on the basis of some user-selected categories and put together a filtered newspaper, where only the most relevant articles are shown to the user. In a similar manner, Flipboard orders the chaotic and highly dynamic world of Twitter into a nicely edited review of news that can be skimmed by the user until she/he finds something worth reading. All these applications have in common two of the key features of wisdom: they filter and support the selection of what is most important.

A complementary scenario is described by Anderson in a recent article published by Wired (Anderson and Wolff 2010). Chris Anderson made the point that the World Wide Web, as we have known it, is dead. The Internet on the contrary, is very much alive, according to him. The distinction made by Anderson is between the Web – as a library of pages to be explored, browsed, and read – and the Internet as a medium to deliver services, like peer-to-peer exchange, or streaming of multimedia contents.

The tangible evidence of such a transition lies in the percentage of bandwidth used to browse the Web (and to search for Web pages), compared to the percentage used by Internet-based services and applications. Around year 2000, Web browsing was using more than 50 % of the total bandwidth. This percentage is now slightly above 20 %. Video and peer-to-peer were around 25 % in year 2000, while now they add up to 75 %. All of that, while the total bandwidth kept expanding.

Anderson sees in this dynamic the transition from the open Web to an Internet of closed gardens, to the use of lean and simple services (i.e., the smartphone apps) which are "less about the searching and more about the getting" (Anderson and Wolff 2010). It is the Internet of walled gardens and well-known and well-protected places in which the user dwells for a while before moving to the next one. Internet is mainly the medium to deliver these services, with no connection left to the founding idea of the World Wide Web as a library of pages to be read.

From the user's perspective, the interaction behavior changes drastically. The Web required a high degree of interaction, each search was a finely crafted piece of strategy, by which fragmented pieces of information were put together. Nowadays, Internet services and apps do not require such a level of active interaction. They are becoming more similar to the lean back attitude of the old-fashioned TV public. Users select a service, or some contents, and then quietly enjoy it. In those cases where we still search for something, Google usually brings us directly to the walled garden of our choice, with no occasion (or very few) for exploration and link browsing.

The user is no longer exploring the open and interconnected Web; she/he is rather moving from one known place to another – the so-called walled (or closed) gardens. For instance, YouTube had recently added channels to its home page, thus complementing the active search modality – by which users view short fragments one after the other, actively deciding what to view next – with a more passive TV mode. The user selects a channel and then leans back to enjoy the preselection of contents. The user can also customize the channel lists, thus preselecting her/his favorite walled gardens. A similar shift was already implicit in the less recent introduction of YouTube music playlists, to stream music continuously without active user intervention, but the channels mark a more radical change of direction towards the analogy of the walled gardens.

12.5 Designing for Reflection

The discipline of HCI has played a major role in shaping the Web world, by making it more user-friendly, engaging, and accessible. It suffices to mention the popularity and wide impact of Jakob Nielsen's usability heuristics (Nielsen 1999). However, the right time might have arrived to critically examine if HCI is properly equipped to support the whole variety of human activities, including those that required focused attention and reflection. It is probably less a matter of having the right methods and techniques available than a need to critically revise some assumptions and move in directions not yet fully explored till now.

The last part of our contribution will present four design directions that may be worthwhile pursuing:

- Design for pauses
- Design for detachment
- Design for serendipity
- Design for action

The underlying idea is that the best way to support reflective thinking is to design spaces and moments where reflection can take place without being constrained by the rhythm of some external "flow" (of experience, of events, of inputs, etc.). These spaces should offer the user the opportunity to "leave the flow" of continuous interaction with technology. Moreover, these spaces should offer action possibilities, since reflection on action is a fundamental source of knowledge.

12.5.1 Design for Pauses

The dialectic interplay of experiential cognition and reflective cognition is a hallmark of human cognition. The issue has been discussed by Norman (1993) but also in the seminal book by Winograd and Flores (1986).

Winograd and Flores analyzed the concept of *breakdown* that is moments where the human-technology interaction does not flow smoothly and the user has to stop and engage in a problem solving activity. Breakdowns were traditionally seen as something to be avoided, being disruptive of the current activity. The authors suggest instead that these moments also play a fundamental role in human cognition, by making it possible for technology to emerge as a thing in itself and not only as a transparent medium. The tool becomes *impossible to use* during a breakdown, thus bringing the user attention on the tool itself and fostering an enhanced understanding of the tool characteristics and of its principles of functioning.

A first design direction might be to explore the means by which "breakdown moments" can be recreated, of course without any actual breakdown. In other words, tools should be able to attract the user's attention on their characteristics before breakdowns occur; they should be able to activate the enhanced understanding triggered by breakdowns as a design feature, not as a side effect of bad functioning.

In this respect, a desirable characteristic of breakdowns that should be recreated is when the user distances herself/himself from the flow of activity, looking at it from a different perspective and restructuring her/his perception of the normal tool functioning. Breakdowns open a space suitable for reasoning, a space that often leads to innovation, as summarized in Petroski's motto "Form follows failure" (Petroski 1994). When confronted with a breakdown, humans try to devise a second (often better) solution. A reflective tool should be able to trigger such an innovation mechanism without relying on actual failure.

Following this line of reasoning, pauses should not be regarded as something to be avoided but as moments where reflective reasoning can more effectively take place. They make it possible for the user to rest and recover from the fatigue of a continuous interaction, and, more importantly, they also offer the possibility to shift our mode of behavior from the experiential one to the reflective mode (Danzico 2010a).

One example is the *debriefing* carried out by aircraft pilots before and after a flight or in flight to prepare for high peak and high demand flight phases (e.g., landing). It is a moment of pause, where the crew prepares itself for the performance moment, when distance is sought from the flow of events to mark a change of rhythm and intensity. Or it may be a transition out of the performance phase, where a collective reflection is carried out to analyze what went well and what could be improved. Debriefings serve a variety of purposes (depending on the domain and on the moment when they are carried out), but it is safe to say that they are characterized by a *problem setting* attitude, as opposed to the *problem solving* one. Problems are redefined during debriefings, which are moments dedicated to reframing the usual into a new form. New problems may also emerge, ones that were not identified before.

Designing for pauses may also imply designing for solitude (Fullerton 2010). Not solitude as a dysfunctional separation from the others (like Robert De Niro in *Taxi Driver*), but solitude as a solid barrier against distraction (Berman et al. 2008) (like Martin Heidegger walking in the woods).

Solitude may be a precondition to avoid continuous interruptions or the constant contact without content that sometimes characterizes Web communities. To enable reflective thinking, pauses may not be enough and physical detachment may also be necessary.

12.5.2 Design for Detachment

There is another way of leaving the flow of activity to reach a space for reflection. It is the one enabled by the change of perspective, by detachment in order to see the problem (or the activity) under a different light.

The example that is currently most prominent is the growing field of *visual analytics*, that the visual representation of huge data sets (*The Economist* 2010). The information deluge has created the need for tools that help graphically summarize complex data sets, in order to enable analysis and comparison without getting lost in infinite minute details.

In this case, turning information into knowledge requires stepping outside the flow of details, to focus on the level of emerging patterns and find the correct interpretation. Knowledge cannot be achieved without detachment, without distancing the interpretation from single events. *Visual analytics* demonstrate how experiential and reflective design can be fruitfully combined. Software tools like *Gapminder* simplify the elaboration of data to make it more experiential, but only in order to then trigger reflection on the emerging patterns.

Another example is the *Change Laboratory* method, developed by Engeström and colleagues (Engeström et al. 1996). The *Change Laboratory* invites workers to use categories derived from the Scandinavian activity theory (Nardi 1996) (i.e., subject, object, tool, rule, division of labor, and community) to reframe everyday working life in abstract categories. The goal is to solve workplace issues by using theory as a form of detachment. For instance, participants are invited to frame problems as *tensions* between the basic six categories: tools may be unfit for the current goals, current rules may be ambiguous or far from reality, and so forth. These tensions cannot be solved if faced directly, while participants find it easier to deal with them by addressing from the meta-level of theory. On this level, most tensions can be solved by referring to common organizational goals.

Videogames also provide some examples of detachment to support reflective thinking. Most *Nintendo Wii* games have been designed to maximize the optimal flow experience. However, other games demand users to increase their self-perception, for instance, to control their body posture while playing a sport (e.g., yoga practice or skiing). *Microsoft* has also delivered a console that can be controlled by body movements and gestures, named *Kinect*. In this case some games are based on the idea of acting (or mimesis), for instance, by playing the part of an animal, moving one's own body, and seeing the animal's body move.

In all these games, the user can rely on the game consoles to operate a form of detachment, to see one's self as in a mirror, thus making it possible to engage in reflective thinking and restructure her/his behavior.

12.5.3 Design for Serendipity

Danzico (2010b) notes how the strict compliance to design guidelines as "less is more" may bring about an unintended drawback: "People may be less exposed to chance or less inclined to try new things; behavior may be planned such that there are no discoveries or surprises. Technology may be increasing the opportunity for specificity, but is it decreasing our chances for serendipity?" By leaving out what is not directly related to the end goal, designers are also diminishing the space for fortuitous discoveries. The tourist armed with her/his smartphone will go straight to her/his hotel but will never stumble upon something unexpected.

The use of serendipity to support creative thinking has deep roots. During the Enlightenment, many authors used to take notes of noticeable quotes, seminal ideas, reflections, or book excerpts, by means of a *commonplace book*. John Locke had even devised a tagging method to make it possible to find notes at a later time, while at the same time leaving them unsorted and mixed. By reading the *commonplace book* after some time, the author was likely to see new connections among all these unsorted thoughts, by reading one note after the other, in an order different than the one in which these had been written.

The *commonplace book* was a loosely organized collector of thoughts, designed to keep together notes but at the same time leaving space for serendipitous connections. By reading the *commonplace book*, the authors could reflect on their own past thoughts and also profit from the mix between order and disorder to trigger new ideas.

As with the other directions we have discussed, serendipity rests on the optimal balance between two polarities: *randomness* and *order*. It is not *all* or *nothing*, *experiential* or *reflective*, or total randomness. We maintain that HCI should pursue this balance by considering both instances, by supporting the users on both dimensions, without reducing human experience to just one dimension. Web services like *Dopplr* or *Hitotoki* combine both goal-directed features (like restaurant recommendations or hints about a new city) with other ones that support serendipity. *Hitotoki* asks users to post online photographs of off-the-beaten-tracks places, to take photos while moving from one famous monument to the next one. *Hitotoki* aims to build maps of serendipity, maps that reflect the unexpected discoveries made by its users. It asks tourists to avoid being enmeshed in the optimal flow, in order to stay detached and find those details often overlooked.

12.5.4 Design for Action

Design is both an active and reflective process. We design by making but also reflect by doing and experimenting with products. This confluence of experiences (action) and thought (reflection) combines to create new knowledge. Both action and reflection are essential ingredients in the construction of meaning.

Donald Schön is one of the first who introduced the idea of design as a reflective practice. He considered the act of reflecting on action as a way to enable designers to develop a useful repertoire of ideas and concepts to be used in future projects (Schön 1983).

On a similar perspective, Bruce Archer (1995) defines research through design as a "systematic enquiry conducted through the medium of practical action, calculated to generate or test new, or newly imported, information, ideas, forms or procedures and to generate communicable knowledge" (p. 15). This kind of research must be knowledge directed, that is, it must produce new knowledge through testing and concretely acting in the context of application. Furthermore, it must be systematic and situation specific, that is, it must be pursued through action in and on the real world, in all its complexity.

This approach is inspired by the phenomenological tradition of considering human action and perception as situated in the world and not abstracted from it (Merleau-Ponty 1962). Social facts emerge from acting in the world and therefore are properties of interactions.

What phenomenology has explored is the relationship between embodied action and meaning. This means that meaning is not a collection of abstract, idealized entities; instead it is to be found in the world in which we act and which acts upon us. It is only through action, and the possibility for action that the world affords us, that we can come to find and make sense of the world, in both its physical and social manifestations.

Over the last 10 years, research in HCI and interaction design has put emphasis on the concepts of action, embodiment, and the fundamental role the physical body plays in shaping our experience and understanding of computation in the world we live in (Dourish 2001). Designers have learned how to develop prototypes that afford embodied interaction to stimulate reflection.

Let's take as an example the AEI lamp designed by Philip Ross (Ross and Wensveen 2010). The lamp is sensitive to touch and to the way people touch it caressingly or not so caressingly. The lamp behaves to be supportive directing the light as expected, but sometimes it needs help. It has to be encouraged and stroked to direct or diffuse its light. One might wonder why to develop a lamp that does not do what it is expected to do. Philip Ross created the lamp to reflect upon values. The lamp is a physical hypothesis that affords action and reflection through the action possibilities offered by the product itself (Overbeeke 2007).

The problem with many electronic devices is that they are not open to our actions and therefore are not open for reflection.

12.6 Concluding Remarks

In the recent years, there has been a flourishing body of academic works increasingly focused on the idea that user-centered design should become person (or human) centered, thus encompassing the person as a whole, not only as a user. This may relate to sociocultural aspects (Harper et al. 2008; Kolko 2010), to serendipity or moments of pause (Danzico 2010a, b), or even to advocating for the design of solitude (Fullerton 2010). In a similar line, Norman has discussed the advantages of emotional approaches to design (Norman 2004), encompassing aspects like physical sensations or values and meanings we attach to products.

The underlying idea of all these works is that by reducing design to just the useful bits (i.e., those aimed at efficiency and efficacy, at achieving goals), we remove aspects that are the hallmark of being humans. When design focuses on what is strictly needed for one task, then the chances of serendipitous encounters, or of explorative behaviors, are very limited.

In our opinion, such emerging approach can be named "design for reflection." We maintain that serendipity, pauses, a certain degree of detachment, and a primary focus on the importance of action are all relevant features to engage in reflective thinking. Examples of the need for reflective thinking can be found in the current patterns of Web use (Anderson and Wolff 2010), where users are alternating a *lean forward* attitude (typical of the Internet of the 1990s) with the *lean back* attitude that marks less interactive media, like TV. This attitude change is coherent with Prensky's *homo sapiens digital* (2009), who shifts away from compulsive interaction modalities to a more balanced use of technology.

In order to orient human-computer interaction towards reflective thinking, we maintain that we should critically revise our implicit assumptions about our users, to address the needs and motivations of the whole person. We should shift from goal-oriented users to persons who pursue both experiences and reflections. The risk we are currently running is to break down the unity of a person into task-oriented fragments.

References

Anderson, C., & Wolff, M. (2010, September). The web is dead. Long live the internet. *Wired*. Retrieved from http://www.wired.com/magazine/2010/08/ff_webrip/

Archer, B. (1995). The nature of research. *CoDesign, 2*, 6–13.

Bagnara, S., Montanari, R., & Pozzi, S. (2009). Designing organisational oblivion. In C. Schlick (Ed.), *Industrial engineering and ergonomics. Visions, concepts, methods and tools* (pp. 233–242). Berlin: Springer.

Bannon, L. J. (2006). Forgetting as a feature, not a bug: The duality of memory and implications for ubiquitous computing. *CoDesign, 2*(1), 3–15.

Berman, M. G., Jonides, J., & Kaplan, S. (2008). The cognitive benefits of interacting with nature. *Psychological Science, 19*(2), 1207–1212.

Blythe, M. A., Overbeeke, K., Monk, A. F., & Wright, P. (Eds.). (2003). *Funology: From usability to enjoyment*. Dordrecht: Kluwer Academic Publishers.

Carr, N. (2008, July–August). Is Google making us stupid? *The Atlantic*, 1–10.

Cheng, J., Bapat, A., Thomas, G., Tse, K., Nawathe, N., Crockett, J., et al. (2011). *GoSlow: Designing for slowness, reflection and solitude*. Paper presented at the CHI 2011.

Csikszentmihalyi, M. (1990). *Flow: The psychology of optimal experience*. New York: Harper & Row.

Danzico, L. (2010a). Adding by leaving out: The power of the pause. *Interactions, 17*(4), 55–57.

Danzico, L. (2010b). The design of serendipity is not by chance. *Interactions, 17*(5), 16–18.

Dourish, P. (2001). *Where the action is: The foundations of embodied interaction*. Cambridge, MA: MIT Press.

Engeström, Y., Virkkunen, J., Helle, M., Pihlaja, J., & Poikela, R. (1996). Change laboratory as a tool for transforming work. *Lifelong Learning in Europe, 1*(2), 10–17.

Fullerton, B. (2010). Designing for solitude. *Interactions, 17*(6), 6–9.

Hallnäs, L., & Redström, J. (2001). Slow technology – Designing for reflection. *Personal and Ubiquitous Computing, 5*(3), 201–212.

Harper, R., Rodden, T., Rogers, Y., & Sellen, A. (Eds.). (2008). *Being human: Human-computer interaction in the year 2020*. Cambridge: Microsoft Research Ltd.

ISO 9241–11. (1998). *Ergonomic requirements for office work with visual display terminals (VDTs), Part 11: Guidance on usability*. Geneva: International Organization for Standardization.

Kolko, J. (2010). On experiences, people, and technology. *Interactions, 17*(6), 80.

McCarthy, J., & Wright, P. (2004). Technology as experience. *Interactions, 11*(5), 42–43.

Merleau-Ponty, M. (1962). *Phenomenology of perception*. London/New York: Routledge.

Nardi, B. A. (1996). *Context and consciousness: Activity theory and human-computer interaction*. Cambridge, MA: MIT Press.

Nielsen, J. (1993). *Usability engineering*. Amsterdam: Morgan Kaufmann.

Nielsen, J. (1999). *Designing web usability: The practice of simplicity*. Indianapolis: New Riders Publishing.

Norman, D. A. (1993). *Things that make us smart: Defending human attributes in the age of the machine*. Reading: Addison-Wesley Publishing Company.

Norman, D. A. (2004). *Emotional design: Why we love (or hate) everyday things*. New York: Basic Books.

Overbeeke, K. (2007). *The aesthetics of the impossible*. Communicatie Service Centrum TU/e.

Petroski, H. (1994). *The evolution of useful things* (2nd ed.). New York: Vintage Books.
Premsky, M. (2009). H. Sapiens Digital: From digital immigrants and digital natives to digital wisdom. *On the Horizon, 9*(5), 1–6.
Ross, P. R., & Wensveen, S. A. G. (2010). Designing aesthetics of behavior in interaction: Using aesthetic experience as a mechanism for design. *International Journal of Design, 4*(2), 3–13.
Schön, D. A. (1983). *The reflective practitioner: How professionals think in action.* London: Temple Smith.
The Economist. (2010, February 25). Data, data everywhere. 1–14.
Turkle, S. (2011). *Alone together: Why we expect more from technology and less from each other.* New York: Basic Books.
Winograd, T., & Flores, F. (1986). *Understanding computers and cognition: A new foundation for design.* Reading: Addison Wesley Publishing Company.

Chapter 13
The Future of ICT and Quality of Working Life: Challenges, Benefits, and Risks

Christian Korunka and Peter Hoonakker

The rapid development of ICT with all its diverse aspects is one of the most fascinating current topics in the world of work. No other recent societal, organizational, or technological change compares with the rapid and wide-reaching impact of these technologies. Any attempt to capture the complexity and wide-ranging aspect of these technologies is limited because it may result only in a selective and momentary picture. On the other hand, after about 30 years of extremely rapid development of ICT in the world of work, we have accumulated many experiences, and many scientific studies have been conducted. Thus, we may be able to capture at least some general trends in how these technologies are affecting the quality of our lives. We do think that the chapters and topics in this book provide an overview on such trends and developments from an international perspective.

The different chapters in this book show how far-reaching the effects of ICT on quality of working life can be. It has become quite obvious that these changes have a potential for a wide range of both positive and negative effects. We do not claim that the different perspectives presented in the book provide an exhaustive overview of the development and the role of ICT for quality of working life. But we think the selection of diverse topics shows at least a somewhat comprehensive and multilayered view of the possible effects of ICT.

First of all, many of the trends and developments as described in these chapters remind us how fast the spreading and development of ICT has been over the last about 30 years. Since the introduction of the first personal computers in the 1980s, we have seen a rapid development which includes the continuous and permanent development of ever "new" information technologies, the improvement of

C. Korunka (✉)
Faculty of Psychology, University of Vienna, Vienna, Austria
e-mail: christian.korunka@univie.ac.at

P. Hoonakker
Center for Quality and Productivity Improvement (CQPI), University of Wisconsin-Madison, Madison, WI, USA
e-mail: phoonakker@cqpi.engr.wisc.edu

C. Korunka and P. Hoonakker (eds.), *The Impact of ICT on Quality of Working Life*, DOI 10.1007/978-94-017-8854-0_13,

communication speed and quality, and the ever-increasing range and impact of these technologies (think, e.g., of the Arab "Twitter" revolutions). Many examples of these developments are described in the chapters of the book. The number of Internet users in 2012 (about 2.5 billion) is about 30 times as big as only 15 years before. There are more cell phones in use at this moment than people are living on this planet. And one of the more recent developments, social media, have changed the communication habits and communication styles of younger generations in developed and developing countries. The terms "digital natives" and "digital immigrants" are used to describe generational patterns in our societies with regard to their differences in ICT use. In nearly all workplaces in developed countries, ICT plays an important role. Most of our work cannot be performed without computers and ICT. If one refers to "social acceleration," as described by Hartmut Rosa in one of the chapters of the book, there is no better example of such acceleration processes than ICT. These technologies are not only triggers but also core elements of social acceleration. Most of the rapid development patterns of ICT follow such an accelerated process. Hartmut Rosa describes some of the acceleration potentials of these technologies when, "...they allow us to speed up activities, to reduce pauses and intervals between activities, and to multitask at the same time." In line with his observation, he describes the development of email communication (as experienced by most of us in our daily lives) as one prototype of technology-related accelerated change. But there are many other patterns of rapid change described in these chapters showing the "acceleration potential" of ICT which, based on the experiences of the last decades, can be expected to continue in our future. Changes related to ICT are expected not only to further advance with accelerated pace but also to pervade with such a pace into all domains of our lives.

In these first 30 years of this development, nearly every part and aspect in the world of work was influenced by ICT. If one takes the rapid and wide-ranging developments of ICT into consideration, it becomes quite obvious that there are many and potentially strong effects on work processes, work design, and work outcomes to be taken into consideration. The chapters of this book show many examples of changes of ICT in the realm of work. In trying to integrate the diverse aspects and approaches, a complex picture of consequences and effects emerges, with at least two most obvious conclusions:

1. Effects of ICT in the world of work are extremely wide-ranging. Implications of ICT development in workplaces are not limited to the work itself but may be found in many other life domains. The permeability of work and nonwork domains, triggered by ICT developments and described by many authors in this book, is only one (but a very important) example for such effects.
2. The other, even more obvious conclusion is the fact that ICT is a double-edged sword and has the potential for both benefits and risks. Pascale Carayon and Michael Smith (Chap. 7) mention the "paradox of IT" in their chapter about the balance theory, a framework for describing numerous potentially positive and negative aspects of new technologies. "Everything comes at a price," the well-known phrase from the German author Theodor Fontane, written nearly

200 years ago, seems to be not only valid for the outcomes of ICT, it may be even bluntly summarize the wide-ranging effects of ICT in one short sentence. Mainly because of the rapid and ever-permeating development of ICT, the coexistence of many potentially (very) positive and many (somewhat or even very) negative effects at the same time seems to be another core characteristic of these technologies.

It is quite obvious that ICT does provide many improvements for us, and these improvements are found in nearly every domain of our lives. Many of us cannot imagine a life without ICT anymore. As a matter of course, there are many positive aspects of these technologies which improve our lives and make many things much easier. The easy availability of all kinds of comprehensive information in nearly every situation of our lives is maybe one of the best examples of positive effects of new information technologies. Information access not only makes our daily lives easier; we are able not only to save time, but it may also allow us to improve the quality of many decision processes in everyday life.

On the other hand, the authors of the different chapters do also describe many potentially negative effects of new information technologies. Increases in work intensification, as described in the chapters by Bettina Kubicek et al. (Chap. 3) and Jörn Hurtienne et al. (Chap. 5), may be one of the most prominent work-related (and at least potentially negative) outcomes of ICT.

As an attempt to integrate the diverse aspects as described in the chapters of this book, we try to classify them along two dimensions. One dimension describes the diverse challenges and the possible positive and negative benefits of ICT.

The other dimension describes the level on which such benefits and risks may occur. Although the main focus of the chapters of this book is the context of work, the changes and effects of ICT implemented at work are not confined to the workplace itself. We therefore summarize these effects in a broader context: the individual level refers to aspects which may have potential effects on individuals and their health and well-being. Effects at the job level describe a wide range of consequences for workplaces, job design, and job-related outcomes. The organizational level describes the potential outcomes for the organizations. Because of the extensive potential for effects of ICT, outcomes at the work-family interface need also to be taken into consideration. On an even more general level, the next group of outcomes is related to potential effects for the whole society. Specific risk groups in the society are included at the societal level.

The following table describes this approach of sorting out the outcomes of ICT development and provides examples for each of the cells. The table clearly shows the strong potential of ICT in influencing many parts of our lives in positive or negative ways (Table 13.1).

Table 13.1 Examples of challenges and possible positive and negative outcomes related to ICT

	Challenges	Potential positive outcomes	Potential negative outcomes
Individual level	Need for ICT-related competencies	Availability and easy access to a wide range of information	Techno strain
	Adequate recovery from work	Increased independence because of better information	Techno addiction
	Finding a personal work-age balance		Alienation
Job	Work intensification	More and better feedback	Burnout
	Work interruptions	Many new opportunities to learn	
	Lack of training		
	Frustration because of technical problems		
Organization	Over controlling	Better service quality	ICT dependency
	Need for development of trust	Increased productivity	Complex interdependencies between subsystems of organizations
	Permanent adaptation needs	Cost reductions	
Work family	Adequate telework design	Enhanced productivity More "quality time"	Reduced privacy
Society and specific risk groups	Need for new forms of learning	Bridging distances	ICT dependency
	Development of opportunities for people with disabilities	Inclusion of all minority groups	

13.1 Individual Level

13.1.1 Challenges

There are many inherent challenges in attaining the possible improvements of ICT. In using the continuously changing ICT, individuals require many "new" ICT-related competencies. Social networks may be a new way to stay in contact, but they also require competent end users. An efficient use of email communication requires effective handling of emails, flexibility and competence in (new) and adequate writing styles, and at least some ICT expertise in using sophisticated mail programs (Hoonakker, Chap. 2).

In a more general sense, by using ICT, individuals are required to find their personal "balance" on many levels. There is the balance between new opportunities in controlling situations and decision processes, on the one hand, and the new demands to reach these new opportunities in an efficient and adequate way (Carayon and Smith, Chap. 7). When using social networks, there is also the challenge to find a personal balance in dealing with flexible timing and location

(Demerouti et al., Chap. 8). Even more general, Hartmut Rosa (Chap. 4) postulates that there is the need for each of us to develop a personal work-life balance into a personal work-age balance.

When developing these "new balances," we have to deal with many barriers. For example, for staying in contact with others, many of us are using ICT always and everywhere. Access to email is simple and easy at every moment and from nearly every location. Thus, bridging distances in time and space may be accompanied by disturbed recovery times and vacation times (Hoonakker, Chap. 2). Permanent and easy access to information and the overabundance of information available in the Internet may quickly lead to information overload (Bagnara et al., Chap. 12). There is not only information overload related to ICT; there may also be ICT-related work overload and "social overload" (Demerouti et al., Chap. 8). Work overload may be not only quantitative but also qualitative and can also be experienced also as ergonomic overload (Salanova et al., Chap. 6). Strong integration into social networks, like Facebook, may easily lead to the reduction of social contacts in "real life" (Carayon and Smith, Chap. 7).

13.1.2 Potential Positive Outcomes

The authors of the chapters also described many potential improvements on the individual level. For instance, ICT clearly improves the access to a wide range of information for every user. Information gathering has become very easy and convenient. ICT allows a convenient access to a wide range of even very specific information. Easy access to information may lead to better and comprehensive knowledge and has at least the potential for a new form of wisdom, entitled by Bagnara et al. in their chapter as "digital wisdom." Better informed persons are more self-contained and may be less dependent of others. Thus, availability and easy access to information may lead an increased sense of independence and autonomy (Demerouti et al., Chap. 8). Another potential benefit for individuals may be found in the social realm. Social media (Facebook as the most widely used example) do have at least the potential for a better social integration. Social media allow the bridging of long distances, and people are able to be in social contact over distances in space and time (Hoonakker, Chap. 2).

13.1.3 Potential Negative Outcomes

As discussed not only by the authors of this book, but also found in many other related publications in the past decades, there are many potential risks for individuals inherent to ICT. Not only physical health but also psychological health may be threatened by use (and overuse) of ICT. The continuous use of many ICT technologies (PCs, laptop computers, tablets, smart phones, etc.) is often accompanied with rigid body postures. As a result, increases of carpal tunnel syndrome and musculoskeletal disorders have been observed since the introduction of ICT (Carayon and Smith, Chap. 7). But the most important ICT-related risk for health seems to emerge in the psychological domain. Techno strain is a new and specific form of a strong and even chronic stress reaction (Salanova et al., Chap. 6). Moreover, the use of ICT may not only increase the dependency of ICT in nearly every moment of our lives; it may lead to new forms of dependencies (Hoonakker, Chap. 2) and even to "techno addiction" (Carayon and Smith, Salanova et al., Chaps. 6 and 7). Furthermore, the alienation aspect of burnout may become predominant (Rosa, Chap. 4); some authors even mention a general alienation of all members of our society because of the increased use of ICT.

As also often discussed in the public media, the use of social media may lead to a strong invasion of privacy (Carayon and Smith, Chap. 7). Individuals may develop a dependency from social networks (Hoonakker, Chap. 2). In the long run, the use of social media may even lead to social isolation (Salanova et al., Chap. 6).

13.2 Job Level

As the job level is the main focus of most of the chapters in this book, it is not surprising that a wide range of effects of ICT were discussed by the authors. There were many challenges and possible positive but also negative aspects described.

13.2.1 Challenges

Learning new things may be an opportunity, but it could easily change into a barrier or even a risk when there is a permanent need to learn too many new things in ever shorter time intervals (Hurtienne et al., Chap. 5). A continuous learning process at work may be necessary in order to cope with the ever-changing technologies and to adapt to new software and hardware. There may be just not enough time for learning when confronted with software and hardware changes at work. Fragmentary learning processes and a general lack of training are two of the reasons that the potential of ICT is not fully exploited in many workplaces (Carayon and Smith, Chap. 7). When the challenges of new ICT are not adequately met, job satisfaction could decrease (Hoonakker, Chap. 2). Thus, keeping job satisfaction – and eventually the quality of work – at least stable is a big challenge in many workplaces. But employees have to deal with many other ICT-related changes. For instance, because of the technological improvements, there is an increased expectation regarding response times at work (Carayon and Smith, Chap. 7). The use of email is a good example here. In many workplaces there exist no clearly defined rules on how quickly to respond to emails from managers and colleagues. Many employees think that they have to respond very fast to email inquiries. Such increased expectations are part of a more general process of social acceleration at work (Rosa, Chap. 4), leading to increases in "working at high speed" and "tight deadlines," as observed in many longitudinal data sets (Hoonakker, Chap. 2), but it also leads to multitasking. ICT seems to be one of the main drivers of a general increase in work intensification, as observed in many workplaces in the Western world (Kubicek et al., Chap. 3). An inherent feature of ICT is permanent connectivity leading to permanent availability (Hurtienne et al., Chap. 5), which, in turn, leads to increases in perceived job pressure (Carayon and Smith). Job pressure and increased workload may be perceived in a quantitative sense (too many things have to be done at the same time in ever-shortening time intervals) but also qualitatively. Employees may not be able to deal with specific demands triggered by ICT. Most of these new demands result from changes in social interactions at work. For instance, ICT lowers the threshold for others for the allocation of new tasks (Hurtienne et al., Chap. 5).

One of the biggest challenges related to ICT at work is coping with new forms of work interruptions (Kubicek et al., Demerouti et al., Hurtienne et al., Chaps. 3, 5, and 8). Email communication makes it very simple to interrupt others or to be interrupted by others. Many observers note that email communication has led to a fragmentation of work. Interruptions and disturbances by email communication are not limited to the working hours. Emails may be received during breaks and at any time and any place outside of the realm of work.

The introduction of new ICT is often accompanied by technical problems. In some cases, the feedback of end users at work is part of the development process of new ICT. On the one hand, this may be experienced as a chance for participation in work design, but on the other hand this again often leads to interruptions and breaks (Hurtienne et al., Chap. 5). The increase of ICT-related errors may diminish the quality of work results. On the other hand, ICT allows for a much better and sophisticated monitoring of worker performance (Hurtienne et al., Chap. 5). Every single step of a task and every break may be easily controlled (even without our knowledge!) by use of new technologies. This leaves the workers not only with a feeling of being permanently controlled, but leads also to experiences of decreases in autonomy and decision freedom.

13.2.2 Potential Positive Outcomes

Most of us know from our daily working experiences that ICT has brought many improvements into the world of work. For many employees, working without the support of ICT would be hard to conceive. First of all, work with ICT has resulted in many areas of work to decline of workload. Even work intensity (which was found to be generally increasing) seems to decrease with ICT at least for certain groups of workers (Kubicek et al., Chap. 3). Improvements in production techniques in the last decades have led to a strong decrease of physical workload in many production areas.

Also with regard to other, central aspects of job design, there are at least potentials for improvements. For instance, ICT can facilitate new ways of feedback (Demerouti et al., Chap. 8). Employees do have many new opportunities for feedback about their work when using ICT. Depending on the type of technology, feedback may not only be continuously available but could be more precise and in general be of a very high quality. There are many examples for high-quality feedback opportunities related to ICT, ranging from the use of word processing software to complex feedback processes over time and space.

The use of ICT also brought to us many opportunities to learn new things (Greenan et al., Chap. 10). Learning at work may be improved by the use of new learning software programs. In a more general sense, there is not only the need to learn new things because of these technologies, but ICT supports new ways of learning at work and facilitates continuous learning processes.

13.2.3 Potential Negative Outcomes

Because ICT seems to play a certain role in the observed general increases in work intensification, there is also the potential of negative work-related health outcomes. Many researchers, but also many practitioners in the field, observe increases in the general risk for burnout and also an increase in the number of burnout cases over the last decades. It is a challenging task to confirm such trends with strong empirical data. The few existing longitudinal data sets show mixed results with regard to increases in burnout over long time periods (see also Kubicek et al., Chap. 3). A detailed analysis of the results of these data sets would be challenging and divert too much from our main topic. But we may conclude that there is at least a certain risk for increases in burnout, related to the rapid development of ICT. Some authors claim that there are also increases in depression as a result of acceleration and alienation processes related to ICT (see Rosa, Chap. 4). Again, it is not easy to quantify such effects because of missing representative longitudinal data and definition problems.

13.3 Organizational Level

Many of the challenges and possible positive and negative outcomes discussed on the job level do also play a certain role at the organizational level. But on this level, there are also new facts to be taken into consideration.

13.3.1 Challenges

The often wide-ranging goals and expectations related to ICT implementations have to be met under the societal condition of social acceleration. Quite often this results in organizations implementing (too) many new ICT-related changes in ever-shortening time intervals. Employees have to continuously adapt to changes related to these implementations. On the employees' side, this leads to many "new" demands at work, such as increased learning demands and the need for increased flexibility.

ICT do also have a strong inherent potential to increase control on all levels. There is even a tendency of "over controlling" in many organizations (Demerouti et al., Chap. 8). For instance, with the support of ICT many organizational parameters can be generated and used for productivity control. Too many comprehensive measures of control of an employee's output can result in a reduction of employee motivation and productivity. Thus, the development of trust on all levels is especially important when using ICT for comprehensive organizational control (Montague and Chiou, Chap. 9). With the introduction of new ICT, there is always the inherent risk for impairment of organizational trust.

ICT allows for fast and efficient communication and supports teamwork even over long distances in space and time (Demerouti et al., Chap. 8). Opportunities for successful teamwork are increased, and the quality of teamwork may be improved. On the other hand, communication conflicts and misunderstandings often increase when using new communication channels and when communicating in virtual teams.

The implementation and use of complex ICT systems also increases the demands put on managers, at all organizational levels. Empirical studies and many practical observations show that in modern organizations, managers have to deal with strong demands regarding organizational targets but have also to deal with demands from the employee's side. New role conflicts are commonly observable. For instance, many managers do have negative opinions towards their employees (especially towards their elder employees) with regard to their ICT flexibility (Greenan et al., Chap. 10). On the other hand, employees may not trust their managers with regard to their ICT competencies but also with regard to their "control ambitions," which, in turn, leads to a decrease of organizational trust (Montague and Chiou, Chap. 9) and an increase of conflicts (Demerouti et al., Chap. 8).

13.3.2 Potential Positive Outcomes

The main reasons for organizations to implement ICT are the reduction of costs and the generation of economic advantages. ICT may help to reach these goals by improving networks and many other communication channels, by implementation of efficient management and administration tools, and by improving the quality of services (Kubicek et al., Chap. 3). In a more general sense, the implementation of ICT may help to improve many aspects of productivity and quality in any organization (Carayon and Smith, Chap. 7).

13.3.3 Potential Negative Outcomes

ICT permeates all organizational levels and processes. There are increasing and complex technological interdependencies (also known as "coupling") in many organizations. Thus, organizations become more and more dependent of ICT. The dependency of ICT may be even the biggest threat at the organizational level.

13.4 Work-Family Interface

As described by the authors in many of the chapters of this book, there are also many challenges and positive and negative effects of ICT on the work-family interface.

13.4.1 Challenges

Many ICT-related challenges that are discussed in the chapters of this book are related to telework. The potential improvements of telework seem to come at a price. Many studies related to telework confirm increased work-family conflicts, higher levels of stress for many teleworkers, and even the potential for a decrease in productivity (Hoonakker, Demerouti et al., Chaps. 2 and 8). An intense use of ICT at home, for both work and private matters, may result in reduced privacy and does have a strong potential for increased work-home conflicts.

A very different challenge of ICT with regard to the work-family interface is the fact that the speed of ICT development may hinder the transfer into retirement (Demerouti et al., Chap. 8). This again may have the potential for negative (overworking) and positive (ICT allows people to work longer, which is considered a general necessity in the Western world) developments.

13.4.2 Potential Positive Outcomes

ICT brought to all of us a much better access to a wide range of information. Shopping, planning of travelling, comprehensive access to news, and many other things are easily and conveniently available from at home which could save us time and enable to spend more "quality time" with the family. More and more people are able to work from home. Telework is one of the biggest changes in job design related to the introduction of ICT. Many positive outcomes of telework are discussed in the literature (Hoonakker, Chap. 2). For instance, telework results in less commuting times and allows for a much better integration of job-related and family-related tasks. Again, there is at least the potential for spending more time at home.

13.5 Society and Specific Risk Groups

Many of the challenges and possible positive or negative outcomes of ICT as discussed on the different levels (individual, job, and organization) add up to even more general effects for our society. Again, there is the potential for many benefits, but they all seem to come at a price. Since the focus of this book is on workplaces, we would like to mention just a few examples here.

The authors of the different chapters also mentioned specific "risk groups" in our societies with regard to ICT implementation. Such risk groups have existed since the introduction of ICT. For instance, in earlier research on effects of ICT, there was a strong focus on older workers and their specific problems with ICT implementations. Now, about 30 years later, most of the older workers are more familiar with ICT (they are at least "digital immigrants"). "Older workers" nowadays do not seem to have any specific problems with the development of ICT (Greenan et al.). On the other hand, we may observe the rise of other, new "risk groups" in relation to ICT developments

13.5.1 Challenges

In reaching the demanding goals of bridging gaps and distances and improving our quality of life, there are many challenges to cope with. For instance, new forms of education may be needed to deal with the ever-increasing demands of new ICT (Weber and Zink, Chap. 11). This leads to new challenges for teachers and educational staff in almost all educational settings. Access to education for a wide range of diverse groups needs to be facilitated. In a more general sense, we need to deal with the "digital divide" which can be observed in many parts of our society (Weber and Zink, Chap. 11). We need to guarantee a similar access to ICT and ICT-related education for people with different socioeconomic backgrounds, for different immigrant groups, for older people, for unemployed workers, and for many other "risk groups." A fair recognition of all groups of workers in a diverse workforce is an important cornerstone when putting the many positive potentials of ICT into practice. As a first step, prejudices against specific group of workers with regard to their ICT competencies need to be dismantled (Greenan et al., Chap. 10).

ICT is a predominant driver of social acceleration processes (Rosa, Chap. 4). This leads not only to increasing competition and information overflow but also to a "subjectification" of work (Hurtienne et al., Chap. 5). Endeavors on many levels will be necessary to deal with such developments and to keep quality of work and the general quality of life high with the rapid further development of ICT.

The authors of the book chapters identified two specific risk groups related to ICT implementation: people with disabilities and people with a low socioeconomic status. For both groups ICT may bring about the potential for many improvements. The development of new interfaces allows people with disabilities a much better "connection to the world." By making specific ICT techniques available, many people with disabilities may have for the first time a chance to be integrated into the workforce. Also, for a very different group of people, namely, people with low socioeconomic status, access to ICT may have the potential to improve their situation. New opportunities for learning and for a better integration in the society may be advanced by ICT. In each of the risk groups, the chance for improvements and the risk for further separation go hand in hand. It will be our common responsibility to take measures to further develop the positive potentials for ICT to better integrate all the groups in our society.

13.5.2 Potential Positive Outcomes

In summing up the diverse improvements as discussed on the previous levels, the biggest potential for improvements of ICT on the societal level may be the opportunity of bridging many gaps and distances. This refers not only to reduced travel and better communication, but also to improved chances for many groups in our society, for better jobs, and, in general, better quality of life.

Over the years ICT has brought many improvements to many specific "risk groups" of employees. Not only has the situation of the older workforce improved over the years. In the early days of ICT implementation, women were also considered a potential "risk group" of ICT. Early studies showed that, when implementing new ICT, the situation of male workers (who were often more familiar with those technologies) improved, whereas the situation for female workers (for instance their opportunities for career advancement) deteriorated. In the meantime, studies confirm that the gender gap in relation to ICT has been strongly reduced or does not exist anymore. New opportunities specifically for women at work may arise when introducing new ICT, for instance a better integration of the work and family domains.

13.5.3 Potential Negative Outcomes

Since ICT permeates many life domains, there is also the threat of ICT dependence on the societal level. Further, one of the most important risks of ICT is that it creates a digital divide.

This short overview has shown that there are many possible positive and negative effects of ICT on all levels. It is not easy to quantify the many challenges and possible positive or negative outcomes in relation to each other. But at least there are many opportunities for accompanying measures to facilitate the positive effects of ICT for every individual of our society.

13.6 Implications for Research and Practice

There are many studies confirming the abovementioned potentially positive and negative effects of ICT on the quality of working life. The chapters in the book refer to results of many of these studies. If one examines the research models used in many of these studies, it is quite obvious that the use of well-established existing research models seems to capture quite well all the potential effects of ICT.

From a research perspective ICT is just another new (although very powerful) tool at work. Thus, research models dealing comprehensively with job demands and stressors, such as Karasek's job strain model, the job demands-resources model, the effort-reward imbalance model, or the effort recovery theory, are used to analyze the wide range of potential effects of ICT. Since some of these effects could be wide-reaching, models focusing on the development of resources, like Hobfoll's Conservation of Resources (COR) theory, seem to capture these effects best. The obvious suitability of the classic stress models for ICT also confirms that all the recommendations regarding good job design will be applicable, even in times of rapid ICT-related changes.

We would like to finish this book with a few thoughts about practical recommendations, as discussed by the chapter authors, aiming at optimizing the positive effects of ICT and minimizing the potential negative effects.

13.6.1 Ergonomics

Good ergonomics is not only good economics (Carayon and Smith, Chap. 7). It is also a basic requirement when using ICT for improving the quality of working life. Because of the rapid development of these technologies, every new ICT tool needs to be designed based on good ergonomic considerations. The ergonomic design should be for everybody (Weber and Zink, Chap. 11); new development of ICT should even be powered by design! Design of "slow" technologies should include design for pauses, detachment, and serendipity (Bagnara et al., Chap. 12).

13.6.2 *Job Design*

For more than 50 years, comprehensive knowledge about good job design has been available. This knowledge can be applied to design "new" jobs with a continuous use of ICT. "Classic" aspects of good jobs, like comprehensive task feedback and enough autonomy, are as important as they always were when designing jobs in the times before the ICT revolution. Thus, job design and job redesign could be implemented with the use of well-established tools (Demerouti et al., Chap. 8). For example, survey feedback could be used to get a better understanding of the perceptions of the employees regarding their jobs and their inherent characteristics. Based on the results of the surveys, employee workshops and participative measures of job redesign are always useful measures for improving the quality of jobs. More generally speaking, participation in job redesign and in organizational decision-making is as important with ICT use as it ever was.

13.6.3 *Workplace and Organizational Learning*

Workplace learning and comprehensive training are important organizational tools when implementing new tasks and new processes. Because of the rapid development of ICT, continuous organizational learning becomes even more important. Learning refers not only to the technical aspects of new technologies but also to a productive and healthy use of these technologies. For example, many workers do not exactly know how quickly they have to respond to email queries within their organization. When responding too slow, this may negatively affect organizational productivity. But in most cases, there is a tendency to respond too fast, which may lead to task interruptions and increased levels of stress. Thus, organizational learning with regard to email use is a wide-ranging concept which affects the improvement of many communication processes within an organization. But there are many other important learning areas related to ICT use. The support of learning processes is especially important when dealing with specific (risk) groups. Older workers often need more learning support to adapt to new technologies. People with disabilities need learning programs which are tailored to their specific needs. Support of learning is a first step to successfully introduce ICT to people with low socioeconomic status and thus may help to reduce the "digital divide." Organizations should stimulate training and learning opportunities, especially in the ICT domain. This will benefit both the organizations and the employees who work for the organization.

13.6.4 Individual Responsibilities

Nowadays, we not only use ICT for work and these technologies permeate all our life domains. In fact, certain characteristics of these technologies are the diffusion into all out life domains and the breakup of the boundaries between our life domains. Workplace support measures, workplace regulations, and organizational policies are related only to the work domain. In coping with the comprehensive effects of ICT on our lives, there is also a strong individual responsibility for each of us. Each individual is requested to find a personal good way in using ICT in different life domains. As the previous chapters have clearly shown, there is a huge potential of ICT for many improvements, but there are also big challenges in achieving these improvements and there are even many risks for the individual quality of life and health. We all are responsible for our personal "quality times," and we need to learn to adequately integrate ICT into our lives for the improvement of our living conditions.

13.6.5 Trust

An inherent characteristic of ICT is the potential for increased control of tasks and processes. Control may enhance quality and help to improve the quality of many services and processes. Increased task feedback is another positive aspect of ICT-related control at work. But in several circumstances, control means the opposite of trust. Not only at workplaces but also in many parts of modern societies we observe increases of control mechanisms at the price of a decrease in trust. Decrease of trust shakes the very foundations of our society. Trust is not only the glue which fits the society together; it is also a personal need for each individual. Thus, the development of trust is maybe the most important task related to the implementation of new ICT. There are many ways to enhance trust, at the level of software programming, the task level, and, most importantly, at the level of social exchange. Teams at workplaces and even whole organizations need to be anchored in trust.

The chapters of this book have described a wide range of benefits but also of risks related to ICT implementation. We believe that the further development of ICT is one of the most fascinating but also one of the most influential aspects of our society which will further affect all our life domains. In the current times of social acceleration, all our knowledge is required to develop measures, tools, and techniques to adequately cope with these technologies and to further improve the quality of work and life.

Index

C. Korunka and P. Hoonakker (eds.), *The Impact of ICT on Quality of Working Life*,
DOI 10.1007/978-94-017-8854-0, © Springer Science+Business Media Dordrecht 2014

MIX
Papier aus verantwortungsvollen Quellen
Paper from responsible sources
FSC® C105338

If you have any concerns about our products,
you can contact us on
ProductSafety@springernature.com

In case Publisher is established outside the EU,
the EU authorized representative is:
Springer Nature Customer Service Center GmbH
Europaplatz 3, 69115 Heidelberg, Germany

Printed by Libri Plureos GmbH
in Hamburg, Germany